CAREER COUNSELING TECHNIQUES

University of North Carolina, Chapel Hill

LINDA BROOKS
University of North Carolina, Chapel Hill

ALLYN AND BACON
Boston London Toronto Sydney Tokyo Singapore

Series Editorial Assistant: Carol Craig
Cover Administrator: Linda K. Dickinson
Cover Designer: Suzanne Harbison
Manufacturing Buyer: Megan Cochran
Production Coordinator: Lisa Feder
Editorial-Production Service: York Production Services

Library of Congress Cataloging-in-Publication Data

Brown, Duane.
    Career counseling techniques / Duane Brown, Linda Brooks.
        p.   cm.
    Includes index.
    ISBN 0-205-12874-2
    1. Vocational guidance.   I. Brooks, Linda.   II. Title.
HF5381.B6758   1990
158.6—dc20   90-1241
                                                    CIP

Printed in the United States of America

10 9 8 7 6 5 4 3 2 1   94 93 92 91 90

Contents

CAREER COUNSELING TECHNIQUES

Preface

Career guidance and probably some form of career counseling have been a part of American culture for well over 100 years. For at least seventy years of that time period career counselors applied trait-and-factor practices to this process, although questions began to be raised about the efficacy of trait-and-factor approaches in the 1950s.

In the last decade, career counselors have seriously questioned the utility of trait-and-factor approaches that focus solely upon the career role to the exclusion of other life roles. Interestingly, practitioners have been far ahead of scholars in this field, because their own research with clients has revealed the inadequacy of traditional approaches. The result has been the adoption of approaches to career counseling that give consideration to the family, leisure, and other life roles.

An even more recent development in career counseling has been the adoption by many counselors of the point of view that mental health issues and career issues are inextricably linked. This point of view holds that career counseling should not proceed without consideration of the possibility that psychological defects may be at the root of career-related problems and that career-related problems may manifest themselves in the kind of symptoms that have long been viewed as resulting from intrapsychic concerns.

We have taken the view that to be effective, career counselors must first be good counselors, including possessing the ability to diagnose and treat psychological problems or, at the very least, refer clients with these problems for treatment. However, we have not stopped with this assumption. We have also assumed that to be successful, a career counselor must also understand the interaction of career with other life roles and be prepared at a minimum to assess interrole relationships.

If problems are identified among the various relationships, we believe that this counselor must (once again) be prepared to either treat those problems or make referrals so that those problems can be ameliorated.

The result of the foregoing rationale is a career counseling techniques book that is aimed at arming the career counselor with the strategies needed to assess and intervene in a wide variety of career problems including those related to planning, adjustment, and change. No attempt has been made to duplicate those books that deal with basic counseling techniques. Nor has an attempt been made to extensively discuss those techniques needed to diagnose and treat mental health problems. However, it will be clear, we hope, that having these skills is a necessary prerequisite to career counseling.

The development of any book is a long and arduous task, and a number of people deserve credit for these contributions. Chief among these are Evelyn Ross, Jane Trexler, and Karen Thigpen, who wrestled mightily with the numerous drafts of this manuscript. Melody Vaitkiss also deserves our thanks because of her work on some of the library research involved. Finally, those students and career consultants who have enrolled in our classes and workshops deserve special consideration for their challenges and for the stimulation they have provided. They have enriched our professional lives just as we hope to enrich the lives of those who read this book.

D.B.
L.B.
February, 1990

PART I

Introduction

1

Career Counseling

THE CURRENT SITUATION

Career counseling is stereotypically viewed as a rather simple process involving helping individuals find out more about themselves and occupations so that they can make a "good" choice. This stereotype, like most, is grounded in a bit of truth and a bit of fiction. It certainly is the case that trait and factor theorizing based on the early thinking of Frank Parsons (1909) has dominated the way that many professionals view career counseling. Parsons held that career choice is a three-step process: (1) develop awareness of self, (2) analyze and understand occupations, and (3) using "true reasoning," choose an occupation. In the 1920s and 30s, under the leadership of differential psychologists, this three-step model evolved because of the development of tests and inventories and the development of a more scientific approach to studying occupations called job analysis. The new model became (1) develop self-awareness using tests, inventories, and various other procedures to identify traits, (2) study occupations to determine which occupations offered a potential match for your traits, and (3) using true reasoning, choose an occupation. This model still dominates thinking about career counseling (Brown, 1984), although this perspective is shifting rapidly.

Self-help books, based largely upon the trait model, have also contributed to current perceptions of career counseling. One "career counselor" was quoted as saying, "I have read Bolles' [1989] book, *What Color Is Your Parachute?*, and that is all I need to know to do career counseling." Bolles, who is not a career counselor, has written an enormously successful book, but it will hardly serve as the basis for career counseling. But his book and dozens like it have been purchased by

3

millions of people who are either making initial career choices or making job changes, and the books have proven to be useful resources.

Another contribution to our current thinking about career counseling comes from noteworthy professionals such as John Holland (1974), who not only developed one of the leading theories of occupational choice but asserted that most people do not need the assistance of a career counselor to make a satisfactory career choice. Holland believes that self-directed activities such as self-scoring and interpreting interest inventories and, presumably, self-help books and computer-assisted guidance programs will be sufficient sources of assistance for most individuals as they make occupational choices. While there is support for Holland's (1974) position, the research in this area is extremely weak.

A NEW AWARENESS

There is increasingly an awareness that while simplistic approaches to career counseling for some individuals may be sufficient, many people bring very complex career-related problems to counselors, and the assistance they need requires the career counselor to be highly skilled in both personal and career counseling. Like the stereotype of career counseling previously described, this awareness is springing from a number of sources. One of these sources is the work that Osipow, Carney, Winer, Yanico, and Koschir (1976) have done in the development of the Career Decision Scale and other research (e.g., Hartman, Fuqua, & Blum, 1985) that suggests at least 16 percent of career decision makers cannot take advantage of typical career counseling activities because of the presence of psychological problems. These persons are classified as indecisive. The remaining 84 percent are categorized as undecided and are characterized as being able to make adequate choices if they get help with finding information, improving their decision making skills, and so on. Clearly, a large number of people who come to career counselors cannot apply "true reasoning" to choosing an occupation.

A second source of our new awareness that we need more complex approaches to career counseling is the life-role perspective. This perspective, advanced by such authors as Okun (1984) and Super (1984), holds that career planning should be conducted in conjunction with the planning of other life roles such as family and leisure. Practicing career counselors more and more call what they do "whole people" career counseling, because they realize that it does little good to assist clients to make an occupational choice if their jobs are incongruent with their family and leisure roles. Planning for one role while not considering the others often creates rather than resolves problems.

Today, career counselors are less concerned with helping people make initial occupational choices and more concerned about planning a career path that will involve a series of occupations. They are also aware that many people who come for career counseling need either concurrent or separate work on psychological problems that inhibit or preclude them from making choices altogether. Moreover, career counselors are increasingly concerned about total life-role integration and, at the very least, helping the client consider the potential impact of career on other life roles. In this light, career counselors should be prepared to assist clients to develop a life plan that will allow for harmony and balance among the life roles.

Although the stereotype of career counseling that developed over three-quarters of a century is not dead, it is changing. As would be expected, our own definition of career counseling deviates considerably from the traditional view and is as follows:

Career counseling is an interpersonal process designed to assist individuals with career development problems. Career development is that process of choosing, entering, adjusting to, and advancing in an occupation. It is a lifelong psychological process that interacts dynamically with other life roles. Career problems include, but are not limited to, career indecision and undecidedness, work performance, stress and adjustment, incongruence of the person and work environment, and inadequate or unsatisfactory integration of life roles with other life roles (e.g., parent, friend, citizen). (Brooks & Brown, 1986, p. 98)

One implication in the foregoing definition is the idea that the career counselor must be able to determine which individuals are undecided and which are indecisive. Indecisive individuals lack cognitive clarity, which can be defined as the ability to objectively assess one's own strengths and weaknesses and relate the assessment to environmental situations. People who have a high degree of cognitive clarity can take data about themselves, assimilate them into their overall view of themselves, and apply this self-knowledge to their environment as they make choices. On the other hand, persons who lack cognitive clarity possess faulty logic systems (Beck, 1976; Ellis, 1962) that can result in what Krumboltz (1983) has described as faulty private rules for career decision making. Consequences of these rules include believing that a problem is nonremediable when in fact it is, failing to exert enough effort actually to solve the problem one has, mistakenly eliminating viable career alternatives, choosing a career alternative for the wrong reason, and suffering because of perceptions that goals are unachievable. Career counselors must be able to distinguish between clients who are hampered by lack of cognitive clarity and those who are undecided.

As is stressed throughout this book, career counselors must be able to discern when difficulties with cognitive clarity are a potential barrier for clients who desire career choices or adjustments within their careers. As also is stressed, once a deficiency in cognitive clarity is established, appropriate action may require postponement of consideration of career-related matters until cognitive clarity is attained in some instances. This matter is discussed in more detail in the following section.

THE PROCESS OF CAREER COUNSELING

It may be obvious from the foregoing discussion that there are at least two fairly distinct views of the process of career counseling. In fact, there are many views of the process. For example, the process of the afore-mentioned trait-oriented approach, if depicted graphically, appears as follows:

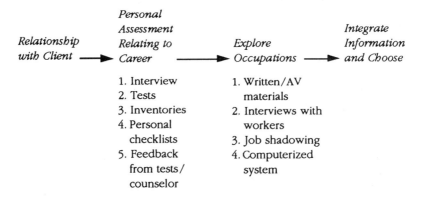

An overview of the career counseling process that we are posing is a bit more complex and is illustrated thusly:

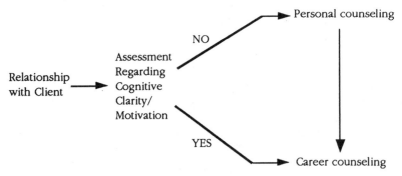

TABLE 1.1 Causes of Cognitive Clarity Problems and Their Disposition

Causes	Career Counseling	Other Intervention Then Career Counseling	Personal Then Career counseling
I Informational Deficits			
A Simple deficit stemming from lack of knowledge of self and occupations	X		
B. Deficit growing out of inability to use information because of reading problems, learning disabilities, etc.	X		
C. Information overload resulting from an inability to discriminate between needed and unneeded information	X		
II. Stereotypical Views			
A. Stereotypical views resulting from experiential deficits (e.g. lack of role models)	X		
B. Stereotyping resulting from deeply held values (i.e., religious teachings)	X		
C. Stereotyping resulting from mild psychological deficits (e.g., low self-esteem results in low risk taking so people "cannot" see themselves in roles other than those they have experienced)	X		
D. Mild injunctions (oughts and shoulds) interfere with consideration of some options	X		
III. Moderate Mental Health Problems			
A. Faulty decision making style precludes thoughtful decision making		X	
B. Low self-esteem precludes consideration of some or many options		X	
C. Illogical thinking results in injunctions or other thought patterns that preclude consideration and selection of options		X	
D. Problems such as phobias or stuttering preclude consideration of some career options (e.g., fear of flying precludes consideration of jobs that require air travel)		X	

(continued)

TABLE 1.1   Continued

Causes	Career Counseling	Other Intervention Then Career Counseling	Personal Then Career counseling
IV. Severe Mental Health Problems			
A Psychoses (e.g., chronic schizophrenia or major affective disorder) that severely impair the individual's ability to consider career options		X	
B.Severe substance abuse disorders		X	
V. External Factors			
A Temporary crises (uncomplicated bereavement or marital discord)			X
B. Stress, either temporary or longterm, precludes focusing on career concerns			X

It might be expected that once problems of cognitive clarity have been addressed, the career counseling process would resemble the trait model. However, this is not the case, as can be seen in the following illustration:

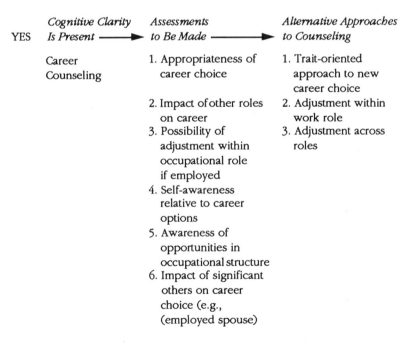

	Cognitive Clarity Is Present ⟶	Assessments to Be Made ⟶	Alternative Approaches to Counseling
YES	Career Counseling	1. Appropriateness of career choice	1. Trait-oriented approach to new career choice
		2. Impact of other roles on career	2. Adjustment within work role
		3. Possibility of adjustment within occupational role if employed	3. Adjustment across roles
		4. Self-awareness relative to career options	
		5. Awareness of opportunities in occupational structure	
		6. Impact of significant others on career choice (e.g., (employed spouse)	

The recommended career counseling process begins with assessing the client's cognitive clarity. For example, clients may temporarily be unable to examine objectively either their personal traits or the options open to them when they are experiencing the grief associated with a loss such as divorce or death. More serious and long-term concerns that may cause cognitive clarity problems include choice anxiety, extreme dependency, debilitating drug or alcohol abuse problems, phobias that preclude certain types of job choices (e.g., fear of flying), low self-esteem, and other psychological problems.

Some cognitive clarity concerns can be handled while career development concerns are being addressed. Those problems that may be addressed simultaneously with the career problem include, but are not limited to, polar thinking (I must be a lawyer or nothing), injunctions (I must find the perfect job), illogical thinking (women who go into business always get divorced), and stereotyping (real men can't be nurses). These types of concerns and techniques for dealing with them will be addressed in Chapter 3. Types of cognitive clarity problems along with recommended action are listed in Table 1-1.

If cognitive clarity is present, the assessment process will focus on a variety of factors depending upon whether the client is making an initial choice, wants to make a career change, or has been displaced and is in immediate economic need. In the third case, the career counselor's immediate concern would be assisting the client to get a job; thus, simply helping the client identify viable job opportunities may be the initial approach of choice. Subsequently, the counselor and the client might consider how this job corresponds to the client's values, the impact that it is making upon her or his other life roles, and the possible need for a change to a more suitable job. If the client's needs are not so immediate, a more holistic approach may be pursued from the outset, including looking at interrelationships of life roles, considering factors that might influence career choice or adjustment, and ascertaining whether the client is stuck in his or her current situation by virtue of the employment of a spouse, other family ties, age, health problems, or other personal circumstances that preclude movement. For the person who is "stuck," the counselor might end up helping the client identify and develop other life roles that could provide life satisfaction (e.g., leisure.) For other clients, the end result might be choosing a new job, making an adjustment within the current job, or making adjustments across roles (e.g., spending less time in leisure so more attention can be paid to the career).

TECHNIQUES NEEDED

Perhaps it is obvious from the discussion thus far that the skills needed in the model advocated here are far more diverse than those required in the trait- oriented model. It is the focus of this book to identify, describe, and illustrate techniques that are used in this more comprehensive approach to career counseling. This discussion includes those techniques that are used in personal or family counseling that have implications for career counseling, as well as the ones that have traditionally been associated with career counseling. What is not discussed are those basic techniques needed by all counselors to establish client relationships and move the client toward problem resolution, since these techniques have already been discussed in other books. These include the techniques that follow:

Relationship-Building Techniques	*Techniques That Facilitate Problem Solving*
Attending/active listening	Confrontation
Responding with empathy	Relationship reparation (immediacy)
Information elicitation and clarification	Additive empathic responses
Demonstrating respect	Summarizing emotional content and problem identification

At the end of this chapter, a number of books are listed that contain excellent presentations regarding these techniques.

The techniques that are discussed in this book include those that can be used to enhance (1) cognitive clarity while simultaneously dealing with career development concerns, (2) self-awareness, (3) goal setting and decision making, (4) career exploration, (5) career and life-role integration, and (6) termination. Techniques for use during the initial stage of career counseling also are discussed, along with some strategies for dealing with the unique career development problems of minorities and women.

This book has been organized around the stages of counseling, starting with the first interview, the assessment of the client's problem, goal setting, and intervention. As the model shown earlier suggests, in reality, career counseling cannot be depicted as a neat set of linear stages. For example, in any career counseling process, there are several assessment points, the initial one being determination of the degree of cognitive clarity. If cognitive clarity is present, then assessment continues as the counselor looks at the totality of the client's existence, *unless* the client has an immediate economic need, in which case assessment is restricted to determining those personal factors that will help secure immediate employment. Goal setting and intervention are also ongoing subprocesses within career counseling. Even though this book is organized linearly for convenience, the career counseling process is not so straightforward.

It should also be noted that although the various career counseling strategies are discussed under the convenient rubrics provided by the stages, they do not fit nicely into "categories that can be used within a given stage." Many of the techniques discussed are useful in many stages. For example, guided fantasy can be used as an assessment, goal-setting, or intervention strategy, and could conceivably be used as a relationship-building technique as well. Books need to be organized in some logical fashion, but the reader should not be misled by the organization of this book.

BECOMING A CAREER COUNSELOR

Many students who enter training programs in counseling and psychology do not want to become career counselors, although there are increasing numbers of students who identify becoming a career counselor as their objective. We believe that anyone who does any type of counseling or therapy should be skilled in identifying and ameliorating career problems and their impact upon other life roles and psychological functioning. However, we also realize that many trainees elect to specialize in personal counseling and to consciously ignore career concerns. Should you decide to become proficient in, or better still, specialize in career counseling, what skills will you need to develop? The National Career Development Association (1985) developed a list of these that can serve as a point of departure in the development of a partial guide to proficiency in career counseling.

Knowledge and Skills Needed for Career Counseling

1. General counseling skills, including knowledge of counseling theories and skills in relationship building.
2. Ability to use counseling skills to assist clients with career development problems.
3. Ability to develop awareness of personal factors such as values, interests, and aptitudes and apply this self-knowledge to career counseling.

4. Ability to help clients recognize their stereotypes about careers and help them overcome them.
5. Ability to assist clients to recognize the importance of other life roles in the career decision making process.
6. Ability to assist clients to improve their decision making.
7. Knowledge of
    a. labor market information, training and employment trends, occupational information.
    b. basic concepts about career development.
    c. career development and decision making theories.
    d. resources and techniques that can be used with special groups.
    e. systems for developing, storing, and using occupational information.
    f. changing roles of men and women and linkages among life roles.
8. Ability to appraise aptitudes, interests, values, and personality traits.
9. Ability to identify appraisal resources for various populations.
10. Ability to evaluate, administer, and interpret appraisal devices.
11. Ability to assist individuals to make their own appraisal of the quality of their lives and their work environment.

This book, if used as directed, can help you develop some of these competencies. As noted in the previous section, it is expected that basic generic knowledge and skills regarding counseling will be studied elsewhere. Similarly, the acquisition of knowledge and skills regarding assessment must be gained in specialized coursework and under the supervision of an authority in the field. The competencies that are addressed, at least partially, in this book are numbers 2, 3, 4, 5, 6,7d, 10, and 11.

Suggestions at the end of each chapter describe approaches to gaining skills and applying them in the career counseling process. These suggestions are aimed primarily at beginners who possess only rudimentary counseling skills. Experienced career counselors may already have learned many of the techniques set forth in this book. For experienced counselors, the suggestions for learning new techniques should be tempered by your own knowledge of yourself and your skills, your awareness of your clients' needs, and your concerns for the ethical standards of your profession.

USING THIS BOOK

Each chapter has been designed to follow a similar pattern. At the outset, the technique to be discussed is defined and its uses in the career counseling process identified. Then a bit of background about the technique is presented. This background provides some of the history of the technique, a description of the populations with which it can be used, and some research regarding the efficacy of the technique. None of these sections is lengthy.

Since this book is intended to be a guide for skill acquisition, a description of how the technique can be personalized to fit the needs of each client typically is embedded in each presentation. Rules or principles for designing and/or applying the techniques are presented, along with outlines of the process. After the technique and its uses have been described, its uses are illustrated by taking excerpts from career counseling sessions. Enough verbal interviews are presented to give the reader a "feel" for how the technique can be utilized in actual practice.

Following the illustration of the technique's utilization, limitations of the strategy are presented. No technique can be used with all clients in all situations. Counselors who attempt to utilize techniques inappropriately or use inappropriate techniques run the risk of doing their clients more damage than good. Suggestions are made regarding a process to help you become skilled in the use of each technique, and a summary of what has been covered about the technique is presented. Finally, chapter references include suggestions for additional readings about the technique.

If you are a career counselor or a trainee enrolled in a field experience, you should make every effort to learn and apply in your work the techniques that you are reading about. Supervisors should typically be consulted by students before using a particular technique. Whether you are a student or a seasoned professional, it is always a good idea to keep some sort of record or log about the strategies you are learning and what you discover in the process of applying them. Following is the outline of a log sheet that may be helpful in this regard.

Date	Technique	Type of Client (e.g., ethnicity, gender, presenting problem, age, etc.)	Results	Suggestions for Future Use

Two aspects of your log or journal are of great importance. The first of these is that you at least informally evaluate the impact of a particular technique on a particular client or type of client. You may find, over time, that a technique works particularly well with one group and not with another. Second, when you are learning any skill, you will find ways of improving the application of the strategy used in your initial efforts. By keeping a record of "suggestions to yourself," you can refine your use of a technique and ensure that you gain the maximum results when you use that technique in the future.

SUMMARY

Trait-oriented counseling, sometimes described as "test 'em and tell 'em," has held and, to a great degree, still holds center stage in career counseling. This approach has led to a devaluing of career counseling by many. However, because of research that shows that many clients do not benefit from traditional approaches and that life roles are interconnected, a new "whole-person" approach to career counseling is developing. This approach requires that the counselor be able to diagnose cognitive difficulties that may impede career decision making to assess how life roles mesh. It also requires that the counselor be able to design interventions that not only can aid career decision making but can facilitate within-work role adjustment and adjustments across life roles. This more comprehensive approach to career counseling requires a wide variety of knowledge bases and skills that only partially are addressed in this book.

REFERENCES AND SUGGESTED READINGS

Beck, A. T. (1976). *Cognitive Therapy and Emotional Disorders*. New York: International University Press.

Bolles, R. N. (1989, revised annually). *What Color Is Your Parachute?* Berkeley, CA: Ten Speed Press.

Brooks, L., and Brown, D. (1986). Career counseling for adults: Implications for mental health counselors. In A. J. Palmo and W. J. Weikel (eds.), *Foundations of Mental Health Counseling*, 95–114. Springfield, IL: Charles C. Thomas.

Brown, D. (1984). Trait and factor theory. In D. Brown, L. Brooks et al., *Career Choice and Development: Applying Contemporary Theory to Practice*, 8–30. San Francisco: Jossey-Bass.

Ellis, A. (1962). *Reason and Emotions in Psychotherapy*. New York: Stuart.

Hartman, B. W., Fuqua, D. R., and Blum, C. R. (1985). A path-analytic model of career indecision. *Vocational Guidance Quarterly* 33:231–40.

Holland, J. L. (1974). Some practical remedies for providing vocational guidance for everyone. *Educational Researcher* 3:9–15.

Krumboltz, J.D. (1983). *Private Rules in Career Decision-Making.* Columbus, OH: National Center for Research in Vocational Education, Ohio State University.

National Career Development Association. (1985). Vocational and career counseling competencies. *Vocational Guidance Quarterly* 24:131–34.

Okun, B. (1984). *Working with Adults: Individual, Family, and Career Dvelopment.* Monterey, CA: Brooks/Cole.

Osipow, S. H., Carney, C. G., Winer, J. L., Yanico, B.J., and Koschir, N.A.(1976). *Career Decision Scale* (2nd ed.). Columbus, OH: Marathon Press.

Parsons, F. (1909). *Choosing a Vocation.* Boston: Houghton-Mifflin.

Super, D. E. (1984). Career and life development. In D. Brown, L. Brooks et al., *Career Choice and Development: Applying Contemporary Theories to Practice,* 192–234. San Francisco: Jossey-Bass.

REFERENCES DEALING WITH BASIC COUNSELING SKILLS

Brammer, L. M. (1988). *The Helping Relationship: Practice and Skills* (4th ed.). Englewood Cliffs, NJ: Prentice-Hall.

Carkhuff, R. R. (1983). *The Art of Helping* (5th ed.). Amherst, MA: Human Resource Development Press.

Egan, G. (1990). *Exercises in Helping Skills: A Training Manual to Accompany the Skilled Helper.* Monterey, CA: Brooks/Cole.

Hutchins, D. E., and Cole, C. G. (1986). *Helping Relationships and Strategies.* Monterey, CA: Brooks/Cole.

CHAPTER 2

The First Interview

The first, or initial, interview is the most crucial interview in the career counseling process. In this interview, the counselor–client counseling contract is set, relationship building and assessment are begun, and the limits of confidentiality are established. Though no exact agenda can ever be established for any counseling interview, the following outline can be considered as a general guide to the first session:

1. Preparation for the interview
2. Meeting the client and building a relationship
3. Structuring: Initial contract setting
4. Structuring: Establishing informal roles
5. Establishing the limits of confidentiality
6. Identifying assessment considerations
7. Housekeeping considerations
8. Termination of the first session

PREPARATION FOR THE INTERVIEW

In some instances, preparation for the first career counseling interview amounts to little more than taking a deep breath, focusing one's self so that clients will receive the attention they deserve, making certain the sessions will not be interrupted by outside intrusions, and waiting.

However, in some agencies such as college counseling centers and private placement offices, the client may have completed a battery of tests,

16

inventories, structured questionnaires, and so on, as a part of an intake procedure or filled out a client data sheet at the time of making the appointment. In public schools, cumulative records are available that contain attendance records, transcripts of courses taken and grades in those courses, and achievement battery profiles, among other records. When data are available, many counselors prefer to carefully review the information so that they can (1) get a preliminary impression of the client, and (2) avoid duplication in the assessment process. Other counselors prefer to review available data after the first interview so that their first impression of the client will come from their interaction with the client. It is recommended that all data be reviewed carefully but that judgment about factors such as client motivation and personality traits be suspended until after face-to-face meetings occur.

Why review client records? One reason is so that duplication of efforts can be avoided. If tests or inventories have been administered previously, there is usually no need to administer them again. Another reason is so that the counselor can demonstrate preparedness for the interview. If clients have taken tests and/or provided information about why they are coming to counseling, they will expect counselors to review that information. Failure to do so may be construed as lack of interest.

Preparation for the first interview may be particularly important if the counselor is white and the client is from an ethnic minority. Although the precise problems associated with ethnic differences in counseling are not well understood (see Sue, 1988), language problems, values differences, and the possibility that the client might prefer a member of his or her own ethnic group should be anticipated. It has also been suggested that clients from some ethnic groups may conceptualize their problems differently from the way a white, middle-class client would, may have different goals, and may have alternate strategies for solving their problems (Sue & Zane, 1987). For example, a client from an ethnic minority may be more likely to see his or her problems as resulting from discrimination, and if he or she is poor, may seek immediate economic relief, as opposed to seeking a career that provides self-actualization. This same client may want answers to the question of how to find a job as opposed to wanting to become engaged in the process of learning how to find a job. These types of problems should be anticipated, and a review of available data may be helpful in this regard.

In summary, a review of available client data can greatly facilitate the counseling process so long as premature conclusions about the client are not drawn on the basis of the data reviewed.

MEETING THE CLIENT AND BUILDING A RELATIONSHIP

It is a basic rule of counseling practice that a counselor should be ready to greet a client once the client arrives for counseling. Failure to observe this principle may communicate lack of interest and impair relationship development.

As Chapter 1 states, techniques regarding relationship development are not discussed in this book. Several excellent sources pertaining to relationship development appear at the end of Chapter 1, however. A good counseling relationship is deemed essential to the success of the career counselor enterprise. Factors that will partially determine whether a facilitative relationship is established are identified in the following list. The counselor

1. Prepares for the counseling sessions.
2. Greets the client and immediately attends to his or her concerns.
3. Communicates, both verbally and nonverbally, warmth, respect, and caring.
4. Is sensitive to cross-cultural and gender concerns of the client.
5. Develops early expectations regarding client's and counselor's roles.
6. Uses good relationship-building strategies.
7. Accurately and efficiently identifies the client's problem and helps the client establish goals.

STRUCTURING: INITIAL CONTRACT SETTING

Contract setting involves exploration of client expectations about counseling outcomes and the counseling process. Clarifying expectations involves securing answers to the following questions:

1. What do you hope will occur as a result of career counseling?
2. How do you expect attainment of these goals to occur within the context of the counseling process?
3. What role do you expect to play in your own goal attainment?
4. What role do you expect the counselor to play in the attainment of your goals?
5. How long do you expect the process to take?

Client expectations may be broken down into two categories: (1)

thoughts about what may happen and (2) thoughts about what ought to happen or must happen if counseling is to be successful.

Just as clients have expectations about the career counseling process, so do counselors. Counselors have expectations that relate to the amount of time that the process may take, the role that the client will play in terms of his or her own change, and the role that the counselor will play in the career counseling process. Again, these expectations can be broken down into (1) thoughts about what may happen during the process, and (2) thoughts about what must happen.

It is probably obvious that a mismatch between the counselor's expectations and the client's expectations will result in an aborted counseling process. Therefore, clarifying the nature of the similarities and differences in this area, particularly with regard to what *must* happen if the process is to be successful, is vital to the success of the enterprise. Then, once expectations are clarified, resolving differences and establishing agreement about what will happen during the process is the essence of contract setting. The following interviews illustrate some of these ideas.

INTERVIEW ONE: ADULT WORKER

After greeting, exchange of pleasantries, and initial exploration of client's concerns, the counselor *(Co:)* begins:

Co: It's important to me to know what you think will happen during our time together.

The client *(Cl:)* responds:

Cl: I'm not sure. I'm hoping to find a more satisfactory job. I was told that you could help me with that. I guess you'll want me to take a few tests and you will want to ask me a few questions. Other than that, I guess I'm not sure what to expect.

Co: So you want to find a more satisfactory job and you're hoping that I can help you with that. I can assure you that I will try, and we may use a few tests and inventories to explore interests and aptitudes.

Another aspect of this that is important to me is that we approach counseling as attacking a problem that will require a great deal of work to solve. That means that we both have to work hard while we are here and that you may have to do some work outside the session such as interviewing workers. What do you think of that?

Cl: I guess it's okay, but I wasn't expecting to do things outside of the counseling sessions. I'm pretty busy on my current job, and time is a real problem.

Co: Well, it's important that we be realistic about outside activities, but some will probably be necessary. You need to do some reading about jobs.

Cl: It seems like this is going to be a bit more involved than I thought, but I'm game. I'll do my best.

Co: Let's summarize a bit just to make sure that we both know what is going to happen here. I'm going to assist you in your search for a more satisfying job. I'll do that by getting to know more about you and your current job and reasons for your dissatisfaction. We may decide you should take some inventories or tests so that we can both enhance our understanding of you as a person and as a worker. I'll also take some of the responsibility of helping you identify resources that may help you find out more about jobs. I'm hoping that you will feel free to share information about yourself as a person and as a worker and why there are problems on your current job. I'm also expecting that you will do certain things outside of counseling that will help the process along.

(Pause)

Co: Is there anything in what I've said that makes you uneasy?

Cl: No. It sounds good to me just so long as we can take my schedule into account. I'm very busy.

INTERVIEW TWO: COLLEGE STUDENT

Co: I read the form you filled out when you made the appointment and you indicated that you want to choose a major.

Cl: Yeah. I've got to declare a major next month at preregistration and I don't have a clue. I've been thinking about it a lot, but so far, I have no good ideas. My roommate thinks I should go into business, but that doesn't sound like a good field to me.

Co: So you have been actively considering majors, but so far you've just drawn a blank, although you haven't completely dismissed business?

Cl: That's right, but I'm just really unsure about that, and my dad told me that you might help.

Co: I'll certainly do my best, and I believe that if we work together, then when preregistration rolls around, you will have some ideas about majors. I usually find that it's a good idea to consider what you might do with a major while you are thinking about choosing one. In other words, what kind of career might result if you choose a particular major?

Cl: That makes sense to me and that's why my roommate suggested business. He said I could get a good job once I graduated. But I'm not sure I'm cut out to go into business.

Co: So the idea of looking at majors in relationship to careers appeals to you. Let's talk about what you expect to occur during counseling.

In interview one, the client's initial goal is fairly clear and, thus, he or she can provide a description of expectations. In interview two, clarification of the initial goal was first conducted, and then roles were discussed. It is quite conceivable that the client in this interview might have declined to participate in career exploration while investigating a college major. Had this occurred, the counselor would have had two courses of action: terminate the session because of incongruity in client/counselor expectations, or work with the client to identify a major. It is not appropriate to establish expectations for counseling and then surreptitiously try to influence the client to pursue the counselor's goals.

Embedded in both interviews one and two is the issue of time. In interview one, the client apparently has a limited amount of time to spend on career counseling and homework activities. In interview two, the student is working against a deadline, which is preregistration. In the latter case, tentative decisions can be made by preregistration and then, if the decision changes, courses can be changed via drop–add. Typically, a counselor will try to work within the time constraints of the client, although this may mean having two sessions a week with the college student or spreading sessions out over a longer period of time for the adult. Regardless of the strategy, some initial agreement (contract) should be reached with each client regarding time. The following excerpts from interviews illustrate this idea:

INTERVIEW ONE: HIGHLY MOTIVATED CLIENT

Co: I'm wondering how many sessions you expect career counseling to take.

Cl: I'm not sure. I had hoped that it wouldn't take long. I'm anxious to get on with a job change.

Co: A lot of factors influence the actual number of session, including your willingness to get involved in activities outside of counseling.

Cl: I'm very willing to get involved. I really want to get started.

Co: I can see how eager you are so, let's look at how often we should meet.

INTERVIEW TWO: CLIENT'S MOTIVATION QUESTIONABLE

Co: Usually, if we deal strictly with the choice of a career, I would expect us to spend one hour per week for from four to six weeks. If other concerns arise, such as how to mesh your career with your spouse's, it might take longer.

Cl: Gee! That sounds like a long time. I had hoped that we could get this over with. I just don't know whether I can come to see you six times.

Co: I can tell that you are reluctant to commit yourself for an extended period of time. I guess I'm wondering if this is the best time to deal with this problem. It seems that there are some other factors in your life that must be dealt with, and that choosing a career is not so important right now.

Cl: Well, it's important, I guess. I just didn't want to spend weeks working on it.

Co: Let's look at some alternative ways to approach the process. One way is to meet twice a week. That means that you have to get very involved in the process both in counseling and the homework assignments that usually grow out of counseling.

Cl: I guess I like that better. I know I need to do it. I just thought it would be easier.

At the culmination of the contract-setting process, an initial goal for career counseling will have been established, the expectations that the client and counselor have of the process will have been clarified and agreed to, and some guidelines regarding the time the process will take will have been established.

An additional statement or two about the initial goal should be made at this point. First, novice counselors often make the mistake of acting as though the initial goal is the final goal of the client. Sometimes it is, but more often it is not. Under all circumstances, the initial goal should be viewed as tentative until a formalized goal-setting process can be instituted. **Do not stop listening to the client to ascertain shifts in goals simply because an initial goal has been established.**

STRUCTURING: ESTABLISHING INFORMAL ROLES

In the foregoing section, the establishment of formal expectations in career counseling was discussed. In this section, the informal establishment of norms that govern career counseling is examined. It is perhaps obvious that it makes little sense for the counselor and client to reach explicit agreement about the goals and process of counseling on one level and then have the counselor undermine those agreements by acting in a manner that is inconsistent with the initial contract. It is obviously counterproductive for the informal aspects of counseling to be incongruent with the formal agreements that have been reached. For example, if the client and the counselor establish that there is to be a continuous series of homework assignments outside the career counseling session, those assignments should be made. Unless the counselor follows through, future agreements with clients will lack credibility. Moreover, and more to the point of this section, certain implicit agreements will develop between the counselor and the client as the counseling process proceeds, and the counselor must follow through on those implicit agreements as well as those established more formally. Consider what type of "agreement" is being reached between the counselor and the client in the following excerpt:

>   *Co:* How old are you?
>   *Cl:* Twenty-one.
>   *Co:* Where were you born?
>   *Cl:* Iowa.
>   *Co:* Where would you like to work?
>   *Cl:* In the Southeast. I'm tired of the cold climate.

Co: You don't like the cold. What do you like best about the Southeast?

Cl: It's warm.

Enough of this ridiculous interview behavior, but what informal agreement is being readied between this client and this counselor? The counselor will ask explicit, closed questions, and the client will give the information provided!

Contrast the foregoing with the following interview:

Co: Tell me a little about yourself.

Cl: I'm twenty-one, and I've lived in Iowa all my life. I'm very interested in moving to a warmer climate, although I'd like to stay in construction. I'm a good mason, and it's something I enjoy.

Co: Even though you enjoy what you do now, you have decided on a move because you are tired of the cold weather. Tell me more about your work.

In this interview, the counselor provides a general stimulus through the use of general leads and open-ended questions, and the client provides the information that will be necessary to fuel the career counseling process.

Other informal agreements stem from the expectations assumed by the counselor. Counselors can assume the expert's role or establish a collaborative role with their clients. It is the authors' opinion that the collaborative role is superior because it empowers the client from the outset. Contrast the following excerpts:

Excerpt One

Cl: I'm hoping to take some tests to find out more about myself.

Co: That's certainly possible. I think the *Self-Directed Search* would be an ideal beginning place.

Excerpt Two

Cl: I'm hoping to take some tests to find out more about myself.

Co: I'm beginning to know a lot about you, but you know yourself better than anyone. Let me describe some inventories and then let you choose the one that will be the most hopeful to you.

Career counselors typically have as their main goal to help the client become an independent decision maker. Certainly, the client in excerpt two is more likely to get the message that he or she is perceived as a person who can make decisions for himself or herself. More important perhaps is the implicit agreement that should develop that the counselor and client are co-equals who bring their own expertise to the counseling process.

Career counselors need to be constantly alert and make certain that their implicit structuring parallels the explicit structuring that has occurred. Similarly, for those aspects of counseling that are primarily implicitly structured, counselors should act in a manner that ensures that the implicit agreements that are reached move the counseling process toward its overall goal of facilitating client growth and problem solving.

ESTABLISHING THE LIMITS OF CONFIDENTIALITY

At some point in the first interview, the matter of confidentiality should be discussed. Essentially, clients should be told that they are entitled to confidentiality unless they or others are in danger. They should also be informed if a supervisor or others will be told the details of the case for supervision purposes. In the excerpt that follows, the counselor is discussing confidentiality with her client.

Co: It is very important that you understand that the things that you tell me will be held in confidence unless there is some evidence that you are about to harm yourself or others. The state of North Carolina also requires that I report cases of child abuse. However, my first concern is always your welfare and I'll act in accordance with that concern. I hope that I have made myself clear in this area.

Cl: I think so. I guess I understand why you'd have to tell others if I was going to hurt myself or others. I don't see any problems.

IDENTIFYING ASSESSMENT CONSIDERATIONS

From the moment test data are consulted prior to the first interview or, if no data are available, from the time of the first meeting, assessment begins.

Test scores and inventory profiles are obvious sources of assessment data. So are the first handshake, eye contact, the manner in which the client is dressed, the nature of the client's speech, nonverbal behavior such as posture, and other sources. In other words, we learn about our clients in a variety of ways. Our work with them requires us to ask a number of questions, not the least of which is "How can we conduct assessments that will enable us to identify those factors that will enable our clients to solve their problems?" This question gets translated into "What information do I need about my client and what specific assessment strategies should I use in assessment?" A partial answer to this question is "I may wish to have information about some or all of the following:

1. Traits including aptitudes, interests, values, and personality variables.
2. Behaviors including interpersonal skills, job skills, work habits, information-seeking skills, test-taking skills, decision-making skills, etc.
3. Cognitions related to either skills, self in general, or perceived ability to perform in a given area (self-efficacy).
4. Knowledge of occupational information, job trends, procedures for securing a job, etc."

Three points should be obvious. First, the strategy used to assess many of the factors on this list is the counseling interview. Second, a variety of other assessment strategies such as the use of tests and inventories may need to be employed in the assessment process. Third, career counselors not only must know how to utilize a variety of assessment strategies, but they must know how to involve their clients in the selection of assessment devices and the utilization of the results from them.

Prior to and during the first career counseling interview, the counselor focuses on the questions posed earlier: "What needs to be assessed?" and "How can it be assessed?"

There are no easy answers to either of the questions of what or how to assess. But in identifying areas that will require assessment, the following suggestions may be helpful:

1. If the client is unaware or unsure about his or her personal behavior or knowledge of an area, assessment of some type is in order.
2. Even if a client possesses a skill (e.g., job interviewing), it is a good idea to discuss his or her self-efficacy regarding the ability to

conduct an interview. A relatively simple way to do this is to ask clients to estimate their ability to conduct a specific act, such as a job interview, on a 1–10 scale (with 1 being very low ability and 10 being very high ability).

3. Very poor decision-making skills (impulsive, dependent), very low levels of self-esteem (I'm just not worth much), or other indicators of cognitive clarity problems indicate that careful consideration needs to be given to whether to proceed with career counseling or switch to personal counseling.

4. Decisions about formal assessment procedures (e.g., tests and inventories) should be made with the client.

HOUSEKEEPING CONSIDERATIONS

For each career counseling process, there are a number of routine concerns that must be dealt with in the first session. Some of these were alluded to earlier. For example, when will we meet? How often will we meet? Where will the meeting occur? And if the client is being charged for the service, either by an agency or a private practitioner, there is the matter of the fee and when and how it is to be paid. There are also concerns about what to do if an appointment is to be missed, where tests and inventories are to be taken if not administered by the counselor, and other details. Satisfactorily dealing with these routine matters can make a great impact on the success of career counseling, and the career counselor needs a checklist to make sure that they are handled adequately. This list might include the following:

1. Appointment slip telling when and where the next appointment is to be held and giving directions for making and breaking counseling appointments.

2. Billing slip stating amount and how it is to be paid (at the session, within thirty days, cash, credit card, etc.).

3. Slip that denotes tests or inventories to be taken and time and place they are to be administered.

TERMINATION OF FIRST SESSION

Termination of the first session should involve a number of activities, including the following:

1. Summary of the content, including the agreements reached by the client and counselor regarding their roles and confidentiality. Either counselor or client can summarize.
2. Homework assignment.
3. "Housekeeping chores" completed.

Two of these activities—summary and homework—are designed to build continuity between session one and subsequent sessions. The summary in session two should focus on both sessions and link them to session three. The summary is then a looking backward ("this is what we have covered") experience. The homework assignment should link what has been covered to what will be covered in the next session (looking forward). The following excerpt illustrates this idea:

Cl: Well, we have agreed that we are going to work together to help me find a more satisfactory job. I understand I will be asked to do a number of things outside of counseling that are supposed to facilitate my getting where I want to go.

Co: That's a good summary. I just want to remind you about confidentiality though.

Cl: Oh yeah, I understand that what I say will be confidential unless I'm going to hurt myself or someone else.

Co: Great, and now I would like to talk about homework to be completed by next week. I'd like for you to make a list of the best and worst times of your job at the end of every day between now and the next time we meet. This will help us develop some insight into your likes and dislikes.

Cl: There won't be many good times.

Co: You're frustrated with your job, but will you be able to make a summary at the end of every workday?

Cl: Sure. I'll just make some notes in my datebook. Who knows, maybe there will be some good times.

Co: Terrific. That's where we'll pick up on May 10 at 6 P.M. right here. I'll put that on a card for you.

SUMMARY OF FIRST INTERVIEW

1. Review all material available regarding the client, being careful not to draw premature conclusions about the client.

2. Prepare yourself mentally by focusing on the client who is coming to see you.

3. Greet the client warmly; use good relationship-building techniques.

4. Establish explicit expectations about roles and the process of career counseling.

5. Conduct yourself so that implicit assumptions do not contradict explicit assumptions.

6. Discuss/explain confidentiality.

7. Begin to identify types of assessment data needed.

8. Determine presenting problem/goal.

9. Assess motivation.

10. Terminate by building a bridge to the next session.

LEARNING TO CONDUCT THE FIRST INTERVIEW

A. Working with a client from your field experience, complete a first interview and incorporate the following exercise:

1. Preview the session by reviewing all case material available. Draw a list of tentative conclusions about the client on the basis of the previous material. *Do not act on these conclusions during counseling.*

2. Meet the client. Notice handshake, eye contact, voice inflection, and posture.

Is the client self-confident? Anxious? Concerned?

3. Identify the client's initial goal. How confident are you that this will be his or her goal when actual goal-setting occurs?

4. Determine the client's expectations of career counseling.

5. How well does the client accept your expectations?

6. Explain confidentiality.

7. Summarize.

8. Handle housekeeping chores.

9. Make homework assignment (e.g., "Think about your interests.")

10. Get feedback from supervisor as appropriate.

B. Answer the following questions:
1. How accurate were your conclusions about the client based on previous data? More important, how many of your conclusions were incorrect?
2. How compatible were the client's expectations of counseling and yours? If these differences had not been clarified, would they have caused a problem in counseling?
3. What client concerns require additional assessment? How do you plan to conduct this assessment?
4. How will you begin the next session?

If you are not e' rolled in a field experience, ask a career counselor for material that has had names and other identifying information removed, and conduct steps A1–10 of the above exercise. Have a career counselor give you feedback on your accuracy.

SUMMARY

There are five aspects of the first interview: preparation; greeting and establishing a relationship with the client; structuring; making a tentative list of assessment considerations; and termination. Confidentiality and routine considerations must also be handled during the first session. For the most part, there is no established way to deal with any of these aspects and, thus, alternative approaches were presented. However, you should evaluate each approach that you try in order to determine which is best for you.

REFERENCES AND SUGGESTED READINGS

Sue, S. (1988). Psychotherapeutic services for ethnic minorities: Two decades of research findings. *American Psychologist* 43:301–08.
Sue, S., and Zane, N. (1987). The role of culture and cultural techniques for psychotherapy: A critique and reformulation. *American Psychologist* 42:37–45

3

Interview-Based Assessment and Pre-Goal-Setting Intervention in Career Counseling

DEFINITIONS

The title of this chapter will be a bit confusing for some readers who are accustomed to thinking about counseling in discrete stages such as relationship development, problem identification, goal setting, intervention to deal with the identified problem, and termination. The model of career counseling that we are proposing is a bit more sophisticated than this five-step model and, as explained in Chapter 1, the process is not expected to follow a linear progression. But the question remains: "What are interview-based assessment and pre-goal-setting intervention?" First, interview-based assessment is one aspect of clinical assessment in which the counselor collects information about the client's problem and arrives at a conclusion (diagnostic label) about the nature of that problem. Data from other sources such as tests and inventories are also used in many instances in that portion of clinical assessment in which the counselor is trying to pinpoint the nature of the client's problem. Interview-based

31

assessment continues throughout the counseling process as the counselor attempts not only to identify the nature of the client's problem but also to monitor the impact of subsequent interventions. This chapter focuses only on the use of the interview to collect and use data to determine the client's main concern.

Second, the idea of pre-goal-setting intervention also deserves some clarification. In the five-stage model, intervention refers to the process engaged in by the client and counselor to solve the career or life-related problems that have been identified and targeted in the previous stages. Pre-goal-setting interventions are those activities engaged in by the counselor and client to facilitate and maintain the counseling relationship. The technique of confrontation (Egan, 1975) is in reality an intervention engaged in by the counselor for the purposes of maintaining and enhancing the counseling relationship and is frequently used prior to goal-setting. Some other pre-goal-setting interventions are discussed later in this chapter.

OVERVIEW

This chapter deals primarily with those interview-based assessment procedures that a counselor may utilize to discern cognitive clarity deficiencies and/or client motivational concerns that may result either in premature termination of counseling or in some way may limit the client's ability to derive maximum benefit from the process (e.g., self-limiting cognitions). Some attention is given to the use of the interview to assess the client's career-related concerns but, for the most part, these considerations have been placed in subsequent chapters. Moreover, discussion of tests and inventories in the assessment process has been placed in a later chapter with one exception: a few inventories that may be useful in assessing the sources of cognitive clarity problems will be discussed.

It is expected that at the conclusion of this chapter the reader will have a thorough understanding of sources of cognitive clarity problems and how they can be assessed and ameliorated. As was noted in Chapter 1, cognitive clarity deficiencies stem from mental health problems. For the most part, strategies for dealing with severe mental health problems are not included in this discussion because literally hundreds of books have been written about this topic.

Another expectation is that the reader will develop some sense of client motivational problems that may impair or abort career counseling and will develop an understanding of how these may be handled in the context of counseling.

Finally, it is worth noting that the rationale for many of the ideas mentioned in this chapter derive from the work of Beck (1976), Bandura (1977; 1982), and to a lesser extent, Super (1990).

INTERVIEW-BASED ASSESSMENT

Throughout the career counseling process, the counselor is continuously generating hypotheses about the client. Some of these hypotheses will develop intuitively, but all will need to be verified with the client The view of the counselor as a hypothesis tester presented in this chapter is not new. As Strohmer and Newman (1983) point out, this perspective goes back more than fifty years. They also indicate that counselors probably use two bases for generating hypotheses about clients: their formal counseling theory and their informal theory of human functioning. Formal theories are those that have been generated by counseling theorists, are taught in theory classes, and have, one hopes, been supported by empirical studies. Informal "theories" spring from counselors' implicit beliefs about the way people function and are probably related to a variety of factors, including perceptions of self, socialization experiences, and so forth. Career counselors should be operating more upon formal than upon informal theories as they assess their clients' difficulties.

Regardless of the "theory" utilized by the counselor, it is important that assessment in career counseling involve a full-blown exploration of the functioning of the client rather than one designed to confirm counselors' perceptions about the way people function. For example, if counselors take the perspective that informational deficits are the basis for all career-related problems, it is likely that interview behavior will focus only on what clients know (or do not know) about themselves and careers. The result is likely to be that many factors relating to career choice or career adjustment will be overlooked.

The process of assessing client concerns is a dynamic one in that the counselor is simultaneously examining cognitive clarity, career problems, the interaction of other life roles and work, and problems within the counseling relationship.

It typically begins with the client's self-diagnosis, which is disclosed to the counselor as the presenting problem. This initial statement of the problem may range from "I don't know what is wrong with me. I just cannot get excited about choosing a career" to "I know exactly what is wrong. This job has me totally stressed out. I need a job where I can work with people under less stressful conditions."

Once the client's self-diagnosis has been presented, career counselors will engage in a variety of strategies designed to develop an information base on which their own diagnosis can rest. As noted earlier, these interview strategies typically are based on the career counselor's theoretical perspective on why individuals have career-related problems. For example, a trait and factor counselor, assuming that a career problem is related to informational deficits, will attempt to discern deficiencies that exist in the client's information about self and the world of work. Counseling leads about interests, values, personality traits, and how these relate to various jobs are sure to characterize the interview behavior of this counselor. Other counselors, operating on different assumptions, will present leads to the clients that are designed to elicit other types of information, such as career maturity (e.g., information about work, decision-making style, attitudes) (Super, 1990) or the bases for self-observed generalizations (e.g., self-efficacy, perception of abilities, etc.) (Mitchell & Krumboltz, 1990).

During the counseling interview(s), career counselors form and, at times, discard hypotheses that relate to reasons for the client's problem. For example, a counselor may assume, on the basis of an early client disclosure, that a college student's inability to "stand up to" a domineering parent is contributing to her inability to make a career choice, since a conflict exists between the parent's and the client's wishes. Later, this hypothesis may be discarded as the counselor learns that the client has indeed asserted herself in the face of parental opposition in the past.

As noted in Chapter 2, career counseling involves not only diagnosing the problem but also includes establishing goals, selecting interventions to attain goals, and evaluating whether the goals have been attained. Counselors must not only assess the career-related problem but must assess problems that will preclude or interfere with the client choosing a career, making an adjustment within his or her current position, or establishing goals that will maximize the client's potential as a worker. Accordingly, career counselors must diagnose and intervene in two overlapping concerns—cognitive clarity and motivation—prior to establishing goals to choose or modify a career. Both of these concerns are discussed in detail subsequently.

ASSUMPTIONS OF ASSESSMENT

There are as many approaches to assessing clients' career problems as there are career counselors, although it is probably the case that there are some common elements in most approaches to assessment. It is the purpose of this chapter to identify what we believe *should be* the common elements in interview-based assessment of career-related problems. This discussion is predicated on several key assumptions, the first of which is that career choice and adjustment decisions cannot be adequately addressed if the client is experiencing a debilitating psychological problem.

For example, a career counselor in a Veteran's Administration Hospital was faced with providing career counseling to a schizophrenic who still suffered from paranoid delusions. In another situation, a high school counselor was faced with a student who "was not college material" even though she had straight A's and an IQ that exceeded 140. The ability to make good decisions about one's career is dependent on the ability to fully understand one's self and environment and how the interaction between self and various aspects of the environment occurs. While there is no such phenomenon as immaculate perception, clients with psychological problems such as very low self-esteem or compulsions to act on injunctions from the past ("you must," "you should") are often not in a position to make choices that will maximize the utilization of their talents and implement their career-related values. These clients either cannot or should not trust their own judgments because their perceptions of their worlds are limited by their problems. Until debilitating problems that limit cognitive clarity are overcome, decision-making about career-related problems should probably be postponed (Brown & Brooks, 1985).

It is undoubtedly a fact that all human beings have some limits on their cognitive clarity. The career counselor's dilemma to know when the problem is severe enough that career counseling should be postponed in favor of addressing the mental health problem. One indicator that career counseling should be postponed is that the psychological problem has limited career choice, change, or advancement in the past. If low self-esteem has precluded risk-taking behavior in choosing college majors, applying for new jobs, or relocation, then it is a virtual certainty that it will restrict decision making in the career counseling process. Depression, severe nonassertiveness, overwhelming grief in the face of a loss, extreme authoritarianism, very poor social skills, phobias that relate to on-the-job behavior, panic attacks, and impulsive or dependent decisionmaking styles are all examples of problems that limit the clients' ability to make good career decisions and, if they have been exhibited in the past and currently appear to be present, career counseling should be postponed.

On the other hand, less severe problems such as low self-efficacy regarding making a "good" choice, or injunctions such as, "I must choose an occupation that is stereotypically associated with my gender," can often be handled within the context of career counseling. Examples of these less-severe types of problems and some suggestions for dealing with them are presented later in this chapter.

The second assumption underpinning this discussion is that client motivation to complete the career counseling process is essential. Motivational problems may result from mental health problems (severe or moderate) and thus may be linked to cognitive clarity. However, persons who have few mental health problems may not have a high degree of motivation to participate in career counseling. For example, it is unlikely that many fifteen-year-olds are developmentally ready to engage in an intense process devoted to discovering their life's work. Motivational problems may also stem from problems with cognitive clarity such as a simple informational deficit, for instance, not recognizing that the time has arrived to choose or change a career, or from a more complex issue associated with the counseling process itself. Some black clients may doubt the ability of a white counselor to assist them with their problems. Regardless of the source of the motivational problem, it must be identified and resolved prior to the process of goal setting.

The third assumption underlying this discussion is that clients' roles as workers are inextricably linked to other life roles: they are interdependent. The implication of this assumption is that change in the work role affects others and thus career planning or readjustment should proceed only in the context of other life roles. If the client is making an initial career choice, the implications of that choice for other life roles needs to be addressed. If the client is considering a job change or adjustment within the current work roles, the change should be considered in light of its impact upon other life roles and vice versa. Career counselors must, therefore, be able to assess, to some degree, the potential interaction of life roles for the career planning and make a definitive diagnosis of these interactions with the career changer. Interrole assessment is discussed in more detail later in the book.

The fourth assumption of this discussion is that the assessment process varies, to some degree, for clients who are making first-time choices and those who are making changes or adjustments in their career status. Clients who fall into the first category are often young and require, along with assistance in career planning, help with defining the relationship of career to other life roles and planning for the integration of these roles. In dealing with a client who is making an initial career choice, the counselor must discern, among other points, (1) degree of self-awareness, (2) knowledge about occupations or world of work, (3) degree of awareness of appropriate career opportunities, (4) deficits that may hinder career selection such as use of poor decision-making strategies, (5) client's confidence in ability to choose a career, and (6) client's skills relating to implementing career choice such as job search and job interviewing skills. With regard to integrating career into other life roles, the counselor needs to assess (1) awareness of the relationship of career to such life roles as leisure, marriage, and citizen; (2) degree to which career and other life roles are planned to be complementary; and (3) skills in planning with significant others to implement a life plan.

Assisting a client who is changing careers involves additional types of assessment. For example, assessing whether a client has a psychological problem is confounded by the realization that symptoms such as mild depression, chronic headaches, lower back pains, reduced motivation, and certain physical problems such as ulcers and heart disease can result from environmental stressors (for a fuller discussion of these issues, see Brown, 1985; Sharif & Salvendy, 1982; and Smith, 1989). It is therefore incumbent upon career counselors not only to assess intrapsychic variables (e.g., cognitions), but also to examine their clients' functioning in various life roles in order to ascertain specific sources of stress and how these are either attenuated or compounded by the relationship of various life roles (e.g., work and its relationship to leisure). This type of assessment requires the counselor to examine what we have called "intrarole congruence" as well as interrole interaction (Brown & Brooks, 1985). For example, a client may have a good job, a good marriage, and a satisfactory leisure life when examined independently. But when the roles are examined collectively, the picture that results is of a person who is overcommitted, under severe stress, and well on his or her way to being burned out. On the other hand, the career counselor may discover that intrarole incongruence in the work role is having a negative impact on other life roles that otherwise would be functioning successfully. The assessment of intrarole congruence and interrole interaction can lead to the determination that a number of problems exist. However, deciding on a course of action requires some additional assessments.

Persons contemplating a job change must determine (1) whether or not they have the needed skills to change to a new career, and if not, if they can acquire those skills; (2) if those with whom they are associated (e.g., spouse and family members) are able to accommodate the change if it requires relocation, a permanent or temporary loss of salary, reduced status, and so on; and (3) if their personal characteristics (age, health, handicaps, etc.) allow them to make a change.

As is obvious at this point, there are many factors to consider when assisting a career changer. To summarize, these are (given that cognitive clarity is present) as follows:

1. Is there intrarole congruence in the job?
2. Is there intrarole incongruence in other life roles (e.g., family) that is influencing the individual's functioning on the job?
3. Has the client allowed his or her skills to become obsolete,

resulting in intrarole incongruence? Can this situation be remedied if the answer is yes?

4. Does the interaction of life roles compound stress?

5. Is it possible to develop compensatory life roles (e.g., leisure) that will offset job stress and thus make the client's job acceptable?

6. Does the client possess the skills needed to move to a more acceptable job? Can these be required if the answer is no?

7. Do significant others, such as family members, make it impossible for the person to make a job change?

8. Do personal variables such as age, health, or handicaps make it difficult or impossible to make a job change?

9. Would a change within the job role be acceptable to the employer and client?

10. What is the degree to which the client is motivated to choose a career or to change an existing one? (Brown & Brooks, 1985)

The fifth and final assumption underpinning this discussion is that, often, prior to the point in the counseling process where the client establishes a goal to choose or change a career, a series of interventions is necessary to correct cognitive clarity problems, to deal with motivational concerns or, if these two problems are not directly interrelated, to do both.

ASSESSMENT AND HYPOTHESIS DEVELOPMENT

As can be seen from the foregoing discussion, assessment within career counseling is quite complex. As was also noted, the career counselor develops a series of hypotheses about both the career-related problems of the client and the likelihood that the client can maximize choices.

The first of these hypotheses has to do with cognitive clarity and the motivation of the counselee. In Chapter 1, two general assessment scenarios are presented in the discussion of the process of career counseling. In the first, the client possesses sufficient cognitive clarity and motivation that career counseling may be pursued directly. In the second, cognitive clarity and/or motivation is lacking. Personal counseling is a prerequisite to career counseling in this case. While these two scenarios provide an outline of the assessment process, several other steps must be included in order to depict the full complexity of the processes.

TABLE 3.1 Assessment in Career Counseling—Simple

Step 1	Cognitive clarity present— yes.
Step 2	Client motivation present— yes.
Step 3	Client self-diagnosis— offered.
Step 4	Client self-diagnosis explored— confirmed.

Table 3.1 contains a skeletal outline of a total but simple assessment process. This table is not intended to provide a temporal depiction of the process, only an outline of what may occur. However, at some point in career counseling, an assessment must be made that cognitive clarity and motivation are present, a client self-diagnosis must occur, and this self-diagnosis must either be confirmed or disconfirmed. That process is illustrated in Table 3.2.

In Table 3.3, illustrative assessment hypotheses are shown for a person exploring the possibility of a job change. As can be seen also in Table 3.3, specific hypotheses are developed and reshaped as the counselor interacts with the client

As also noted in Table 3.3 (e.g., steps 5.3 and 6.0), the client plays a crucial role in shaping the assessment and final goal. As shown, the counselor *develops hypotheses*. These are often shared with the client for acceptance or rejection. Acceptance of the counselor's hypothesis about the problem is a prerequisite to goal setting. Rejection of the counselor's hypotheses suggests the need to expand the database about the client until an assessment of the nature of the problem is generated.

The actual process of taking the assessment and shaping counseling goals is discussed in Chapter 9. In the remainder of this chapter, some strategies for assessing and intervening in cognitive clarity, client motivation, intrarole congruence, and interrole relationships are discussed.

TABLE 3.2 Assessment in Career Counseling—Complex

Step 1	Self-diagnosis presented.
Step 2	Self-diagnosis disconfirmed; cognitive clarity diagnosed as a problem.
Step 3	Personal problem addressed.
Step 4	Client self-diagnosis represented.
Step 5	Self-diagnosis disconfirmed; counselor shares diagnostic hypothesis.
Step 6	Client accepts counselor view.

TABLE 3.3   Assessment Hypothesis: Development with Employed Worker

1.0	No cognitive clarity problems.
2.0	Motivational problem— individual discouraged about lack of options.
3.0	Motivational problem resolved—stress has resulted in "burnout." Client seems to make poor personal decisions and admittedly made poor career decision at the outset.
4.0	New data suggest decision-making skills satisfactory. Client has difficulty with self-awareness (e.g., understanding what is really right for him or her).
5.0	Other information presented:
5.1	Spouse inflexible—relocation not possible.
5.2	Client has unique skills— not transferable to other job
5.3	Client rejects retraining because of age.
6.0	Counselor suggests need to develop more self-awareness—client agrees.
7.0	Exploration suggests some aspects of current job consistent with values.
8.0	Goal becomes readjustment *within* work role and the development of compensatory life roles that are related to values.

ASSESSING AND CORRECTING COGNITIVE CLARITY WITHIN CAREER COUNSELING

It is outside the scope of this book to discuss the assessment of severe mental illness, although examples of mental health problems that might result in postponing career counseling are given earlier in this chapter and in Chapter 2. What is discussed in this section is assessing indicators of cognitive clarity that can and should be handled within the context of career counseling.

Krumboltz (1983) lists nearly a dozen ways of assessing cognitive clarity including structured and unstructured interviews, free association, reconstructing prior events, self-monitoring, drawing inferences from behavior, and the uses of psychometric instruments. Of these, the most commonly used approach is the approach we discuss here, the unstructured interview. What follows is a list of indicators that cognitive clarity may be deficient, followed by a client verbalization that portrays the presence of the indicator. The client verbalization is followed first by a suggested strategy for intervening with the problem portrayed, and then by a brief excerpt from a counseling session illustrating how the career counselor might approach a client who lacks cognitive clarity.

1. Misinformation [Simple]

Cl: Only rich kids can go to that university. I wouldn't want to go there anyway. They're just a bunch of snobs. Most of them are from the Northeast and couldn't get into Ivy League schools.

Intervention: Information Giving

Co: You have developed some pretty strong negative feeling about X University, but the university does have an extensive scholarship program, and while many of the students have been from the Northeast in the past, that picture is changing. So is the fact that X is a "second choice" school.

2. Misinformation [Complex]

Cl: (From No.1) I still don't buy it. X seems like a school for Northeastern snobs to me. I've met four students from there and they are all the same.

Intervention: Logical Analysis (Ellis, 1973)

A. Logically analyze problems
B. Provide analysis
C. Restructure faulty logic system

Co: Let's look at what you just said from a logical perspective. First, there are well over 5000 students at X. You have met four of them. That's a limited sample from which to draw conclusions. Let's look at the total picture. You may not like X after the examination, but it's important to make decisions based on facts, not stereotypes.

3. Lack of Specificity

Cl: They say it's impossible to get a good teaching job these days.

Intervention: Concreteness [Specification]

Co: I'm wondering who "they" are?
Cl.: Well, everyone—my advisor, my professors, even my relatives who teach.
Co: Well, let's look at the facts.

4. Assumed Impossibility/Inevitability

Cl: I could never make it through medical school.
Co.: But your grades here have been quite good.
Cl: But I'd flunk. My friend Jim went over there and he had to drop out because of grades.

Intervention: Logical Analysis (Ellis, 1973); Encouragement (Bandura, 1977)

Co: You are certain that you are going to fail in medical school, partially because your friend Jim did. Let's look at the similarities between yourself and Jim.

5. Cause-and-Effect Errors

Cl: I've considered going into business, but most women in that field end up getting divorced.

Intervention: Logical Analysis (Ellis, 1973)

Co: You are afraid that you will end up being divorced if you enter business. Let's look at some statistics regarding divorce for women in business and for those who go into other fields.

6. Sabotaged Communication [Yet, but]

Co: You have told me that you are having a great deal of difficulty following through on the homework assignments I have made. I wonder if it would be helpful if I make a call or two myself to arrange for some job shadowing opportunities?

Cl: That sounds great! Did you know there could still be some problems because of my work schedule, and my car isn't that reliable?

Intervention: Refocus on Resistance

Co: I'm wondering if career problems may not be your major concern. It seems that each time I make a suggestion, you reject it. Let's talk about how you feel when you think of the problem being solved.

7. Injunctions

Cl: I've got to be a lawyer. My dad's a lawyer, my grandfather is a lawyer, and my brothers and sisters are lawyers.

Co: It sort of feels inevitable that you will become a lawyer.

Cl: Yeah. It's definitely expected.

Co: What would happen if you didn't become a lawyer?

Cl: All hell would break loose, and I would feel terrible.

Intervention: RET Techniques (Ellis, 1973)

    A. Identify irrational thoughts
       1. Life should be as I want it to be
       2. If I feel upset, it is awful
       3. I am worthless, undeserving of self-respect
    B. Explain ABC's
       1. A = precipitating event (turned down by employer; fail to get promotion)
       2. B = irrational thought (I am worthless)
       3. C = emotional and behavioral consequence

    C. Teach them that they feel bad not because of A, but because of B, that is, their beliefs about A
      1. They will feel bad as long as they hold beliefs
      2. Model alternative beliefs
      3. Challenge beliefs
      4. Ask for commitments to change

Co: In other words, you would feel terrible if you didn't do what others wanted you to do. Let's look at that statement from an ABC perspective.

8. Polarized Thinking

Cl: For me, it's engineering or nothing. I just cannot imagine myself doing anything else.

Co: Sounds as though it would be a disaster if you cannot fulfill your goal of being an engineer. But your grades have not been satisfactory in engineering.

Cl: It scares me to death. I'm about to flunk out and that's it for me.

Co: I'm sure it is scary when you think of a life with no alternative.

Intervention: Paradoxical Thinking—Prescribing the Symptom (DeBord, 1989)

    A. Identify thinking to be changed
    B. Contract to change thinking
    C. Then urge person to continue thinking

Co: I think that you would agree that you need to change your thinking about engineering.

Cl: Yeah, but I don't seem to be able to do it.

Co: I have a suggestion for you. I want you to hold this thought in your mind: "It's engineering or nothing." Every waking hour of every day until next week, you are to think that thought over and over again or constantly, if you can.

I know we have agreed that you need to change thinking, but try not to. I'm sure you can maintain that thought.

9. Filtering—Hearing Only the Bad or Good

Cl: My supervisor never says anything good to me. She is always on my tail about something. The other day, she did give me a left-handed compliment—said my desk was clean. Really meant I wasn't doing anything.

Co: Seems like your supervisor is on your case all the time.

Intervention: Reframing [Changing Perceptions] (DeBord, 1989; Haley, 1976).
Also, paradoxical techniques (see No. 8). Reframing attempts to change a perceptual set about a person or activity by emphasizing the positive.

Co: Let's look at an alternative view. Maybe your supervisor's comments are keeping you on task regardless of her intentions. Her behavior may not be pleasant, but it keeps you performing at a high level, and I'm sure others notice.

10. Heaven Will Be My Reward [Martyr]

Cl: My life at this point doesn't matter. I know that if I just do what I'm supposed to, things will be better in the future. It's tough sometimes—but I just have to hang in there.

Co: You feel like there is a way that you should respond, and if you do, your life will get better.

Intervention: Logical Analysis

Co: Let's examine your logic. You state that if you just continue with the same approach to your career, things will get better. However, you also state that the situation in the job has remained the same for you.

11. Blaming

Cl: I'm just like my dad. He drank on the job too. People have always told me that I'm just like him. And with every passing day, I know that it's true.

Intervention: Confrontation, Logical Analysis

Co: Sounds like you have decided to blame your dad for your drinking problem. Let's look at how true that statement may be. Since alcoholism may have a genetic component, your father may have inadvertently been a contributor. But what about your role...?

12. Faulty Decision-Making Style

Cl: I can't help it. When I've got an important decision to make, I just want to get it made and get it over with. Did you know that I chose this school because it was the first one that I received an application for?

Co: Sounds like making decisions causes a lot of anxiety, and you make a choice rather than deal with the discomfort.

Intervention: Deep breathing to cope with anxiety; use decision-making aids (see Chapter 12)

Co: Let's first look at the anxiety that arises from certain decisions and deal with that. Then let's look at some systematic ways to make decisions.

13. Lack of Self-Awareness

Cl: It's hard for me to understand why people react to me as they do. I mean well. But it seems that I'm always stepping on someone's toes.

Co: It's a bit upsetting when people's reactions to you don't meet with your own expectations.

Cl: It's downright depressing. I'm an outcast at the office.

Intervention: Metaphor or Parables—Stories that reframe or develop insight into person's cognitions (Wessler & Wessler, 1980)

Co: Tell me a story/joke/nursery rhyme that depicts how people see you.

Cl: This may seem strange, but I feel like the ugly duckling. Every time I do something I get punished for it.

Co: Do you remember how that nursery rhyme ended?

Cl: No.

Co: Well, the ugly duckling turned into a beautiful swan that was accepted by all.

Cl: That's not going to happen to me.

Co: Since we are on nursery rhymes, do you remember the story about the little train that couldn't?

Cl: Sure, when he started saying "I can," he did climb the hill.

Co: It seems to me that you are always saying to yourself "I can't."

14. Low Self-Esteem Resulting from High, Unachievable Standards

Cl: I do well, but I always feel bad because it just never seems to be enough. I know that I can do better. Even when people tell me I've done well, I know that what I did wasn't really that good.

Intervention: Disputing Irrational Beliefs (Ellis, 1973); Paradoxical Techniques (DeBord, 1989); Fantasy (see Chapter 19)

Co: It sounds to me as though you want to be perfect, and it's just terrible when you aren't.

Cl: What do you mean?

Co: Well, you are never satisfied. But is it rational to expect perfection?

or

Would you agree that you need to start giving yourself credit for your accomplishments?

Cl: Yes, so long as they are really good work.

Co: OK, I want you to hold this thought until we meet again. "I must be perfect in all that I do."

Cl: That seems to contradict what you have been saying to me.

Co: We'll talk about the reasons next time. Just hold the thought and try to apply it. Remember: "I must be perfect."

15. Powerlessness

Cl: I just cannot deal with all of this. I've got my family and I have to get a job. I'm so frustrated by the whole situation—partially because I can never cope with the problem.

Intervention: Guided Fantasy (see Chapter 19)

Co: You're frustrated, as well as feeling overwhelmed. I would like to try a technique known as guided fantasy as one way to help you deal with your feelings of powerlessness.

Cl: OK.

Co: I'm going to have you relax and then introduce you to a fantasy that will emphasize your personal power.

16. Stereotyping

Cl: Some people have suggested that I consider nursing, but I just cannot see me working with all those women.

Intervention: Information: Challenging Assumptions

Co: You seem to think that only women go into nursing.
Cl: That's right. I've never seen a male nurse, although I have seen men in the hospital.
Co: Let's take a close look at nursing and the number of men involved. (Give information.)
Cl: But what about those guys? I'm not sure that I want to be like they are.
Co: You're not sure that the men who do go into nursing are the same type of man that you see yourself as being. Tell me a bit more about how you see those men, and contrast your perceptions with how you see yourself.

The foregoing presentation is not an exhaustive list of verbalizations that indicate the presence of cognitive clarity deficiencies. Neither is the list of interventions presented meant to encompass the only approaches that can be utilized by the counselor to cope with these concerns.

OTHER COGNITIVE CLARITY ASSESSMENT STRATEGIES

Several other cognitive clarity assessment strategies tested by Krumboltz (1983) appear potentially useful and will be discussed here. For example, Krumboltz suggests that clients test their thoughts about their career plans with a counselor. These thoughts may provide some insight into possible cognitive clarity problems, particularly if they are negative. Similarly, clients might be asked to think out loud as they consider information about certain careers or as they consider various aspects of the decision-making process (e.g., choosing). Both thought-listing and think-aloud strategies *require* clients to vocalize their thoughts either in simulations of or while involved in real career decision-making activities. Once thoughts are verbalized, they can be examined for their rational, counterproductive contents.

Krumboltz also suggests that a technique developed by Hollon and Kendall (1981) called Dysfunctional Thought Record (DTR) may be useful in career counseling. Use of the DTR requires the client to describe a problem such as choosing a career or choosing among alternatives and then identify the emotions and thoughts associated with the problem. In the DTR approach, clients are also asked to counter their irrational thoughts using techniques developed by Ellis (1973), although this intervention phase would not have to be employed as a part of the assessment strategy.

Finally, Krumboltz (1983, pp. 23–24) lists a number of psychometric instruments that may be useful in assessing cognitive clarity. This list and the description provided by Krumboltz follow:

a) *A Questionnaire to Determine Beliefs About Career Decision Making (Mitchell and Krumboltz, cited by Mitchell, 1980).* This thirty-nine-item questionnaire asks subjects to assess the degree to which they believe their current interests, values, skills, and personality traits are constant over time. They are asked to rate their capabilities to succeed and to plan a career. They report their degree of anxiety about career planning, describe the way in which they think a career decision should be made, and report the extent to which they endorse certain irrational attitudes. Eight subscores are calculated: rigid behavior, rigid beliefs, confidence in beliefs, desire to change beliefs, fear of failure, nonrational career decision-making style, maladaptive emotionality, and overgeneralization.

b) *Inventory of Anxiety in Decision Making (Mendonca, 1974).* This inventory is in two parts. The first part presents ten common types of vocational decisions and asks respondents to write specific instances of current decision problems and rate their difficulty. In the second part subjects respond on a 5-point scale to descriptions of possible emotional reactions to the process of wrestling with a vocational problem.

c) *An Attitudinal Assessment of Decision Making (item wording by Clarke Carney, instructions and rating scales devised by Mitchell, 1980).* Fifty-one items are presented, and two subscores are derived: maladaptive behavior (e.g., "I avoid responsibility for the choice") and maladaptive belief (e.g., "Others know what's best for me").

d) *Efficacy Questionnaire (Mitchell, Krumboltz, and Kinnier, cited in Mitchell [1980]).* This questionnaire was designed to evaluate the effectiveness of a career decision-making workshop. Subjects identify which particular skills have been learned, which decisions they are currently in the process of making, the extent to which they have learned any useful skills for making those decisions, the degree to which they are satisfied with the outcomes of the decisions they have already made, and the extent to which they are confident that they can make each decision produce satisfying outcomes. Representative decision situations include "deciding on an expensive purchase," "deciding on a summer job," and "deciding on a program of study for the next year."

e) *My Vocational Situation (Holland, Daiger, & Power, 1980)*. Three subscores are derived from this inventory: the identity scale (e.g., "I don't know what my major strengths and weaknesses are"), the information scale (e.g., "I need the following information: how to find a job in my chosen field"), and the barriers scale (e.g., "I lack the special talents to follow my first choice"). Holland, Gottfredson, and Power (1980) have presented some evidence for the construct validity of these scales.

f) *The Career Decision Scale (3rd ed.) (Osipow et al., 1976)*. This short eighteen-item questionnaire is designed to identify specific reasons why people might be undecided about a career choice (e.g., lack of information, need to satisfy others). A manual summarizing some of the research that has been done on the instrument has been prepared by Osipow (1980).

ASSESSING CLIENT MOTIVATION

Client motivation, or the willingness of the client to participate in and follow through to completion, is always a problem for career and other types of counselors. Lack of motivation can be tied to a variety of factors, including lack of cognitive clarity. For example, the persons who suffer from low self-esteem because they have set unattainable personal goals may not be highly motivated to follow through to completion in career counseling. Similarly, the person who engages in polarized thinking ("it's medical school or failure") may not continue in career counseling once medicine is eliminated as a career option. Career counselors must learn to anticipate motivational problems and eliminate them if they are to keep many of their clients from prematurely terminating the counseling process. In addition to assessing cognitive clarity deficiencies, the following assessments should be made. (This discussion is based on Bandura, 1977; 1982).

1. How important is choosing a career/changing an existing career at this point? (Appraisal of the importance of the situation)
2. How confident is the client that he or she can successfully choose a career or change his or her current career? (Self-efficacy expectations)

3. How confident is the client that he or she will improve his or her situation?

Does the client feel that there is a possibility that he or she will be worse off than he or she is now? (Outcome expectations)

4. How important is it to the client to do a "good job" in choosing or changing his or her career? (Standards of performance)

Much of the assessment of motivational influences can be conducted merely by attending to key client disclosures about motivation. Some examples of these follow.

1. Importance Attached to Decision

Low

(a)   *Cl:*   My father said I needed to choose a career.

(b)   *Cl:*   Well, it's time to choose a major. I suppose I should also consider what I'm going to do with my education.

Medium

(a)   *Cl:*   My unemployment payments are running out. I need to get another job.

(b)   *Cl:*   All my friends are making decisions about their lives. I should be doing the same thing.

High

(a)   *Cl:*   I just feel like I'll be more motivated to do well in school if I know where this is all leading. I'm that kind of person.

(b)   *Cl:*   I know that I'm worth more than I'm making. I want to find a job that will allow me to earn what I'm worth.

(c)   *Cl:*   The last thing I want to do is end my career in that place. I'd like one shot at doing something really important.

2. Confidence in Ability

(a)   *Cl:*   I've never been very good at figuring things out for myself. I just cannot get things right.

(b)   *Cl:*   My mother told me to get some help because I'd screw it up and she's probably right.

Medium

(a)   *Cl:*   I have some ideas about choosing a career, but I still feel like I need a lot of help.

(b)   *Cl:*   My friends tell me I have a lot of personal insight and they are right, to some degree. However, I feel like I'm going to need a lot of help in choosing the right job for me.

High

(a)   *Cl:*   I'm pretty sure I know what I want to do, but I would like to confirm that nursing is the right choice for me.

(b)   *Cl:*   I don't think this will take very long. I've already talked things over with my wife, and she agrees that I'm on the right track.

3. Confidence in Outcomes

Low

(a)   *Cl:*   I'm not very sure that things can get better. The job market seems pretty bleak right now.

(b)   *Cl:*   I've got a good job. I'm just unhappy doing it. I don't see how I can improve my situation, but the thought keeps nagging at me that I should try.

Medium

(a)   *Cl:*   I'd estimate that my chances of getting a better job would be fifty-fifty.

(b)   *Cl:*   I'm not sure this is going to work out. I believe that I may find a job, but with my handicap, it's going to fairly tough. Of course, I have been successful in the past.

High

(a)   *Cl:*   Any job would be better than this one. I know I'll be better off.

(b)   *Cl:*   I'm just dying to get into another job, and I'm sure I'll find one in my field.

4. *Personal Standards of Performance*

Low

(a) *Cl:* I really don't want to spend a lot of time at this. I know from experience that I won't keep this job very long.

(b) *Cl:* I want to make a choice now, but I'm sure I'll change my choice before I graduate.

Medium

(a) *Cl:* I can't give my all to choosing a career with two more years of school left. But it is important to have some idea where I'm going.

(b) Cl. Well, I suppose I could interview some workers to see what they do. That sounds like a good way to find out exactly what they do.

High

(a) *Cl:* This is it. I have set aside a lot of time to make sure that I do all the right things. I really want to make a good choice.

(b) *Cl:* Let's get this right, doc. The last time I made the wrong choice. No more mistakes for me.

If the degree of motivation is not readily apparent from the contextual cues provided by the client, level of motivation can be assessed directly. For example, the following questions could be posed: "On a 1 to 10 scale, with 1 being very low and 10 being very high, how would you rate:

1. The importance of making a career choice/change at this time?
2. Your ability to make an adequate career choice at this time?
3. Your confidence that the choice you make will improve your situation (e.g., increase your motivation, lead to a better job, etc.)?
4. The importance of doing a really good job in exploring career options available to you?"

USING MOTIVATIONAL ASSESSMENT DATA

Clients with high motivation to succeed are *typically not a problem* in career counseling unless the motivation is so excessive that it causes anxiety that moves the client toward premature closure in the process. This situation is a rarity and can be dealt with by helping the client to systematically deal with the problem at hand by utilizing a decision aid such as the ones described in Chapter 17.

Low motivation, as was suggested earlier, poses a threat to the career counseling process and must be raised with the client, since failure to do so may result in premature termination or an inadequate choice. The following are suggestions for coping with low motivation.

1. Increasing the importance of making a career choice at this time:
   a. Use live or videotaped models to discuss how they were motivated by having a well-considered career choice.
   b. Confront underlying logic that career choice can be postponed with no harm.
2. Increasing self-efficacy that good choices/changes can be made:
   a. Use live or videotaped models similar to the client to discuss how they successfully made career choices.
   b. Encourage clients by focusing upon their strengths.
   c. Reinforce positive steps.
   d. Teach clients to self-reinforce when they accomplish a planning/ decision-making task (e.g., "I did a good job").
3. Increasing confidence that career counseling can lead to desired outcomes:
   a. Have live or videotaped models tell of their successes *as a result* of career planning.
   b. Tell of past clients who have experienced success as a result of career planning.
4. Increasing standards to ensure that client applies sufficient effort to maximize results for career counseling:
   a. Help person with low standards of performance identify the necessity for high standards of performance in career counseling.
   b. Reinforce high levels of performance.
   c. Have client engage in goal setting that will increase the level of performance.

ASSESSING INTRAROLE CONGRUENCE

In the context of career counseling, intrarole congruence indicates the degree to which the client now fits or will fit into an occupation. Lofquist and Dawis (1969) suggest that there are two aspects of worker-workplace congruence: worker satisfaction and satisfactoriness of performance. Worker satisfaction occurs when the individual's interests, values, or personality characteristics are reinforced. Satisfactoriness occurs whenever the worker or individual possesses the abilities needed to perform the job at a level deemed appropriate by supervisors and others in the work environment.

Chapters 4 through 9 of this book are devoted to assessing some of those characteristics of the individual that relate to finding a job that will be satisfying. Some counselors try to help clients to identify jobs that will reinforce a client's interests as measured by an inventory, whereas others look at personality variables or values. Most career counselors assess all of these variables using standardized inventories, interview strategies, and nonstandardized instruments. They also attempt to discern whether a client possesses the prerequisite ability to perform a job at a satisfactory level by assessing aptitudes and skills and matching these in some way to the jobs of interest to their client. This is typically done by using occupational information that describes the demands of the job, having the individual observe (shadow) workers, or using work samples that have been devised to assess a potential worker's ability to perform on the job. Chapters 15 and 16 are devoted to this process.

The end result of intrarole congruence assessment should be some estimates of why the current job may be problematic and/or some estimates of how well the individual will function and be satisfied in a variety of occupations or interests. It would be erroneous to say that the matching process is one characterized by a high degree of precision, because our individual assessment devices (e.g., inventories and tests) are imprecise, and our descriptions of jobs are less reliable than we would like. However, the alternative to intrarole assessment is random trial and error, and it is certain that we can improve on randomness with a careful intrarole congruence assessment.

ASSESSING INTERROLE RELATIONSHIPS

Interrole relationships are important in career counseling for several reasons, the most important of which may be that stress across roles can be cumulative (Wierwille, 1979) and, thus, when an individual makes a poor career choice, other life roles may be negatively affected. A second concern arises when an individual is "stuck" in his or her current position because of personal factors such as health, age, or significant others who cannot or will not accommodate a change because of the perceived impact upon them. In these situations, compensatory roles may need to be developed to help the client offset the dissatisfaction and stress stemming from the work role. Finally, from a life-planning perspective, it would be ideal to help a client choose a job that would be complementary with all other life roles. For example, an ideal job might provide the monetary support and time to engage in family roles, enhance opportunity for travel, and afford opportunities to develop a role as citizen. Assessing role interaction is discussed in detail in Chapter 9.

LEARNING TO ASSESS CAREER-RELATED PROBLEMS

1. Develop an understanding of tests, inventories, and nonstandardized instruments, including their strengths and weaknesses.
2. Develop a full understanding of normal, and perhaps to a lesser degree, abnormal functioning.
3. Adopt and use a theory of counseling, examining it from time to see if it actually "fits" you as a person.
4. Visit career development classes in community colleges, continuing education centers, high schools, and/or universities, and listen to the types of career-related problems people present.
5. Conduct in-depth interviews with career choosers and career changers to determine the problems they are experiencing.
6. Develop an understanding of at least two theories of career development. Use these theories to assess the problems inherent in one case. What differences in the assessment do you observe?
7. Get feedback on your interview behavior to make certain that you have good listening skills.
8. Read about as many career counseling cases as you can. During the past few years, the *Career Development Quarterly* has contained career counseling cases along with the recommendations of "expert" career counselors.
9. Begin to do career counseling under supervision. With one of your clients, have your supervisor review a tape with the client to determine his or her reaction to your career counseling strategies.

LIMITATIONS OF ASSESSMENT

1. The ability to conduct a thorough clinical assessment will depend upon your ability to establish a good relationship with your client, your understanding of human development, and your ability to focus counseling and career development theory in the analysis of your client's concern. Inability in any of these areas will be a major limitation.

2. Time is a definite limitation. Good career counseling takes more than one or two sessions. If clients come with the expectation that they are going to be "tested and told," they may he unwilling to spend the time needed to take a full look at their career concerns.

SUMMARY

There are many facets of the assessment process in career counseling, and all must be conducted if the outcome of the process is to be maximized. Assessing degree of cognitive clarity is the beginning point of assessment. If the client has severe mental health problems, cognitive clarity will be impaired, and career counseling must be postponed in favor of personal counseling. Many issues that limit cognitive clarity can be handled within the context of career counseling, however.

Client motivation can be tied to certain aspects of cognitive clarity, but other factors such as appraisal of the importance of the situation, outcome expectations, self-confidence, and personal standards of performance may also influence motivation. If problems exist in this area, they must be resolved, or the likelihood that premature termination will occur is very real.

Finally, current or future intrarole congruence and interrole interaction must be assessed. In the past, career counselors focused primarily upon intrarole congruence, but contemporary career counselors tend to work with all facets of the client's life because of their realization that life roles impinge upon one another. The contemporary counselor is aware that strengthening the work role may exacerbate a problem in another area and that the work role may be positively influenced by strengthening another life role.

REFERENCES AND SUGGESTED READINGS

Bandura, A. (1977). *Social Learning Theory.* Englewood Cliffs, NJ: Prentice-Hall.

Bandura, A. (1982). The assessment of predictive generality of self-precepts of efficacy. *Journal of Behavior Therapy and Experimental Psychiatry* 13: 195–99.

Beck, A. T. (1976). *Cognitive Therapy of Emotional Disorders.* New York: International University Press.

Brown, D. (1985). Career counseling: Before, after, or instead of personal counseling. *Vocational Guidance Quarterly* 33: 197–201.

Brown, D. (1988, January). Life-role development and counseling. Paper presented at the National Career Development Association Conference, Orlando, Florida.

Brown, D., & Brooks, L. (1985). Career counseling as a mental health intervention. *Professional Psychology: Research and Practice* 16: 860–67.

DeBord, J. B. (1989). Paradoxical interventions: A review of recent literature. *Journal of Counseling and Development* 67: 394–98.

Egan, (1975). *Exercises in Helping Skills.* Monterey, CA: Brooks/Cole.

Ellis, A. (1973). *Humanistic Psychotherapy: The Rational-Emotive Approach.* New York: Julian Press

Glass, C. R. (1980, September). Advances and issues in cognitive assessment. Paper presented at the annual meeting of American Psychological Association, Montreal.

Haley, J. (1976). *Problem Solving Therapy.* New York: Harper Colophon Books.

Holland, J. E., Daiger, D. C., & Power, P. G. (1980) *My Vocational Situation.* Odessa, FL: Psychological Assessment Resources.

Hollon, S. D., & Kendall, P. C. (1981). Assessment techniques for cognitive-behavioral process. In P. C. Kendall & S. D. Hollon (eds.), *Assessment Strategies for Cognitive-Behavioral Interventions,* 319–62. New York: Academic Press

Krumboltz, J. D. (1983). *Private Rules in Career Decision Making.* Columbus, OH: National Center for Research in Vocational Education. The Ohio State University.

Loesch, L. C., & Wheeler, P. T. (1982). *Principles of Leisure Counseling.* Minneapolis: Educational Media Corp.

Lofquist, L. H., & Dawis, R. V. (1969). *Adjustment to Work.* New York: Appleton-Century-Crofts.

Medonca, J. (1974). Effectiveness of problem solving and anxiety management training in modifying vocational indecision. Ph.D. dissertation, University of Western Ontario.

Mitchell, L. K. (1980). The effects of training in cognitive restructuring and decision making skills in career decision making behavior, cognition, and affect. Ph.D. dissertation, Stanford University.

Osipow, S.H. (1980). *The Career Decision Scale Manual.* Columbus, OH: Marathon Press.

Osipow, S. H., Carney, C. G., Winer, J., & Koschir, N. A. (1976). *The Career Decision Scale* (3rd ed.) Columbus, OH: Marathon Press.

Sharif, J., & Salvendy, G. (1982). Occupational stress: Review and reappraisal. *Human Factors,* 24: 129–62.

Smith, R. L. (1989). Work and mental health: Stress as a major factor. In D. Brown & C. Minor (eds.), *Working in America: A Status Report on Planning and Problems*, 83–96. Alexandria, VA: National Career Development Association.

Strohmer, D. C., & Newman, L. J. (1983). Counselor hypothesis-testing strategies. *Journal of Counseling Psychology* 30: 557–65.

Super, D. E. (1990). Career and life development. In D. Brown & L. Brooks, and Associates, *Career Choice and Development: Applying Contemporary Theories to Practice* (2nd ed.). San Francisco: Jossey-Bass.

Wessler, R. A., & Wessler, R. L. (1980). *The Principles and Practice of Rational-Emotive Therapy*. San Francisco: Jossey-Bass.

Wierwille, W. W. (1979). Psychological measures of aircrew workload. *Human Factors* 21: 575–93.

PART II

Assessment

4

Using Inventories
and Tests

A test can be defined as a systematic, objective measure of a sample of behavior that has correct and incorrect answers. A standardized inventory is also an objective measure of behavior, but responses are not considered either right or wrong; rather, answers are compared with those of individuals who constitute a norm group. In general, career counselors are more likely to use inventories than tests.

USES OF TESTS AND INVENTORIES

Probably the most frequent type of inventory used by career counselors is a vocational interest inventory, although personality and values inventories and aptitude or ability tests are used on occasion. Insofar as the career counselor's role is to help clients gather and interpret information relevant to career decision-making, tests and inventories should be viewed as only one possible source of data and as only one component of the ongoing career counseling process.

1. Identify areas of occupational interest.
2. Confirm occupational choice or preference.
3. Identify possible college majors/programs of study in vocational technical program.
4. Determine general aptitudes or abilities.
5. Expand or narrow range of occupations for further exploration.
6. Identify personality strengths and weaknesses.
7. Determine sources of occupational dissatisfaction.

8. Identify sources or causes of vocational undecidedness/indecision.

9. Identify work values.

BACKGROUND OF TESTING AND USE OF INVENTORIES

One of the earliest inventories available for purposes of self-assessment was the Strong Vocational Interest Blank (SVIB) (Strong, 1927). A wide variety of instruments has been developed since the first version of the SVIB and, at this time, career counselors make widespread use of tests and inventories. This practice will no doubt continue into the future.

Nevertheless, the use of tests and inventories has been frequently criticized. Some writers complain that career counselors overly on tests and equate them with counseling. Another criticism is that testing interferes with the counseling relationship. Others charge that tests encourage client dependency on external sources for answers to their problems. Still others assert that tests are frequently inaccurate and, in particular, are guilty of gender and cultural bias. Finally, almost everyone can cite an example of test results that have had a negative impact on himself or herself or someone he or she knows. A quite capable student in a graduate class in counseling, for example, complained that his high school counselor proclaimed that he would never be able to complete college since his intelligence test scores were so low.

A thoughtful analysis of the criticisms just noted reveals that they are primarily directed at the misuse of tests rather than at tests per se. And most experts agree that the misuse of tests is a frequent problem.

The proper use of tests and inventories requires that career counselors be familiar with ethical guidelines regarding test use (American Education Research Association et al., 1985). In addition, counselors have a responsibility to obtain the technical knowledge necessary to (1) evaluate, select, and administer psychometrically sound tests and inventories that are appropriate and relevant to the client's goals and characteristics, and (2) interpret test results in an appropriate and adequate manner.

Space does not permit a thorough discussion of the necessary technical knowledge. Rather, it is assumed that the reader has completed a graduate level introductory course in testing and has some familiarity with the concepts of reliability, measurement error, validity, and norm-referenced testing. The emphasis of this chapter is on selecting and interpreting tests appropriate for the client's goals and characteristics within the context of ongoing career counseling. The stance taken here is that tests should (1) be viewed as only one component of the ongoing counseling process, (2) used as a tool to obtain information that will be helpful in client decision making, (3) selected in collaboration with the client who is expected to be an active rather than passive participant, and (4) interpreted or shared directly with the client.

PURPOSE OF TESTING

Career counselors primarily use inventories to help clients obtain self-assessment information that will facilitate decision making about initial career choice or change. In this sense, inventories are used as one means of helping clients construct a model or image of themselves (Zytowski & Borgen, 1983) and can help answer such questions as: "What are my interests? My values? What are my strengths and weaknesses?"

Tests can also be used, however, to assist the counselor and the client in identifying the nature, extent, and/or causes of the decision-making difficulty. In this sense, we might think of tests and inventories as diagnostic tools that can help answer the question "Why is this person having a decision-making problem?" For example, some possible but by no means exhaustive reasons a college student might be experiencing difficulty making an initial career choice include career immaturity, lack of autonomy from parents, unclear identity (vocational or otherwise), difficulty making decisions in general, cognitions that immobilize the client ("This is an irrevocable decision—I can't ever change my mind"), inability to separate personal wishes from those of others, lack of self-awareness, and lack of information regarding the world of work. Although more frequently than not the counselor relies on interview techniques to answer diagnostic questions, inventories can also be helpful in some instances. In the case of the college student, a career maturity inventory (e.g., Crites, 1978; Super et al., 1983); and/or a career indecision scale (e.g., Osipow, et al., 1980; Holland et al., 1980) might help identify sources of indecision, vocational identity difficulties, and/or external and internal barriers to decision making.

A career maturity measure such as the Career Development Inventory (CDI) (Super et al., 1983), for example, might indicate that the client has adequate knowledge about the World of Work (one of the subscales of the CDI) but has been unable to apply this information to himself or herself, as indicated by low scores on the Career Planning, Career Exploration, and Knowledge of Preferred Occupations subscales. The results of a career indecision scale such as My Vocational Situation (MVS) (Holland et al., 1980) might show low scores on the Vocational Identity scale, suggesting the decision-making difficulty could be caused by the lack of clarity regarding goals, interests, personality, and talents.

A slightly different example is that of an adult client with a career adjustment or dissatisfaction problem. Some possible sources or causes of this kind of concern are person-environment incompatibility, unrealized values, life-role–work incompatibility, or interpersonal relationship problems. Some assessment tools that could help diagnose these difficulties are interest inventories, role salience inventories, and values and personality inventories. For example, a personality inventory might reveal that the person is very introverted but is in a job, such as sales, that requires extreme extroversion. Interest inventories might show that the person is very socially oriented but is in an (incompatible) work environment that requires concentrated, independent work and provides few opportunities for social contact. A role salience measure might indicate that work is a very important role for the person, but the client is in an occupation that requires minimal commitment or personal investment.

In summary, tests and inventories can be used for both self-assessment and diagnostic purposes, although the former is more common than the latter.

SELECTION

This section considers the following issues in test selection: (1) whether to use a test; (2) the psychometric properties of tests in relation to the goals and characteristics of the client; and (3) involving the client in test selection.

Would Testing Be Useful and/or Necessary?

One of the first issues to consider is whether to use tests at all. Cottle and Downie (1960) assert that two reasons counselors use tests are to save time or to compensate for unavailability of information from any other source. For example, with some very self-aware clients, a clear pattern of their vocational interests, personality characteristics, and work values can be obtained quite efficiently through interview techniques. Administering inventories in these cases would be inefficient and costly in terms of both time and money.

It is not infrequently that clients enter career counseling asking to "take one of these tests that will tell me what I would be good at." More often than not, these clients have interest inventories in mind, which, of course, can help to clarify and identify interests but not abilities. Numerous examples could be cited to illustrate that clients frequently have unrealistic expectations and/or misconceptions about tests and inventories. The important point here is that clients' goals regarding tests need to be thoroughly explored before deciding whether assessment inventories are appropriate or relevant, as the following vignette illustrates.

Co: What brings you here?

Cl: Well, a friend of mind came to see you and she took a test that told her what job she would be good at. So, since I don't know what kind of job I want, I'd like to take that same test.

Co: It's true that we do have some inventories that might help you identify your vocational interests, although they won't tell you what jobs you would be good at. I'll explain more about how tests might help you later, but first, in order to decide what might be most helpful to you, it's important that we talk some about your particular situation. I gather from what you said that you're having difficulty deciding what kind of occupation you would be interested in. Could you tell me more about your thoughts about that?

Cl: Well, I'm majoring in education but I don't like it. My parents, especially my father, think I should be a teacher, but I'm just not so sure that I want to do that. I just finished a semester of observing in a classroom and that just sort of did it. The teacher was really good and the kids were wonderful, so it was a good situation. But I just can't see me doing that—I think I would hate it. Deep down, I've never thought I would like teaching, but now I don't know what else to do either. I just haven't ever considered anything else. I was hoping a test could tell me what to do.

Co: Sounds like you're facing a bit of a dilemma. You thought you had a plan, and now that doesn't feel right to you. You said you've just never thought of any other possibilities. Let's explore that a bit more. Sometimes people really have thought about other options but they have dismissed them because they thought they were unrealistic, perhaps too fanciful. What about you—have you had any ideas at any time of what you might like to do, whether it seems realistic to you or not?

(The counselor begins to act on a hunch that the client might have some ideas, contrary to what she says. For now, the counselor is storing the additional hunch that the problem might be a conflict between the parent and daughter.)

Cl: Well—uh—I used to fantasize about being an artist. But Dad thinks art is a waste of time—he thinks they all just become Bohemians and don't make any contribution to society. He doesn't even want me to take an art course—he thinks it's a waste of money.

Co: You sound a bit frustrated with Dad.

Cl: You can say that again! I've tried to tell him that majoring in education just wasn't right for me, but he wouldn't listen. When my friend told me about taking that test, I thought—well—I was thinking maybe that would convince him.

Co: In other words, your hope is that the test would show in black and white terms that you're not suited for teaching. And you could show that to Dad, hoping it would convince him.

Cl: Right!

Clearly, this is a situation in which testing would be inappropriate—at least immediately. First, the client is likely to approach the test with the attitude of making it "come out right." In this case, the validity of the test would be questionable. Second, the client may want to use the test (and perhaps the counselor) as ammunition to confront her father. Thus, the test would be used as a weapon rather than a source of information. Rather than administer a test at this time, a more appropriate direction would be to further explore the situation between parent and daughter.

This case may seem extreme and may occur infrequently, yet it illustrates the important point that counselors need to conduct a thorough assessment of client goals prior to selecting and administering inventories.

In contrast to the foregoing, suppose a client's goal is to identify occupations that might be appropriate to consider. Vocational interest inventories are usually, although not always, helpful. Personality inventories are less directly helpful for this purpose. Though some test developers have tried to relate personality characteristics to specific occupations, the results thus far are unimpressive. Personality inventories, however, can help clients develop general self-awareness and might be useful in suggesting specific roles and/or functions the person may prefer in work situations (Kunce & Cope, 1987). Similarly, aptitude tests relating abilities to specific occupations are also rather limited—a fact that often disappoints clients who hope that an aptitude test is available that will tell them with pinpoint accuracy and a high level of specificity that, for example, "You have the ability to be a successful landscape architect." Nevertheless, aptitude tests can be helpful in some more general ways. For example, the Differential Aptitude Test (DAT), the Scholastic Aptitude Test (SAT), or the Graduate Record Examination (GRE), could be helpful in predicting whether the client could successfully complete the training required for some occupations. The DAT manual, for example, contains a table showing the relationship of the mechanical reasoning subscale to grades in an auto mechanics course. To the extent that a given occupation requires a particular level of education or training, aptitude data can provide information regarding the realism of a client's preferences (Walsh & Betz, 1985). A client with a very low score on the quantitative scale of the SAT, for example, could be expected, at best, to experience great difficulty completing the requirements in engineering school. In this instance (and all other instances where aptitude test results are available, for that matter), the results of the SAT should be considered only in the context of other data that could have bearing on success in training, such as grades in school and the client's motivation.

This section on whether to use tests can be summarized with the statement: Consider using tests if they might provide information that is unavailable through other means, if they save time, and if they are appropriate for the client's goals.

PSYCHOMETRIC PROPERTIES OF TESTS

In order for tests and inventories to be useful for the client's goals, they must meet certain technical requirements, usually referred to as the psychometric properties of a test. As noted before, to adequately evaluate the technical properties of a test, a beginning course in tests and measurement is an essential prerequisite. Again, space does not permit a thorough discussion of the technical requirements, so only brief mention is made here of the most salient issues as they relate to the goals and characteristics of the client.

One technical concern is whether an inventory has adequate validity for the purpose at hand and for the particular client. Suppose, for example, a client wants to know whether his or her personality characteristics are compatible with the field of dentistry. The test manual of XYZ personality inventory indicates that the construct validity of the inventory is excellent (e.g., the measure correlates with other measures in directions that conform to theoretical predictions). However, though the test manual reports the predictive validity of the measure for some occupations, dentistry is not among them . Thus, whereas this inventory appears to have good validity for some purposes, it is inadequate for this client's purpose. Similarly, suppose a client is thirty-five years old and is interested in assessing his or her mechanical aptitude. You know that the ABC Aptitude Test has a mechanical aptitude scale. However, closer inspection of the manual shows that validity studies have not been conducted with clients over eighteen. Thus, the usefulness of this test for this particular client is highly questionable.

Another important technical property of an inventory is the appropriateness of the norm group. To use the same example cited above, if the client is thirty-five and the norms for the test are provided only for those who are eighteen and younger, then the test is probably not very useful for the client, unless for some reason the client wants to compare himself or herself with eighteen-year olds! To cite another example, some tests have not developed norms for certain ethnic minority groups (e.g., Native Americans). Thus, in these cases, it may be best to rely on the interview to gather information for these clients rather than risk providing misleading results from an inventory.

A third technical property of importance is the reliability of the test. Reliability is related to the degree of confidence we can place in the accuracy of the test for use with individuals. Tests with low reliability may be sufficient for research purposes when the interest is in predicting group differences but would not be precise enough to make a good estimate of an individual's true score.

In summary, the main technical qualities of the test that are important in selection are reliability, validity, and norms. There are also some practical considerations involved in proper test selection, however. Among these are the costs of the tests (which could be prohibitive in some situations), the readability of the test (the reading level of some tests is too high for some populations), the time involved in taking the test, and ease of scoring.

Involving the Client in Test Selection

In some important ways, proper interpretation of test data begins with the test selection process, which is done in collaboration with the client. Once rapport and trust are established between counselor and client, and the client's goals have been identified, the actual selection of tests or inventories can begin.

In order to engage the client in the selection process, the counselor, of course, must be able to suggest appropriate instruments that might be helpful and relevant for the particular client. Also, the counselor needs to be able to clearly describe the kinds of results that tests can provide. An important point to emphasize is that tests and inventories will not provide precise answers; rather, in the case of vocational interest inventories, for example, they might identify areas of interest worth considering by showing how the client's interests compare with the interests of workers in various occupational groups. In the case of personality inventories, it would be important to clarify that the results might help increase the client's self-awareness but will not necessarily point to any particular occupation.

One method that can be used to help clients understand a particular test is to show them a blank profile that indicates the dimensions that will be measured. Several different personality inventories, for example, plot scores on a profile sheet that clearly labels the scales (e.g., Jackson Personality Inventory). By reviewing several such profile sheets, the client can choose which one(s) he or she thinks would be most helpful.

Once some clear descriptions of the possible alternative, relevant instruments have been made, the counselor then makes it clear that it is the client's decision as to whether he or she believes the results might be helpful in providing additional information or confirming information about which the client is uncertain. In most instances, it is a good idea to inquire further about how the client thinks the tests might be helpful. Client responses can help the counselor determine if there are any gaps in understanding and/or misperceptions regarding the kind of information that tests can provide. Actively involving clients in the selection process should help them approach tests in a conscientious, honest manner because the main purpose of using assessment instruments is to be helpful to the client.

The following vignette illustrates involving the client in the selection of assessment instruments. The client is the same one we met previously— the one who wanted a test to prove to her father that education was wrong for her. At this point, the counselor has worked with her for several sessions to help clarify the relationship between her parents and her choice of major. The client has had several conversations with her parents, and they have agreed, albeit reluctantly, that it is important for her to freely explore career interests that would be satisfying to her rather than to them.

Co: Where would you like to begin today?

Cl: Well, I've been thinking about when I first came in here and how lost I was about what to major in once I decided that education was the wrong thing. Now I feel much clearer about the fact that my upset was partly because I didn't know how to talk to my Dad, and I was afraid he would throw a tantrum. Now we see more eye-to-eye about things, but I'm still lost about what I should major in. So, could we work on that now?

Co: That seems appropriate to me, too. How would you like to begin?

Cl: I'm not exactly sure. I thought you could tell me.

Co: Ok. I'll give you an overview of how we might work together. First, I see this as a puzzle-solving process that we will work on together. There are no magical answers that I or anyone else can provide. Rather, what we need to do is to find out what you know about the factors that would be important for you about a major and how that major might relate to occupations. What I have in mind here are such things as your interests, your work values, your abilities—your strengths and weaknesses—and generally, what kinds of things would be important to you in the future in terms of how you live and work. We can go through a self-assessment process first, and then try to put all of the information together in a way that will help you make some decisions about what areas to explore. Does that make sense so far?

Cl: Well, I guess so, but how do we do that? Is this where tests come in?

Co: Good question. There are a number of ways. I might give you some homework—some questions, for example, that you might write out between our meetings. And, yes, some tests or inventories might also be helpful. One kind of test is what's called a vocational interest inventory. These instruments can tell you something about how your interests compare with those of people who are working in various occupations, but they won't tell you anything about your abilities in occupations.

Cl: I thought there were some tests that would tell you what you'd be good at.

Co: Not really. What you're talking about here is aptitude or ability, which is different from interests. One way we could identify your aptitudes or abilities would be to look at your grades, SAT scores, and past achievements, but there aren't really any tests that will tell you directly what occupations you could be successful in. An interest inventory might help you identify some potential areas, however. Are you familiar with any of them?

Cl: No, although as I told you before, I do have a friend who took a test, and I guess that is what it was. She thought it was useful.

Co: Do you know in what ways she found it useful? (The counselor checks for expectations.)

Cl: I think she found some interests that she didn't know she had.

Co: Sometimes that is what happens. Before we decide whether an interest test might be helpful, I'd like to hear more from you about what you know about your interests. Sometimes tests don't tell a person anything they don't already know, and then the person is disappointed.

(The counselor then explores what the client knows about her interests. This discussion suggests the client has several ideas, but she is not committed to any of them. In some ways, she feels there are many possibilities, but she's not sure how to narrow them down.)

> Co: Well, it does sound like an interest inventory might help us figure out what interests are the strongest. Let me tell you about those that are available.

(The counselor briefly describes three interest inventories, and then asks which ones the client would prefer. The counselor goes through a similar process with the decision about whether to use values or personality inventories, showing the client blank profile sheets where possible. The client and the counselor decide the client will take two interest inventories and one values inventory.)

TEST INTERPRETATION

Perhaps the most important aspect of using formal assessment instruments is the interpretation to and with the client. Because results can be confusing, surprising, and "magical" to clients, careful, sensitive interpretation is essential. This section discusses preparing for the interpretative session and delivering the interpretation.

Preparing for the Test Interpretation

Perhaps it is obvious that counselors need to review inventory results before interpreting them to clients. But what does this review entail? Tinsley and Bradley (1986) discuss two steps. The first is Understanding. In essence, the counselor tries to answer the question "What do these scores mean?" In addition to getting a synthesis of the main themes in mind, the counselor needs to ask "What might these scores mean to the client?" It is here that information gained from the client in previous sessions is extremely important. Keeping in mind that inventories are, in essence, statements that clients make about themselves, the counselor can review the results in light of information provided by clients in previous interviews and develop ideas or hypotheses about the meaning to be discussed in the interpretive session. During this preparation, the counselor can make notes to take into the session with the client in order not to forget important details.

The second stage in the preparation stage is Integration. Here the task is to integrate the test results with other information the counselor has about the client, such as family background, previous work experience, client statements about self, and so on. As Tinsley and Bradley (1986) note, one of the tasks here is to determine the consistency of data. If inconsistencies are apparent, the first step is to check for technical errors. For example, was the inventory scored correctly? Did the client answer every question? Are there errors in transcribing scores? If no errors are found, then the counselor develops hypotheses and ideas about the inconsistencies to explore with the client. Tinsley and Bradley caution that the counselor should neither automatically accept the scores if they contradict other data nor reject the scores if they do not affirm expectations. Instead, what is needed is a healthy skepticism about the results combined with the attitude that the purpose is to make sense of the results in collaboration with the client.

Interpretative Session

It is seldom if ever appropriate to begin a session by immediately launching into an interpretation of a test; rather the counselor should first explore the client's agenda for the day. The client may have some more pressing concern he or she wants to discuss first. Again, it bears repeating that tests should not interrupt the process of counseling. Once it is determined that the interpretation is appropriate for that session, an important first step is to inquire about the client's feelings toward the inventory. This inquiry may reveal important information about the client's attitudes toward the test and may influence the interpretation. Contrast, for example, the client who says "I hated having to choose between two alternatives, neither of which I liked. I can't believe that test will tell me anything important" versus the one who says "I really enjoyed taking this inventory. It made me think about me." Clearly, the interpretative task will be different with these two clients. Also, if the counselor was not present when the client completed the inventory, which is often the case, it is important to inquire about the testing conditions. If the client didn't feel well or some other distraction interfered with the client's concentration, the results may have been affected.

In addition to inquiring about the client's attitude toward the test(s), it is a good idea to briefly review the inventory in terms of why it was taken and the types of information it will provide. In some cases, especially if more than one inventory was administered, the counselor may need to briefly review the types of items and the format of the test(s) to jog the client's memory.

During the interpretation per se, several principles are important to keep in mind.

The Do's of Test Interpretation

1. Keep the client actively involved during the interpretation. Remember, an inventory is only meaningful in relation to the client, and interpretation is best seen as a collaborative effort to make sense of the scores. Thus, rather than plopping the entire results of a multiscale inventory on the client all at once, do it in stages and keep checking the client's reactions. For example, after indicating to a client that the results show that "compared with men in general, your interest in writing is above average, and your interest in medical service is very low," an inquiry can be made about the client's reaction. "How do these results fit with how you see yourself? How do you feel about these results?" Some clients will respond to the results spontaneously, but for those who don't, it is important to be continually sensitive to their possible reactions as well as possible misinterpretations or misunderstandings of the meaning of the results. It is not uncommon for clients to find the results surprising or incongruent with their view of themselves. In these cases, the counselor and client must then embark on a puzzle-solving expedition to make sense of the discrepancies. Here, there is no substitute for a counselor's thorough knowledge of the test, the test manual, and any other interpretative materials provided by the test publisher. Also important, however, is the counselor's rapport with the client, as discussion of discrepancies can sometimes be quite threatening. In some cases, no ready explanation can be found, other than the imprecision of tests.

2. Use language the client can understand. While many inventories translate technical scores (for example, standard scores) into terms that are clear to most people (e.g., very low, average, above average), some do not, and it is the counselor's responsibility to convey the results in language that is meaningful. Percentile rank, for example, may be translated as "that point below which a certain percentage of the norm group falls. Your rank of 75 means that you scored higher than 75 percent of the individuals in the norm group."

3. Keep in mind that scores are not exact, but give the range within which the client's true score probably falls. This is not the place to thoroughly explore the technicalities of scores, but counselors must remember that no score should be thought of as a point but rather a band or range. Many instruments, such as the Differential Aptitude Test, provide profile sheets showing score bands. If not provided, then counselors can consult the test manual for the standard error of measurement and construct profiles themselves

or phrase the results in terms of a band or range. For example, a client's T-score of 70 with a standard error of 5 could be translated to the client as "we can be reasonably confident that your true score falls between 65 and 75 and very confident that it falls between 60 and 80."

4. Assume a neutral stance about test results and avoid an impression of evaluating the client. An important point here is that the counselor cannot always anticipate how the client will react to the test results. What may seem negative to the counselor may not seem so to the client and vice versa. One counselor, for example, was particularly hesitant to tell a graduate student client that the results of his interest inventory showed that his comfort with academic situations was more similar to high school students than graduate students. Contrary to the counselor's expectation, the client was not upset with these results; rather they provided him with some clues as to why he was finding graduate school a "grind." Another counselor was fearful that her very independent female client would be disturbed with her high score on domestic activities. Instead the client's rather matter-of-fact reaction was, "That makes sense. I love to cook and decorate." In both of these instances, the counselors' values were interfering with objectivity. Clearly, counselors need to continually scrutinize their reactions toward test scores for any indication of positive or negative feelings toward the scores to prevent a judgmental or "watered-down" interpretation. "Embarrassment in interpreting low or negative scores signifies a problem the counselor, not the client, needs to address, " sum up Tinsley and Bradley (1986, p. 464).

5. While it is important that counselors' attitudes toward the results are neutral and nonjudgmental, they do need to be alert to client reactions to low or threatening scores and conduct the interpretative session in a way that will minimize defensiveness (Tinsley & Bradley, 1986). Here again, it is important to keep clients involved, encourage their feedback, and help them make sense of the scores in a way that is useful. One client expressed distress that his scores on a personality inventory indicated that he was "average" on assertiveness. Further inquiry from the counselor revealed that he had been frequently berated since childhood for nonassertiveness, had engaged in a self-improvement program to increase his assertiveness, and was interested in marketing—a field he perceived as requiring high assertiveness. It is easy to understand why this client was disappointed with his results. In this case, the counselor helped the client see that "average" does not mean nonassertive. Also, the counselor suggested that the client explore whether

marketing did indeed require high assertiveness and if so, then he had at least two choices: continue to work on assertiveness by joining an assertiveness training group run by an expert, or look for other fields that might be of interest to him.

6. Be clear about what an inventory measures and does not measure (Tyler, 1984). Intelligence tests, for example, do not measure innate ability—research has not been able to separate the effects of genetics from those of the environment. Vocational interest inventories do not measure motivation or ability; rather, they measure the degree of similarity of the client's likes and dislikes to the likes and dislikes of people in selected occupational groups. Achievement tests, as is true of all tests, measure only a sample of behaviors—not all of the client's knowledge.

LIMITATIONS OF TESTS AND INVENTORIES

Throughout the previous discussion, some limitations have already been identified. Among them are that tests are imprecise and always contain some error. Some additional cautions are the following:

1. Tests and inventories can reinforce the client's wish for magical answers. Counselors can help to demythologize tests by emphasizing the collaborative nature of counseling and that tests simply provide one piece of information among many others that will be used to help clients with decisions. It is also important to point out (once again) that inventories cannot be precise and cannot measure all of the possibilities. For example, interest inventories typically include less than 200 occupations out of a possible total of more than 10,000. Thus, it can be emphasized that inventories can only provide clues—not definitive answers. Another method that can be used to reduce the "magical" quality of tests is to give two inventories measuring the same phenomenon. The results are seldom exactly the same.

2. Some types of clients will be able to make better use of tests than others. Clients who are not inclined toward introspection, for example, may dismiss the value of tests. Clients' attitudes toward tests in general should be explored before making the initial decision to use tests.

3. Tests and inventories can be gender- and culturally biased. For example, earlier editions of interest inventories used sexist job titles such as "policeman" and "airline stewardess." To judge a test as gender- or culturally biased requires more than a perusal of individual items, however. Rather, the issue of test bias is an

extremely complex issue on both social and psychometric grounds, and thus beyond the scope of this chapter. Nevertheless, counselors need to be knowledgeable about these issues in order to make an informed judgment (see Walsh & Betz, 1985, pp. 379–83 for an excellent overview). Neither the stance of assuming that all tests are biased and therefore useless nor that of assuming that all tests provide a fair evaluation of all groups is a healthy or informed position. Once again there is no substitute for technical knowledge regarding the construction, reliability, and validity of tests and inventories in order to evaluate individual instruments regarding cultural and gender bias. Simply observing that one group scores lower than another group does not necessarily mean that the test is biased—the issue is much more complex and in some instances has more to do with the way the test is used than the adequacy of the test per se.

LEARNING TO USE TESTS AND INVENTORIES

1. As has been mentioned several times, a course in tests and measurements is a necessary but not sufficient prerequisite to using tests. Using tests without this training is unethical.
2. Before using a test or inventory with a client, take it yourself. First, this will enable you to gain some personal knowledge about the test. Second, you will be better able to understand client reactions to the test. Third, you can more directly evaluate the possibilities and limitations of the test. Try to be objective in your evaluation, however. If you don't like your results, try to separate your reactions to the results from the characteristics of the test. Some clients will like tests that you don't. Nevertheless, if you're unable to be objective about the test, it's probably best to refrain from using it with clients until you can be. Both overly positive and negative reactions on your part can interfere with the neutral stance needed in test interpretation.
3. Thoroughly study the test manual and any other interpretive materials available on the test. If you have completed a course on testing, and the professor has reviewed the test in class, don't assume that is enough. It would be impossible for a professor to thoroughly cover all aspects of a test that might be important. Further, many, if not most, test manuals provide several examples of test profiles with narrative interpretations that can be extremely useful in getting a sense of some of the nuances of the test. It is important to stay up to date—tests and their manuals are revised

periodically. Don't assume because you once were familiar with the test that your study is completed.

4. Give the test to as many clients as possible, within the bounds of relevance to the client and ethics of the profession. Some counselors-in-training become quite enthusiastic about tests and want to give them to all their family members and friends. Remember, testing is simply part of ongoing counseling—a relationship that requires initial objectivity. Thus, giving tests to important people in one's life is a highly questionable practice and in most instances unethical. Nevertheless, there is simply no substitute for experience in giving and interpreting tests with as many different types of clients as possible. Such experience can help you, at a minimum, to (1) see recurring patterns and their meaning, (2) obtain some sense of the types of clients who will find tests helpful, (3) discover the kinds of issues that clients raise about tests and their results, and (4) of course, help you gain proficiency. Initially, of course, you should administer and interpret tests only under the supervision of a qualified person who has training and experience with the test.

5. Thoroughly review what experts have said about the test. A primary source here is the *Mental Measurement Yearbook* (Conoley & Kramer, 1989) which contains evaluations of the majority of published, standardized tests. The *Yearbook* will also cite other reviews of the test that are available, usually in professional journals. Another resource is *A Counselor's Guide to Career Assessment Instruments* (Kapes & Mastie, 1988).

SUMMARY

A test is a systematic, objective measure of a sample of behavior. Career counselors often use vocational interest, personality, and values inventories to help clients make career decisions. Aptitude tests are also helpful in some instances.

In order to use tests properly, it is essential that, as a minimum, counselors complete an introductory course in tests and measurements. Tests and inventories may be used if they will provide information that is not available from other sources, if they save time, and if they are relevant to the client's goals. The selection of tests should be a collaborative process between counselors and clients, and only those tests and inventories that are sufficiently reliable and valid for the purpose and client at hand should be selected.

Adequate test interpretation requires that the counselor be thoroughly familiar with the test and any available interpretive materials and carefully plan for the interpretation before meeting with the client. It is also important that the counselor involve the client in the interpretation, use understandable language, and assume a neutral stance toward the results.

REFERENCES AND SUGGESTED READINGS

American Education Research Association, American Psychological Association, and National Council on Measurement in Education. (1985). *Standards for Educational and Psychological Testing*. Washington, DC: American Psychological Association.

Anastasi, A. (1988). *Psychological Testing* (6th ed.). New York: Macmillan.

Bradley, R.W. (1978). Person-referenced test interpretation: A learning process. *Measurement and Evaluation in Guidance* 10: 201–10.

Conoley, J.C., & Kramer, J.J. (eds). (1989). *The Tenth Mental Measurements Yearbook*. Lincoln: University of Nebraska.

Cottle, W.C., & Downie, N.M. (1960). *Procedures and Preparation for Counseling*. Englewood Cliffs, NJ: Prentice-Hall.

Crites, J.0. (1978). Career *Maturity Inventory*. Monterey, CA: CTB/McGraw-Hill.

Holland, J.L. (1985). *Making Vocational Choices*. Englewood Cliffs, NJ: Prentice-Hall.

Holland, J.L., Daiger, D.C., & Power, P. G. (1980). *My Vocational Situation*. Palo Alto, CA: Consulting Psychologists Press.

Issacson, L. E. (1985). *Basics of Career Counseling*. Boston: Allyn and Bacon.

Kapes, J.T., & Mastie, M.M. (eds.) (1988). *A Counselor's Guide to Career Assessment Instruments* (2nd ed.) Alexandria, VA: National Career Development Association.

Kunce, J.T., & Cope, C.S. (1987). Personal styles analysis. In N.C. Gysbers, & E.J. Moore. *Career Counseling*. Englewood Cliffs, NJ: Prentice-Hall.

Lyman, H.B. (1971). *Test Scores and What They Mean* (2nd ed.). Englewood Cliffs, NJ: Prentice-Hall.

Mehrens, W.A., & Lehmann, I.J. (1985). Interpreting test scores to clients: What scores should one use? *Journal of Counseling and Development* 63: 317–20.

Osipow, S.H., et al. (1980). *The Career Decision Scale* (3rd ed.). Columbus, OH: Marathon Press.

Strong, E.K., Jr. (1927). *Vocational Interest Blank*. Palo Alto, CA: Stanford University Press.

Super, D. E. (1983). *Career Development Inventory*. Palo Alto, CA: Consulting Psychologists Press.

Tinsley, H.E.A., & Bradley, R W. (1986). Test interpretation. *Journal of Counseling and Development* 64: 462–66.

Tyler, L.E. (1984). What tests don't measure. *Journal of Counseling and Development* 63: 48–50.

Walsh, W.B., & Betz, N.E. (1985). *Tests and Assessment.* Englewood Cliffs, NJ: Prentice-Hall.

Zytowski, D.G., & Borgen, F.H. (1983). Assessment. In W.B. Walsh & S.H. Osipow (eds.). *Handbook of Vocational Psychology* (vol. 2), 5–40. Hillsdale, NJ: Lawrence Erlbaum.

CHAPTER 5

Assessing
Interests

An interest can be defined as something that arouses or holds one's attention or curiosity. Interests are indications of what individuals want to do or what they enjoy or like.

Information about a person's interests, likes and dislikes, and preferences for activities may be obtained in a variety of ways. Over forty years ago, Super (1949) distinguished three methods of assessing interests. The first—*expressed interests*—simply involves asking the person to state likes and dislikes regarding activities or occupations. The second—*manifested interests*—involves inquiring about or observing people's participation in activities or how they spend their time. The assumption of this method is that people become involved in activities that they enjoy or like. The third method—*inventoried interests*—is perhaps the most frequently used approach to assessing interests. Individuals complete a standardized inventory that asks about their likes and dislikes for a variety of activities. On most inventories, individual responses are then compared for their similarity to the interests of people employed in specific occupations. The focus of this chapter is on methods to assess expressed, manifested, and inventoried interests.

USES OF ASSESSMENT OF INTEREST

Five frequent uses of assessing interest are to:

1. Develop self-awareness.
2. Identify occupational alternatives.
3. Differentiate occupational from leisure preferences.

4. Identify sources of occupational/educational dissatisfaction.

5. Stimulate occupational exploration.

BACKGROUND OF ASSESSING INTERESTS

The assessment of interests is synonymous in many ways with the history of career counseling. In 1908, Frank Parsons, the parent of vocational guidance, founded the Vocation Bureau in Boston and asserted that individuals needed a clear understanding of their "aptitudes, abilities, interests, ambitions, resources, limitations and their causes" (Parsons, 1909, p. 5). Despite Parsons' emphasis on a broad range of client characteristics, interests have typically captured the most attention from career counselors. This emphasis was no doubt stimulated by the early introduction of the measurement of interests by E.K. Strong, Jr. As is well known, Strong published the Strong Vocational Interest Blank for Men (SVIB) in 1927. The inventory compared a person's likes and dislikes to those of people employed in a variety of occupations. Strong believed at the time that interests were strongly tied to abilities, but later research did not support his conclusion. The SVIB, of course, has been revised many times since 1927, most recently in 1985, and is probably the most frequently used standardized interest inventory. Another early interest inventory was the Kuder Preference Record, first published in 1934 and most recently revised in 1985. Currently, over 200 interest inventories with reasonable reliability and validity are available (Walsh & Betz, 1985).

Despite the popularity of interest inventories in assessing interests, there are several reasons why additional approaches should be considered. First, as Yost and Corbishley (1987) state, many clients view inventories as magical instruments that will provide definitive answers. Even though counselors can explain the fallibility of inventories, some clients are not easily dissuaded from their perspective. Eliciting indications of interest in ways other than inventories can help reduce the "magic," as can administering more than one inventory, because no two inventories will produce the exact same results. Second, research suggests that expressed interests have equal or superior predictive validity to measured or inventoried interests. In a seminal paper written over twenty years ago, Dolliver (1969) concluded that the SVIB, in particular, was not superior to expressed choices. Several subsequent studies provided additional support for this conclusion (see Holland, 1985; Slaney & Russell, 1981). Moreover, additional research has shown that when expressed choices disagree with measured interests, the predictive validity of the former is often superior to the latter (e.g., Bartling & Hood, 1981; Borgen & Seling,

1978). Third, the reading level and/or language of the client may preclude the use of an inventory. Finally, other methods such as verbal reports can be more efficient.

SOME ISSUES IN INTEREST ASSESSMENT

Before discussing techniques to assess interests, some important issues related to that aspect of career counseling need to be identified. First, traditional career counseling has probably overemphasized the importance and role of interests in career decision making. The practice of confining career counseling to the administration and interpretation of an interest inventory, for example, is based on the erroneous assumption that intrinsic interest in an activity is the primary source of satisfaction in occupations (Katz, 1987). That assumption does not hold in many instances, however. For example, one former client on the "fast track" in a large company felt extremely satisfied with his current job because of the opportunity it provided for high income, financial security, advancement, and so on. He was not, however, intrinsically interested in the activities or duties of his current job. This case illustrates the point that the source of satisfaction may be related more to fulfilling one's values.

The distinction between values and interests is not always an easy one to make. As Osipow (1983) noted, some authors take the position that interests, values, and needs are not separate dimensions. Katz , however, takes the opposite position and asserts that interests and values "represent different sources of satisfaction: People's values express what they want and desire and what outcome or state is important to them; their interests indicate preferences for various ways of obtaining what is important, a liking for one activity more than another." (1987, p. 34.) For example, a client may say, "I want to help people" (a value). *How* clients prefer helping people (e.g., assisting them with travel plans, counseling, advocating for community services, or planning and implementing employee benefit plans) is a function of interest.

To further complicate matters, interests and values also may be closely intertwined with skills or abilities. People may be interested in and value an activity because they are good at it. Sports participation enthusiasts may play golf more than tennis because they perform better at the former than the latter. On the other hand, people may enjoy and/ or be skilled in certain activities that they do not wish to pursue in their occupation. Since it is sometimes difficult to differentiate conceptually between interests, values, and skills, and because client occupational decisions may be based more or less on one or the other, as well as a variety of other realistic factors (e.g., opportunities in the local community, family restraints, etc.), it is often inefficient as well as impossible to try to assess the various characteristics of the client (e.g., interests, values, skills, role congruence) as separate, unrelated dimensions. Nevertheless, this chapter is focused on interests as if they were a separate domain, and that approach is also taken in upcoming chapters as well, for example, values (Chapter 6) and skills (Chapter 16). This approach has been taken for purposes of convenience and clarity of discussion. The reader should keep in mind, however, as noted in Chapter 1, that the authors believe that career counseling should involve a more holistic than piecemeal approach.

A second issue in assessing interests is which technique(s) should be used with which client. Multiple techniques are often needed with clients who have little self-awareness or work experience, or a constricted view of their possibilities caused by, for example, low self-confidence, or racial or gender role stereotypes. Other clients who know themselves quite well can readily identify their interests with minimal input from the counselor. In these situations a comprehensive battery of inventories or exercises would be inefficient and in some situations irritating. For example, one introspective client in her forties with twenty years of work experience and several years of psychotherapy scoffed at the counselor's suggestion that a comprehensive self-assessment approach would be taken. "I don't need self-assessment!" she exclaimed. "I've been assessing myself for years!" It would be impossible to try to identify all of the different client situations and then be prescriptive about what kind of approach should be taken with each client. Rather, this chapter suggests a few techniques; which ones are selected with which client is left to the sensitivity and good judgment of the career counselor.

ELICITING EXPRESSED AND MANIFESTED INTERESTS

With some very self-aware clients, assessment of both expressed and manifested interests can be completed quite readily in the context of a counseling session through such open-ended questions as:

What occupations have you been thinking about?
What occupations have been of interest to you throughout your life, from childhood to now?

What types of activities do you enjoy doing?

What subjects do you like most in school? What least?

If you could have your ideal job, what would it be?

If you had the weekend free to do anything you like, how would you spend your time?

Clients who have difficulty answering these types of questions or who produce a very small list of interests will clearly need additional techniques or questions. See the following list for some additional stimuli that counselors might use.

Techniques to Assess Interests

1. Alphabet exercise: Have the client write the letters of the alphabet on a sheet of paper and write down interests that correspond to each letter. This list can be retained and added to as counseling proceeds. Then instruct the client to look for themes and interests that have been important in the past. These listings can also be used in developing a preferred job description (Carlsen, 1988).
2. Role models: Have the client generate a list of models who have been important because the client admires them or they do things the client likes. The models can be real or fantasy, living or dead, characters in a book, and so on (Carlsen, 1988).
3. Have the client review the stages of his or her life and identify activities that captured his or her interest.
4. Have the client generate a list of occupations considered and rejected over the years and the reasons why.
5. Have the client indicate what kind of work he or she would do if he or she had only ten years to live. (Yost & Corbishley, 1987).
6. Using the environment as a stimulus: Have the client watch TV, read newspapers and magazines, and make a list of jobs portrayed that are of interest. Family and friends can be asked for their suggestions regarding jobs the client might enjoy.

Additional approaches to working with clients who have few or no interests are discussed in chapter 12. Two strategies that require a more detailed explanation—analysis of work experience and occupational card sorts—are described below.

Analyzing Work Experiences.

In this strategy, work is defined broadly to include paid and nonpaid, full- and part-time, and for younger clients, tasks around the home and educational experiences. While the focus here is on the assessment of interests, this technique could be used more broadly to identify also the client's values, skills, life-style preferences, life-career themes, and other work-related preferences (Gysbers & Moore, 1987; Yost & Corbishley, 1987). The analysis of each experience can often be completed rather quickly during an interview with adult clients who have considerable self-knowledge or who have given a great deal of thought to their likes and dislikes in work situations. Others may need more assistance and more time to complete this task. Assigning the work analysis as homework (see Table 5.1) can save interview time as well as money for the clients in fee-for-service situations.

The work-analysis technique involves four steps. First, clients identify all jobs they have had, or in the case of clients who have held a large number of jobs, perhaps the jobs held in the last five to ten years. Second, the tasks of each job are described. Third, clients indicate which tasks they liked and disliked. Fourth, together the counselor and client summarize the information looking for themes (e.g., likes structured situations) and inconsistencies. (E.g., client expresses desire for time with family but takes jobs with long hours.) The following vignette illustrates

FIGURE 5.1 Work Analysis

List all the tasks involved in all jobs you have had. Experience can include full- or part-time salaried jobs, volunteer work, home responsibilities or school activities. Indicate what you liked and disliked about each task.

Description of Job and Tasks	What I Liked
Job: Executive Director of Nonprofit Organization	
Tasks:	
1. Fund raising	Working with a variety of people
2. Coordinating volunteers	Skill training

the beginning of a work analysis during an interview. Notice that the counselor summarizes the themes, which helps the client gain insight and provides building-blocks toward a final summary.

> *Co:* You've identified some general interests you have and now I think it would be helpful if we talked more specifically about your work experience and what you have liked and disliked about the various jobs you've had. Let's begin with your current job. What does it involve?
>
> *Cl:* I sell frozen gourmet food to individual households. The company sets up appointments for me, and I go to people's houses and try to convince them to buy the products. Usually the appointments are in the late afternoon or early evening—and, that's about it.
>
> *Co:* What do you like about this job?
>
> *Cl:* I meet some very interesting people, and it's a great thrill to make a sale. I like trying to figure out what strategy to use with different people to try to convince them to buy.
>
> *Co:* What would you say you like most?
>
> *Cl:* The charge I get out of making a sale.
>
> *Co::* What are some of the things you dislike about the job?
>
> *Cl:* It's a real downer when I fail to make the sale, although I'm handling that better now than I used to. I hate the hours. I don't feel like I'm living in the real world. When I'm off, everyone else is working, and when I'm working, everyone is off. So there isn't much time to see my friends. And sometimes it's hard to make myself meet those appointments—anxiety I guess—but once I get there the people are usually so interesting that I end up enjoying it. I do feel bad sometimes because I've been successful at convincing people who seem to have very little money to buy a huge stock of food.
>
> *Co:* It sounds like you enjoy selling, particularly the interaction with people and the sense of achievement you get from convincing them to buy. You stated earlier that you were extremely unhappy with this job but your dissatisfaction doesn't seem to be caused by selling per se.
>
> *Cl:* Right - I like the selling part. I hadn't realized that as clearly as I see it now. Sometimes when my boss gets on my back or I don't get a few sales, I become disgruntled and discouraged and begin to think I don't like anything about the job.

The interview continues with an examination of likes and dislikes about previous jobs. A useful question to ask during this process is "What one or two changes might have made these jobs more or less enjoyable?" (Yost and Corbishley, 1987). The results of this strategy should be a summarization of recurring interests, as well as a general picture of activities that are disliked.

Occupational Card Sort.

The card-sort strategy, originated by Tyler (1961) and adapted by Dolliver (1967) asks the client to sort a set of cards, each of which contains a separate job title on one side and, in some versions, a brief description of the job on the other. Though several card sorts are available for purchase (e.g., Holland, 1980; Jones, 1979; Knowdell, 1982), counselors can easily construct their own (see Gysbers & Moore, 1987, for an excellent discussion of guidelines to use in selecting occupations to be included). Typically, the occupations used in the card sort are coded according to Holland's (1985) typology, although other occupational classification systems could be used as the underlying framework (see later discussion in this chapter of classification systems). More than one set of cards that include occupations which differ in skill and educational level would enable counselors to use this strategy with a wide variety of clients. Jones (1979), for example, provides three different versions. In addition, as suggested by Dewey (1974) and extended by Cooper (1976), a card sort that includes occupations that are gender typical and atypical can be useful in assessing the role that gender role stereotypes play in clients' interests (Brooks, 1988).

Occupational card sorts can be assigned as homework or completed within a counseling session. If clients are asked to "talk out loud" as they sort, ("I like this occupation because———"), the counselor can directly observe the dimensions the client uses to sort the occupations. The disadvantage of this approach, however, is that it can become tedious.

The exercise can be approached in a variety of ways, although the following steps are common.

1. The client sorts the cards into three piles: (a) Would Choose, (b) In Question, and (c) Would Not Choose.
2. The client identifies the reasons behind choosing and not choosing each occupation. This process usually starts with the Would Choose pile first, then the Would Not Choose, and finally the In Question pile. Gysbers and Moore (1987) suggest using a worksheet

with three columns for this process. Notes are made about the reasons clients like and dislike each occupation, and tallies are noted beside the entries mentioned more than once. More frequently than not, the reasons noted by clients will cover the range of interests, skills, and values. For example, clients might indicate that the occupation of carpenter is in the "Would Choose" list because the client likes to make things with wood, values seeing a finished, tangible product, and views the job as requiring abilities he or she possesses.

3. The preferred occupations (Would Choose) are sorted into related categories. For example, Tyler's (1961) original version asked the clients to sort the preferred occupations into categories on the basis of their similarities and differences. The counselor then elicited the client's schema or basis for clustering the occupations.

Another approach that can be used instead, or in addition, is to code each preferred occupation according to one of the occupational classification systems described later in this chapter.

Though the card-sort method is particularly useful in identifying client's occupational interests, the strategy may also reveal conflicts and problems that may not have been recognized heretofore. One female college freshman, for example, presented herself as someone who was quite intent on pursuing an occupation that would capture her interest and commitment. The counselor was surprised to find that the occupations she selected from the card sort to be of most interest to her were the following: Executive Housekeeper, Optometry Assistant, Dental Assistant, Secretary. Clearly none of these occupations require a college degree, which she seemed intent on pursuing. Further inquiry revealed that the client was very naive about the world of work, but more important, the client recently had become involved with a senior whom she planned to marry. Her thinking was that she needed to support him while he went to medical school, so she had selected "helper" occupations. Additional inquiry revealed that the couple had never discussed their future together; she was simply assuming that she would support him and that *her* career interests would have to be put aside.

INVENTORIED INTERESTS

It is beyond the scope of this book to describe interest inventories in detail; thus only some commonly used inventories are listed in this section. More extensive information about the inventories on the list can be found in the manuals that accompany each inventory, in Kapes and Mastie (1982;

1988), in Conoley & Kramer (1989), and in various textbooks on tests and measurements (e.g., Walsh & Betz, 1985). Selection of an interest inventory will depend on a variety of factors, including the psychometric properties (e.g., reliability and validity), relevance to the individual client, the counselor's preference and/or knowledge about the instrument, and its cost, availability, and so on. As noted in Chapter 4, both adequate selection and interpretation of interest inventories require that the counselor has had the appropriate technical training and has adequately studied the specific inventory.

Hansen, J.C., & Campbell, D.P. (1985). *Manual for the SVIB-SCII.* 4th ed. Stanford, CA: Stanford University Press.

D'Costa, A.G., et al. (1981). *Ohio Vocational Interest Survey.* New York: The Psychological Corporation.

Harrington, T.F., & O'Shea, A.J. (1984). *Manual for the Harrington-O'Shea Career Decision-Making System.* Circle Pines, MN: American Guidance Service.

Holland, J.L. (1985). *The Self-Directed Search Professional Manual.* Odessa, FL: Psychological Assessment Resources, Inc.

Jackson, D.J. (1977). *Jackson Vocational Interest Survey.* Port Huron, MI: Research Psychologists Press.

Johannson, C.B. (1976). *Manual, the Career Assessment Inventory.* Minneapolis: National Computer Systems Interpretive Scoring System.

Knapp, L., & Knapp, R.R. (1982). *California Occupational Preference System Interest Inventory, Revised Form R.* San Diego: Educational and Industrial Testing Service.

Kuder, G.F., & Diamond, E.E. (1979). *Kuder DD Occupational Interest Survey. General Manual 2nd ed.* Chicago: Science Research Associates.

RELATING INTERESTS TO CAREERS

One difficult task in interest assessment facing the counselor is helping clients determine the relationship of their interests to occupations. A client may have a long list of interests, preferred activities, and likes and dislikes, but without some schema to organize the list, it simply remains a confusing sometimes unrelated set of activities or preferences. Some interest inventories listed in the preceding section do use a system that connects interests to the world of work (Self-Directed Search, SVIB, CAI, Harrington–O'Shea) but others do not. Moreover, nonstandardized or informal methods of assessing interests typically yield a seemingly random list unless the counselor uses some organizing schema in the process. Described in this section are several occupational classification systems that can be used by the counselor and taught to the client. Counselors will need to study each of these systems beyond the material provided here if they are to become proficient at using them. The selection of a system will depend on the counselors' personal preferences, although the kind of occupational information systems that are locally available may also be a consideration.

Dictionary of Occupational Titles (DOT).

The DOT (U.S. Department of Labor, 1965; 1977), which contains a description of over 20,000 separate occupations, classifies occupations into nine broad categories. Volume I of the 1965 edition of the DOT provides a brief definition of the occupations in alphabetical order. Volume II classifies the occupations in Volume I by nature of the work (Occupational Group Arrangement) and the requirements of workers (Worker Trait Arrangement) The Occupational Group Arrangement classifies occupations into the following nine broad categories:

Professional, technical, and managerial occupations
Clerical and sales occupations
Service occupations
Farming, fishing, forestry, and related occupations
Processing occupations
Machine trade occupations
Bench work occupations
Structural work occupations
Miscellaneous occupations

These nine categories are further subdivided into two additional levels, yielding 84 divisions and 603 groups. For example, the professional, technical, and managerial occupational category is subdivided into fifteen groupings (e. g., occupations in architecture and engineering, mathematics and physical sciences; medicine and health; education; religion; art; etc.). Each of these groups is in turn further subdivided into additional categories. For example, architecture and engineering subdivides into civil engineering, architecture, drafting, etc.

The Worker Trait Arrangement classifies occupations on the basis of the requirements of occupations for the worker; that is, the traits, abilities, and other characteristics needed to perform the work. The arrangement assumes that each occupation requires the worker to be involved in varying degrees with data, people, and things.

The 1977 edition of the DOT excludes the Worker Trait Arrangement classification. Instead, it appears as a supplement, *Guide for Occupational Exploration* (GOE) (U.S. Department of Labor, 1979), which uses an occupational-cluster approach (see below).

Occupational Cluster

An occupational-cluster approach to classifying occupations has been developed by the U.S. Department of Labor (USDL). The USDL cluster, used in the GOE, organizes occupations into the following twelve interest clusters:

Artistic
Scientific
Plants and Animals
Protective
Mechanical
Industrial
Business Detail
Selling
Accommodating
Humanitarian
Leading/Influencing
Physical Performing

These twelve interest areas are divided into 600 work groups that are further subdivided into 348 subgroups.

Roe's System.

Roe (1956) developed a two-dimensional classification system. The horizontal dimension is concerned with the primary focus of activities and the vertical dimension is concerned with the level of function (i.e., degree of responsibility, capacity, and skill). More specifically, the eight areas on the horizontal dimension are:

Service
Business
Organization
Technology

Outdoor
Science
General culture
Arts and entertainment

The six levels of function on the vertical axis are:

Professional and managerial—independent responsibility
Professional and managerial—other
Semiprofessional and small business
Skilled
Semiskilled
Unskilled

A table showing the categorization of typical occupations using this two-dimensional system may be found in Roe (1956) and Roe & Lunneborg, (1990).

Holland's Typology

Holland's (1985) classification system is based on his more general theory that there are six types of persons and six types of corresponding work environments. A brief description of the six types and some representative occupations are provided below.

1. *Realistic (R)*: Occupations involving working outdoors or with tools, such as auto mechanic, surveyor, farmer, and electrician.
2. *Investigative (I)*: Occupations that involve scientific activities and solving abstract problems, such as biologist, design engineer, or physicist.
3. *Artistic (A)*: Occupations that involve creativity or writing, music, or artistic skills, such as writer, interior decorator, and music composer.
4. *Social (S):* Occupations that involve working with and helping people, such as teacher, counselor, and religious worker.
5. *Enterprising (E)*: Occupations that involve persuading, leading, and speaking abilities, such as salesperson, business executive, and lawyer.
6. *Conventional (C)*: Occupations that involve working with numbers, details, and data, such as clerical worker, banker, and tax expert.

Few occupations are purely one type or another, so most occupations are coded by two or three letters arranged according to order of influence. For example, career counselor is coded "SAE", indicating that the work is a social occupation that includes enterprising and artistic components. The *Occupations Finder* that accompanies the SDS provides the codes for 1156 occupations in the United States—a list that comprises more than 99 percent of the labor force. In addition, Gottfredson, Holland, and Ogawa (1982) have classified all the occupations listed in the DOT according to Holland's system.

Using Occupational Classification Systems

As noted previously, the counselor needs to assist clients in relating their interests to occupations. In the case of interest inventories, this task is relatively simple. For example, the Strong–Campbell Interest Inventory provides scores on over 100 occupations, each coded according to Holland's system. The Self-Directed Search (SDS) and the Harrington–O'Shea provide clients with a Holland code. The *Occupations Finder* and the *Dictionary of Holland Occupational Codes* (Gottfredson, et al., 1982) provide the DOT number for each occupation, and the client can easily access the DOT.

When more informal interest assessment techniques are used, counselors will need to use their preferred system of classification to categorize clients' identified interests. For example, suppose a client generates the following list of general interests: working with data, fixing things, seeing results, being outdoors, working with plants and animals. An understanding of Holland's system would suggest to the counselor that occupations of interest to this client would probably fall in the Realistic or Conventional categories. On the other hand, if the occupational cluster approach of the *Guide for Occupational Exploration* was used, the occupations of interest would most likely fall in one or more of the following clusters: Plants and Animals, Mechanical, Business Detail, or Physical Performing. The GOE could then be used to help the client generate a list of occupational alternatives that fit the pattern of expressed interests.

LIMITATIONS OF INTERESTS ASSESSMENT

Some limitations to interest assessment are:

1. Informal assessment techniques and some interest inventories do not yield information that shows the relationship between interests and occupations.

2. Too much focus on interest assessment, without putting the process in the context of a larger model of career decision-making, can overemphasize the role of interests.
3. Clients have a tendency to attribute magical qualities to interest inventories.
4. Interests are limited by experience.

LEARNING TO ASSESS INTERESTS

The following list contains suggestions for increasing your ability to assess interests:

1. Assess your own interests using the techniques listed in Table 5.1. Which ones were most helpful? Create additional techniques.
2. Using one of the occupational classification systems described in this chapter, organize your list of interests according to one or more of these systems.
3. Complete two standardized interest inventories. Review your results. Are they similar? Are there any conflicts?
4. Review some self-help career planning workbooks for additional ideas for assessing interests. Complete the exercises using yourself as a "client."
5. Assess the interests of a friend or colleague.
6. Assess the interests of a client using both formal and informal devices. Get feedback from the client and a supervisor.

REFERENCES AND SUGGESTED READINGS

Bartling, H.C., & Hood, A.B. (1981). An 11-year follow-up of measured interests and vocational choice. *Journal of Counseling Psychology* 28: 27–35.
Borgen, F.H., & Seling, M.J. (1978). Expressed and inventoried interests revisited: Perspicacity in the person. *Journal of Counseling Psychology* 25: 536–43.
Brooks, L. (1988). Encouraging women's motivation for nontraditional career and lifestyle options: A model for assessment and intervention. *Journal of Career Development* 14: 223–41.
Carlsen, M.B. (1988). *Meaning-Making*. New York: W.W. Norton.
Conoley, J.C., & Kramer, J.J. (eds) (1989). *The Tenth Mental Measurements Yearbook*.

Lincoln: University of Nebraska Press.

Cooper, J.F. (1976). Comparative impact of the SCII and Vocational Card Sort on career salience and career exploration of women. *Journal of Counseling Psychology* 23: 348–51.

Dewey, C.R. (1974). Exploring interests: A non-sexist method. *Personnel and Guidance Journal* 52: 311–15.

Dolliver, R.H. (1967). An adaptation of the Tyler Vocational Card Sort. *Personnel and Guidance Journal* 45: 916–20.

Dolliver, R.H. (1969) Strong Vocational Interest Blank versus expressed occupational interests: A review. *Psychological Bulletin* 52: 94–107.

Gottfredson, G.D., Holland, J.L., & Ogawa, D.K. (1982). *Dictionary of Holland Occupational Codes*. Palo Alto, CA: Consulting Psychologists Press.

Gysbers, N.C., & Moore, E.J. (1987). *Career Counseling: Skills and Techniques for Practitioners*. Englewood Cliffs, NJ: Prentice-Hall.

Holland, J.L. (1985). *The Self-Directed Search Professional Manual*. Odessa, FL: Psychological Assessment Resources.

Holland, J.L., et al. (1980). *The Vocational Exploration and Insight Kit (VIEK)*. Palo Alto, CA: Consulting Psychologists Press.

Jones, L.K. (1979), Occu-Sort:. Development and evaluation of an occupational card sort system. *Vocational Guidance Quarterly* 28, 56–62.

Kapes, J.T., and Mastie, M.M. (eds.) (1982). *A Counselor's Guide to Vocational Guidance Instruments*. Falls Church, VA: National Guidance Association.

Kapes, J.T., & Mastie, M.M. (eds.) (1988). *A Counselor's Guide to Career Assessment Instruments*. Falls Church, VA: National Career Development Association.

Katz, M.R. (1987). Theory and Practice: The rationale for a career guidance workbook. *Career Development Quarterly* 36: 31–44.

Knowdell, R.L. (1982). *Career Assessment Instruments*. San Jose, CA: Career Research and Testing.

Osipow, S.H. (1983). *Theories of Career Development* (3rd ed.). Englewood Cliffs, NJ: Prentice-Hall.

Parsons, F. (1909). *Choosing a Vocation*. Boston: Houghton-Mifflin.

Roe, A. (1956). *The Psychology of Occupations*. New York: John Wiley.

Roe, A., & Lunneborg, P. (1990). Personality development and career choice. In D. Brown, L. Brooks, & Associates, *Career Choice and Development* (2nd ed.) 68–101. San Francisco: Jossey-Bass.

Slaney, R.B., & Russell, J.E.A. (1981). An investigation of different levels of agreement between expressed and inventory vocational interests among college women. *Journal of Counseling Psychology* 28: 221–28.

Super, D.E. (1949). *Appraising Vocational Fitness*. New York: Harper.

Tyler, L.E. (1961). Research explorations in the realm of choice. *Journal of Counseling Psychology* 8: 195–202.

U.S. Department of Labor. (1965). *Dictionary of Occupational Titles*. Vol. I. 3rd ed. Washington, DC: U.S. Government Printing Office.

U.S. Department of Labor. (1977). *Dictionary of Occupational Titles*. 4th ed. Washington, DC: U.S. Government Printing Office.

U.S. Department of Labor. (1979). *Guide for Occupational Exploration*. Washington, DC: U.S. Government Printing Office.

U.S. Department of Labor. (1988). *Occupational Outlook Handbook*. (Revised biennially) Washington, DC: U.S. Government Printing Office. .

Walsh, W.B., & Betz, N.E. (1985). *Tests and Assessment*. Englewood Cliffs, NJ: Prentice-Hall.

Yost, E.B., & Corbishley, M.A. (1987). *Career Counseling*. San Francisco: Jossey-Bass.

6

Assessing Values

Values are the basic beliefs of people, the beliefs they hold most sacred. They are the source of motivation and the basis for personal fulfillment. They are also the sources of personal standards of performance in a given area and an individual's goals for overall achievement. Values manifest themselves in both the avoidance and pursuit of tangibles and intangibles such as money, power, or spirituality.

USES OF ASSESSMENTS OF VALUES

Assessment of values has the following uses:

1. Develop of self-awareness.
2. Determine the basis of current occupational dissatisfaction.
3. Determine the basis for conflicts among roles (e.g., work and family).
4. Determine the basis for low motivation and/or achievement.
5. As a preliminary step to assessing other aspects of the person, such as interests or personality type.
6. As a strategy for "clinching" the correctness of a job choice or change.

BACKGROUND OF VALUE ASSESSMENT

All values do not possess the same strength or valence. As just noted, tangibles and intangibles may have positive or negative valences, that is, they may be something to be pursued or avoided. Similarly, values may have a high or low positive or negative valence. Objects or states of mind that have high positive valences will be pursued most vigorously, while those with high negative values will be avoided (Rokeach, 1973; 1979).

Both values that have positive and negative valences are of interest to career counselors. Unfortunately, the formal measurement of values, either positive or negative, has not advanced to the same level of sophistication as has the measurement of interests. Therefore, career counselors typically use informal methods of assessing values during the career counseling process. Six informal methods of assessing values will be discussed in this chapter. A list of potentially useful inventories will also be provided. The informal values assessment strategies to be discussed include (1) ranking values on checklists, (2) recalling past choices, (3) examining peak experiences, (4) using discretionary time and money, (5) telling daydreams, and (6) describing people who are admired.

DESCRIPTION OF INFORMAL VALUES
ASSESSMENT METHODS

Checklists

Clients may be given a checklist such as Table 6.1 and asked to complete it by placing a plus after important values, a minus after unimportant values, and then identifying their most important values by ranking the top five from among those marked with a plus. An alternative to the ranking exercise is to give clients an imaginary $10,000 and then ask them to spend it by purchasing values. If the entire amount is spent on increasing security this would be a very important value. Another alternative is to have clients rank order the entire list of values. In the following list there are only twenty work values and, thus, ranking the entire list would be relatively easy for most clients. It would also be important to determine which of the values listed had the strongest negative valence. Again, a ranking exercise could be employed to make this determination.

TABLE 6.1   Work Values

Place a (+) by important values and a (−) by those that are unimportant.

Variety in my life	_____
Routine activities	_____
Nurturance (helping others)	_____
Independence (autonomy on the job)	_____
Friendship (collegiality)	_____
Moral fulfillment	_____
Affiliation (recognition as part of a work group)	_____
Security	_____
Power and authority	_____
Balance with other life roles	_____
Artistic creativity	_____
Stability	_____
Excitement/ Risk-taking	_____
Profit/ Money	_____
Ambience of surroundings (e.g., climate)	_____
Social status	_____
Intellectual status	_____
Competition	_____
Influencing others	_____
Altruism (contributing to others)	_____

Rank order your top five values from among those that have a (+) after them.

1. _____

2. _____

3. _____

4. _____

5. _____

Rank your bottom five values from among those that have a (−) after them. Begin your list with the value that is most negative.

1. _____

2. _____

3. _____

4. _____

5. _____

Finally, you can construct your own values checklists using the following list of positive human values which was compiled by Crace and Brown (1989).

Being accountable to those around me
Being successful
Flexibility in my life
Control of my life
Control of others
Being respected by others
Being loved by others
Standing up for my point of view
Being liked by others
Being myself/Acting natural
Concern for others
Helping others grow and develop
Open communication
Feeling supported by those around me
Competence/Feeling I can do a task well
Competing against others
Feeling I belong
Quiet contemplation
Self-discipline
Working collaboratively with others
Being courteous and respectful
Creating new things or ideas
Being rational and logical
Working under pressure
Initiating things
Having system and order in my life
Discovering new ideas or things
Duty to country
Duty to family
Making money
Physical beauty
Beauty in nature

Educational attainment
Being efficient
Feeling my life is in balance
Equality for all
Being ethical
Being my own evaluator
Personal freedom of expression
Taking risks
Religious faith
Punctuality
Leadership
Personal safety
Giving generously to others
Personal growth
My physical health
Having priorities in my life
Personal integrity
Human dignity
Interdependence with others
Intimacy with others
Justice/Fairness
Discovery of new knowledge
Law and order
Loyalty
Respecting others
Belonging to clubs and groups
Being goal-oriented
Obedience
Being objective
Patriotism
Simplicity
Power
Social status/Societal prestige
Being productive
Having prosperity/Financial security
The opportunity to relax
Originality
Tradition/Heritage
Ritual

Family security
Sensory pleasure
Service to others
Prestige among peers
Truth/Honesty
Wisdom
God
Hard work
Doing a job well
Worship
Curiosity
Saving/Conserving
Self-worth
Being forthright/direct
Technological advancement
The beauty of art
Relying on intuition to solve
    problems
Adventure
Wealth
Devotion/Fidelity
Reverence
Solitude
Privacy
Being physically attractive to
    others
Being taken care of
Being compatible with others
Being physically active
Attending to detail
Being precise or exactly on
    target
Relying on facts to solve prob-
    lems
Challenges from others
Difficult problems
Spontaneity
Playfulness/Having lots of fun
Danger
Being physically comfortable
Winning
Teamwork
Individual effort
Expressing emotion
Scientific knowledge

Literary expression
Historical knowledge
Working with my hands
Mathematical knowledge
Aggressive physical contact
Having parental responsibility
Contributing to society
Having many friendships
Stability
Benevolence/Kindness
Urban development
Being future-oriented
Diversity
Being culturally refined
Influencing others
Creative self-expression
Commitment/Being totally in-
    volved
Luck
Political involvement
National security
Ambition
Open-mindedness
Cleanliness
Forgiveness
Being nonconforming
Physical prowess
Equity/Being rewarded ac-
    cording to the amount of
    contribution made
Taking care of loved ones
Being reliable
Cheerfulness
Consistency
Affection
Being politically conservative
Environmental preservation
Closure/Completion of tasks
Advancement/Making prog-
    ress in an organization
Being politically liberal
The beauty of music
Taking responsibility
Ownership of property

Past Choices

Values can also be assessed by having clients examine choices they have made in the past. The following questions can be useful as a guide to examining the values embedded in past choices.

1. When you could choose from among courses in school, what did you choose? Why?
2. What types of people did you choose to spend time with? Why?
3. What types of jobs have you chosen to pursue? Why?
4. What types of leisure activities do you pursue? Why?
5. If you have chosen a school or college, which one did you choose? Why?
6. If you have purchased an automobile, which one did you choose? Why?
7. When you choose friends, what characteristics do you hope they will possess?
8. If you have volunteered your time, what activities have you chosen? Why?
9. When you purchase personal items such as clothing, what guides your purchases? Why?
10. Do you choose to dress, act, and look like others? Why or why not?
11. What is the most important decision you have ever made? What guide did you use in making that decision?
12. What was your worst decision? Why?
13. What was your best decision? Why?

The answers to these questions can provide valuable insights into the values of your client.

Peak Experiences

Peak experiences are those times when we feel most excited, aroused, alive, or fulfilled. They are the ultimate in human experience. Clients can be asked to identify the most exciting, fulfilling times in their lives and asked to explain why they were excited or fulfilled. What was it about those experiences or events that aroused feelings of excitement or fulfillment?

One difficulty with this type of approach to values identification is that some clients may have never had what they consider a peak experience: They have never have been thoroughly excited, aroused, or the little aspects of their lives that make them feel happy to be alive or that excite them in some way. These experiences can yield valuable information about values.

Another approach to examining peak experiences is to have your clients fantasize about the ultimate experience they could have. This question might be phrased as follows:

> Co: You are walking down a path in a woods. Suddenly, you come upon a clearing where the sun is shining very brightly. A voice tells you that you have been chosen to receive three wishes. You are told that these wishes must relate to the things you believe in most or they will not be given and you will lose that wish. Think about your wishes. What would they be?

Use of Discretionary Time and Money

One important cue about personal values is how we choose to use our discretionary or free time. Clients can be asked to think about those times when they have free time and what they choose to do with that time. They can also be asked to keep a log of their activities to see how they use their free time. Some clients have no discretionary time. In these situations, the client should be asked to respond to the question: "If you had one hour of free time a day, what would you do?"

A similar approach can be used in looking at the expenditure of discretionary money. Clients can be asked how they spend their money that is not obligated to paying bills. If the client has no discretionary money, he or she can be asked: "If you had $50 a week to spend on anything you like, how would you spend it?"

Daydreams

It has long been recognized that our personal fantasies about ourselves have relevance for career planning and are a relatively good predictor of vocational choice (e.g., Touchton & Magoon, 1977; Yanico, 1981). Career counselors can tap fantasies by having their clients relate their daydreams and then analyze these for values. The following is a sample daydream that was provided in response to a career counselor's questions about career fantasies:

> Co: Sometimes the things we daydream about tell us more about ourselves than what we think we ought to be doing

or even what our logical selves tell us. Do you ever have any daydreams about your career?

Cl: Sure, but they don't make any sense.

Co: Let's not worry about them making sense. I'd like to hear them.

Cl: Well, I often think of myself as leaving this secretarial position and becoming a manager. I can imagine how I would treat people, the decisions I would make, and how I would go about solving the problems in our office. I know that I would try to help people rather than criticize them. I would also be much more understanding when people are having personal problems. People will do a good job if you just try to help them out.

Co: It seems that when you daydream about management, your major concern is with regard to helping others as opposed to managing others or making more money, which you have said is not important to you.

Cl: I guess that's right. I'm not concerned about power, at least not the getting of power and using it the way I see some people using it.

Co: Are there any other aspects of your fantasy?

Cl: Just one other. If I became a manager, I'd be a lot freer. Sometimes I can just see myself saying to the staff, "I'm going to take the afternoon off." No more 8:00 to 5:00 for me.

Co: So, having more control over your time and your life are important, or so it seems from your fantasy.

Cl: I think that's right. Sometimes I feel like I'm suffocating behind that desk. It's as though I have a chain around my neck and it's tied to that word processor.

Co: It certainly seems that two of your work values are autonomy and helping others, perhaps in the role of a manager. Let's look at some other indicators of values.

Admired Others

Sometimes the people that our clients admire and would like to emulate can provide clues to their values. Clients can either be asked to make lists of the people they admire or respond to lists of persons such as the following:

TABLE 6.2   Famous People

From among the following list of famous people, select three that you would most like to be like. Then write a brief paragraph telling why you made the choices you did.

	Most	Least
Elvis Presley	_____	_____
Abraham Lincoln	_____	_____
Joan of Arc	_____	_____
Martin Luther King	_____	_____
Michael Jackson	_____	_____
Michael Jordan	_____	_____
Gandhi	_____	_____
Leonardo Da Vinci	_____	_____
Geraldine Ferraro	_____	_____
Richard Nixon	_____	_____
George Washington Carver	_____	_____
George Washington	_____	_____
Mick Jagger	_____	_____
Lee Iacocca	_____	_____
Donald Trump	_____	_____
Mother Teresa	_____	_____
Madame Curie	_____	_____
Madonna	_____	_____
Barbra Streisand	_____	_____
Leonard Bernstein	_____	_____
Beethoven	_____	_____
Michelangelo	_____	_____
Pope John	_____	_____
Billy Graham	_____	_____

responding to the names will be familiar with them. Actually, the names selected are much less important than the paragraph about why they selected the names. The following paragraphs were written by a seventeen-year-old.

> I wouldn't like to be like any of the dead people. But I would like to be as rich as Michael Jackson. I'd also like to have crowds of people come and see me and that's why I chose Madonna and Michael Jackson. They are also very rich.
>
> I wouldn't want to be like Richard Nixon because my dad said he's a crook. Billy Graham is a good guy, but he tells people how to live their lives and I wouldn't like that. I read that Barbra Streisand is very hard to get along with so I wouldn't like to be like she is

Obviously, that was written by a fairly immature individual who will need some help clarifying his or her work values. Most teenagers value money and adulation and, thus, the more important statements may be in the second paragraph. This student is against dishonesty, telling people how to live their lives, and being difficult in interpersonal situations. All of these values would warrant further exploration.

VALUES INVENTORIES

Career counselors may choose to use a values inventory as a supplement to the informal assessment approaches described in the preceding section. The following inventories may be useful in this regard:

Allport, G.W., Vernon, P. E., and Lindzey, G. (1951). *The Study of Values: A Scale for Measuring the Dominant Interests in Personality* (3rd ed.). Boston: Houghton-Mifflin.

Nevill, D.D., and Super, D.E. (1986). *Salience Inventory,* Palo Alto, CA: Consulting Psychologists Press.

Rokeach, M. (1982). *Rokeach Values Inventory.* Palo Alto, CA: CPP.

Super, D.E. and Nevill, D.D. (1986). *Values Scale.* Palo Alto, CA: Consulting Psychologists Press.

SUMMARIZING VALUES ASSESSMENT DATA

Data about values constitute only one aspect of the assessment of factors relating to career choice and adjustment. As such, the data must be placed in the context of the other data available. In order to accomplish this, a clear-cut list of values must first be identified. In order to complete the clear-cut list of values must first be identified. In order to complete the development of this list, the following procedure is recommended:

1. Complete three or four of the informal values assessment techniques discussed earlier in this chapter. On the basis of each exercise, compile a list of values. Once this list is compiled, compare the values included for discrepancies. Reconcile the discrepancies by discussing them with the client. Discuss the impact that contradictory values (work vs. leisure) can have on decision making, motivation, and so on.

2. If discrepancies in lists of values cannot be reconciled, administer a values inventory and compare the profile growing out of the inventory with the profiles developed using the informal procedures.

3. Develop a tentative list of values that relate to career choice.

Once a list has been developed, values data should be integrated into other available information. This integration can be accomplished by the following:

1. First, compare values data to interest data. Are there any obvious discrepancies (e.g., a person who values money and power has interests in low-paying jobs)? Reconcile these lists with the client by determining which measures seem to be most accurate.

2. Compare interest and values data from reconciled list to aptitudes, including test data and self-estimates of aptitudes and skills.

3. Identify aspects of the client's life roles that are in conflict with values as they have been identified.

4. Identify the extent to which values are being reinforced on the job and in other life roles.

5. If client is a potential job changer, look at possible alternatives for involvement in activities that will result in reinforcement of values such as a new job, adjustment within the job, and spending more time in a role other than work.

6. If the client is choosing a first job, look at the potential for jobs to provide reinforcement for values. Also, look at other life roles as potential sources of values reinforcement.

WHAT IF VALUES CANNOT BE CLARIFIED?

It is certainly the case that some individuals, either because of lack of experience, contradictory learning experiences, or the failure to adequately focus on self-exploration, are unable to articulate a clear set of values. In this situation, values clarification is in order. For a fuller discussion of values clarification, books by Kirschenbaum (1977), and Simon, Howe, and Kirschenbaum (1972) may be consulted. These are listed in the reference section. However, Kinnier and Krumboltz (1984, p. 317) suggest that a basic six-step process underpins most values clarification processes. These are paraphrased here:

1. Identify the values related to the choices involved and begin to estimate the personal meaning of living with the values associated with each choice ("My life will be this way if——").
2. Identify problems similar to the current one that have occurred in the past and determine how you have dealt with those problems. Determine if patterns emerge with regard to values-based decisions ("I acted this way in the past").
3. Ask important others how they view the situation and the values involved. Project yourself into their positions and values ("If I take your position, I would believe——").
4. Take a stand on an issue and then, taking the other side, argue with yourself ("I know you believe this, but if you look at it from the opposite view——").
5. Take time to escape from the immediate problem so you can think clearly ("I need to get away and think").
6. Make a choice based on your best estimate of your values ("I've looked at this from every angle. My values are——and, thus, I'm going to make this decision").

It is also possible that psychological problems such as choice anxiety are interfering with values clarification. If this is the case, then the career counseling process may need to be suspended while these problems are eliminated.

A CASE ILLUSTRATION

J came to the career counseling because of a growing dissatisfaction with his job. He entered the insurance business when he graduated from college and had worked as a successful insurance salesperson for fifteen years. For each of the last ten years, he had been a member of the company's million-dollar round table and had been the top salesperson in the company for five of those years. His income was well into six figures as a result, and he lived comfortably with his wife, who worked as a branch bank manager, and two children in a Midwestern city of 85,000. His opening statement to the career counselor was "I've achieved everything I ever hoped for, but there is an emptiness—there has to be more."

An assessment of J's values revealed the following as being the strongest:

1. Achievement—high standard of performance
2. Collegiality
3. Family well-being
4. Personal autonomy with regard to work roles
5. Nurturance

His weakest values tended to fall in the following areas:

1. Material goods
2. Power and authority
3. Recognition
4. Completing routine tasks
5. Artistic pursuits

J revealed to the counselor that the money he was making was great, but that he "could live without it." He also indicated that the money was probably more important to his wife and, certainly, the things that it could bring such as houses, cars, clothes, and so on, were important to his wife. Further, he indicated that she was more excited about his income than he was. He suggested that the reasons he continued to sell insurance so well were that (1) his wife wanted him to, (2) he always tried to do a good job, and (3) he really believed that having a good solid insurance plan was helpful to people. He also stated that "the most satisfying thing that I do is helping people lay out their life plans. When I do that, it is the one time when my job seems really worthwhile."

An analysis of J's work and other life roles revealed that his primary values, when rated on a 1 to 10 scale, were being reinforced at the following "rate":

Achievement	8
Collegiality	2 (I'm the lone ranger)
Family well-being	9
Personal autonomy	8 (I sell when I want to)
Nurturance	4 (especially now that the kids are getting bigger)

An analysis of J's life revealed that he spent about fifty hours per week selling insurance or working on other job-related activities; fifteen hours a week on family matters such as going to church, eating together, helping with homework, and so on; ten hours a week in house maintenance and other routine activities; two to three hours on leisure (fishing/tennis); and the remainder in travel, and so on.

Possible ways for making his life-style more congruent with values that were identified included the following:

1. Change to a helping occupation such as counseling.
2. Make a work-role adjustment to help new insurance agents be more successful (mentoring).
3. Volunteer for community services such as Meals-on-Wheels, a program where meals are delivered to the elderly.
4. Become a Big Brother.
5. Develop a leisure outlet that is "people-oriented."

All of these adjustments would result in reduced income, and adjustments 2 through 5 would result in a reduced number of hours being spent on the current job.

SUMMARY OF VALUES IDENTIFICATION PROCESS

1. Stress importance of values in decision-making, job satisfaction, motivation, and so on.
2. Complete formal/informal values identification exercise.
3. Construct list of values.
4. Clarify values as necessary.
5. Discuss implications of values for choices, changes, and selection of other life roles.

LIMITATIONS OF VALUES ASSESSMENT

1. Psychometric instruments are weak, and informal assessment procedures may not produce reliable information.
2. There is no immediate "bridge" between information about personal values and various types of jobs as there is with interests. Since these links must be constructed by the counselor and the client, this can be time-consuming.

LEARNING TO ASSESS VALUES

1. Start by assessing your own values. Make a list of the values you believe you hold by looking at the list presented at the beginning of the chapter. Then take one or more of the inventories listed in this chapter. Finally, analyze your values by looking at your use of discretionary time and money.

2. Read several news stories in two different newspapers. Can you tell anything about the authors' values based upon the way that the stories are written? People's reports about their lives are like newspaper stories. Voice intonation, shadings in stories, and points of emphasis reflect values.

3. Pick up two or three of the self-help guides available to career changers. Look at how each author proposes to measure values. Try to improve their systems.

4. Assess the values of a colleague or fellow student.

5. Try some of the exercises from this book or from other sources with a client. Get feedback from the client, and from a supervisor if one is available.

SUMMARY

Values are those beliefs that motivate us, to either pursue or avoid an activity or a state of mind. As such, their assessment is essential to the career counseling process. Assessment can be conducted either formally or informally, although there are relatively few values inventories available, and those may not be as relevant to career choice as are values estimates derived from informal means. Once values are assessed, the values data need to be integrated with other assessment data such as information about interests and aptitudes. Finally, some preliminary estimates need to be made about choices or adjustments that will lead to reinforcement of the client's values.

REFERENCES AND SUGGESTED READINGS

Crace, K. & Brown, D. (1989) Positive human values. *Unpublished Paper*. School of
Education, UNC-CH, Chapel Hill, NC.
Kinnier, R.T., & Krumboltz, J.D. (1984). Procedures for successful career counseling.
In N. Gysbers (ed.), *Designing Careers*, 307–35. San Francisco: Jossey-Bass.

Kirschenbaum, H. (1977). *Advanced Value Clarification*. La Jolla, CA: University Associates.

Rokeach, M. (1973). *The Nature of Human Values*. New York: Free Press.

Rokeach, M. (1979). *Understanding Human Values: Individual and Societal*. New York Free Press.

Simon, S.B., Howe, L.W., & Kirschenbaum, H. (1972). *Values Clarification: A Handbook of Practical Strengths for Teachers and Students*. New York: Hart.

Touchton, J.G., & Magoon, T.M. (1977). Occupational daydreams as predictors of vocation plans of college women. *Journal of Vocational Behavior* 10: 156–66.

Yanico, B.J. (1981). Sex-role self-concept and attitudes related to occupational daydreams and future fantasies of college women. *Journal of Vocational Behavior* 19: 190–201.

7

Assessing Personality

The term *personality* has dozens of meanings (Allport, 1937; Hall & Lindzey, 1970). People on the street typically of personality as the totality or pattern of qualities of individuals that make them more or less socially desirable. The phrase "He has a good personality," reflects this view. Personality theorists and researchers, however, have not reached a consensus about the definition of personality. This state of affairs was highlighted by Hall and Lindzey (1970) in their classic text on personality theory: "[I]t is our conviction that *no substantive definition of personality can be applied with any generality... [P]ersonality is defined by the particular empirical concepts which are a part of the theory of personality employed by the observer*" (p. 9; emphasis in the original). In essence, Hall and Lindzey's message is that diverse theoretical approaches to the meaning of personality prevent a common definition. Trait theorists, for example, view personality as a collection of traits and assume that these characteristics are relatively stable across situations. Interactional theorists, on the other hand, reject the stability hypothesis of trait theorists and assert that personality is best viewed as a person–environment interaction, whereas situational approaches define personality in terms of overt behavior that is assumed to be a function of antecedent conditions and prior learning. Psychodynamic views of personality focus on the inner needs of the individual, whereas phenomenological theorists concern themselves with the individual's subjective view of himself or herself (e.g., self-concept).

Despite the existence of several theoretical approaches, the trait model has been the dominant force in personality research and assessment. One measurement text, for example, reflects the trait view when it

115

defines personality as *"an individual's unique constellation of psychological traits and* states Accordingly, *personality assessment* entails the measurement of traits and states" (Cohen, et al., 1988, pp. 286–87; emphasis in original).

Most of the 350 published personality inventories listed in *The Ninth Mental Measurements Yearbook* (Mitchell, 1985) are products of the trait approach. Only a handful are used in career counseling, however. One reason for this limited use is that many of these personality assessment instruments are used to diagnose severe psychological problems; thus they are less relevant to career concerns and can be offensive to clients. A second reason for the limited use of personality measures is that they do not predict occupational choice with satisfactory validity. As one measurement text states: "Current personality inventory scores have generally been of little or no value for predicting future success either in school, on the job, or in personal life" (Hopkins, Stanley, & Hopkins, 1990, p. 448). However, though low predictive validity renders personality measures of limited use in generating specific occupational options of interest to clients, some can be very useful in helping clients to develop general self-awareness and to construct self-images that can then be related to preferences for work environments, roles, or functions. For example, a client with an extroverted personality would usually want to look for occupations that entail considerable involvement with people.

Although career counselors may use few formal personality assessment devices, informal assessment of personality is probably quite common, although it may not be labeled as such. For example, one counselor observed that his client was quite introverted and wondered whether her plan to pursue public relations was wise. Another counselor hypothesized that her client's abrasive style might be partly responsible for his inability to get along with his co-workers. Further, counselors who rely on Holland's (1985a) typology are, in essence, engaging in personality appraisal.

USES OF PERSONALITY ASSESSMENT

Three common uses of personality assessment are:

1. Increase self-awareness.
2. Identify preferred work roles, functions, and environments.
3. Determine source of work dissatisfaction.

BACKGROUND OF PERSONALITY ASSESSMENT

Common sense tells us that personality is a central explanatory variable in career choice and adjustment. "Sales persons must be extroverts." "Counselors must be nurturant." "Stockbrokers must be risk-takers." Even though these assertions contain a bit of truth, they also reflect a bit of fiction. Research has not supported the idea that certain personality characteristics are prerequisites for occupations. Rather, what is closer to the "truth" is that occupations tolerate a variety of personality types. Individuals with similar personality characteristics can find satisfaction and perform adequately in different occupations, and those with different characteristics can enjoy the same or similar jobs. Thus, personality is not necessarily a constricting variable in career development.

Interestingly, books on career counseling devote little if any attention to personality assessment per se, although they typically give considerable space to career-development theory. Paradoxically, most of these theories assert that personality variables are central to occupational choice and development. Similar to the variety of approaches to defining personality noted earlier, these theories reflect different theoretical traditions, as the following demonstrates.

Holland (1985a), closely associated with the trait model of personality, proposes that people develop a personality or set of behaviors that are persistent and relatively permanent, and that they express this personality in the choice of an occupation. Holland posits six basic personality types (Realistic, Investigative, Artistic, Social, Enterprising, and Conventional). Roe (Roe & Lunneborg, 1990) and Bordin (1990), on the other hand, follow the psychodynamic "needs" approach. More specifically, Roe's model, derived from her research on the characteristics of eminent scientists, proposes that people develop orientations either toward or away from people. Those who are oriented toward people are more likely to select occupations involving, for example, service and business contact, whereas those with an orientation away from people will favor, for example, technological, outdoor, or scientific occupations. Bordin hypothesizes that intrinsic motivations (e.g., curiosity, precision, power, or expressiveness) drive people toward certain occupations and away from others. A theoretical approach that in part reflects the phenomenological approach is that of Super (1990). One of his key concepts is that the career development process involves the implementation of one's self-concept.

Despite the centrality of personality in career development theory, only Holland has developed instruments to measure his personality constructs. Counselors who wish to assess personality using other theoretical systems will need to rely on informal approaches [see Brown &

Brooks, (1990) for suggestions] or extrapolate from standardized personality measures.

This chapter focuses on two approaches to personality assessment.
One is theoretical, using Holland's model. This model can be useful in
identifying occupational alternatives, as well as determining sources of
career-choice and work-adjustment problems. The second approach is the
use of a standardized personality measure, specifically the Myers–Briggs
Type Indicator (MBTI). The MBTI can be particularly useful in identifying
clients' preferred work roles, functions, and environments and can also
point to possible sources of work-adjustment or dissatisfaction concerns.
Both approaches can, of course, be used to help clients increase general
self-awareness by providing them with a schema with which to think
about themselves. Several other personality measures besides the MBTI
could be discussed; the MBTI has been selected because of its increasing
popularity in career counseling.

HOLLAND'S TYPES

A variety of interest inventories based on Holland's model can be used to
assess a client's typology (e.g., Strong–Campbell Interest Inventory, Self-
Directed Search, or Vocational Preference Inventory). A client's typology
can also be assessed informally with a listing of adjectives that describe
each type, such as Table 7.1. Clients are instructed to circle all those words
that describe them.

Once the client circles the most relevant descriptors, each category
can be tallied and a two- to three-letter code calculated, using the highest
totals. One client's totals, for example, were the following: Conventional—
12; Realistic—9; Investigative—7; Social—6; Artistic—1; Enterprising —0.
In this instance, the client's two letter code is CR (conventional-realistic)
and the three letter code is CRI (conventional-realisitic-investigative). Based
on these numbers alone, the difference between I and S may be
insignificant. In this situation, the client can be asked to globally review
the lists and determine if one category seems to fit better overall.
Alternatively, the results could be checked against an interest inventory,
such as the Self-Directed Search (SDS) (Holland, 1985c). Another method
to identify a Holland code would be to classify a client's expressed
interests, abilities, work experiences, preferred subjects in school, and so
on, and look for the most frequent letters.

Once the Holland code is determined, the Occupations Finder
(Holland, 1985b) that accompanies the SDS might be used to generate
occupations that are congruent with the code. All permutations of the
three-letter code should be used to generate possible occupational

TABLE 7.1   Holland's Personality Types

Circle all words that describe you.

Realistic	Investigative	Artistic
Conforming	Analytical	Complicated
Frank	Cautious	Disorderly
Honest	Critical	Emotional
Humble	Curious	Expressive
Materialistic	Independent	Idealistic
Natural	Intellectual	Imaginative
Persistent	Introverted	Impractical
Practical	Methodical	Impulsive
Modest	Modest	Independent
Shy	Precise	Intuitive
Stable	Rational	Nonconforming
Thrifty	Reserved	Original

Social	Enterprising	Conventional
Convincing	Adventurous	Conforming
Cooperative	Ambitious	Conscientious
Friendly	Attention-getting	Careful
Generous	Domineering	Conservative
Helpful	Energetic	Inhibited
Idealistic	Impulsive	Obedient
Insightful	Optimistic	Orderly
Kind	Pleasure-seeking	Persistent
Responsible	Popular	Practical
Sociable	Self-confident	Self-controlled (calm)
Tactful	Sociable	Unimaginative
Understanding	Talkative	Efficient

alternatives. For example, if a code is RIS (Realistic, Investigative, Social), the client would search for occupations under RIS, RSI, ISR, IRS, SRI, and SIR.

In addition to using the client's typology to generate occupational alternatives, the code can also be used to explore sources of career-choice or work-adjustment problems. One high school male, for example, described himself as Artistic and Conventional. According to Holland's theory, this is an inconsistent code. Further exploration with the client revealed that he and his parents had conflicting ideas about the career he should pursue. More specifically, his parents believed strongly that he should follow in his father's footsteps and pursue a career in accounting (a C occupation). The client, however, had dreams of becoming an actor (an A occupation). Another client, who described himself as primarily Social and secondarily Investigative, was extremely dissatisfied with his job as the director of a sheltered workshop. An analysis of his job duties showed that a large component of his job was not direct service to clients (i.e., S), but rather personnel management and solicitation of work contracts with large companies, a largely Enterprising endeavor.

MYERS–BRIGGS TYPE INDICATOR

The MBTI, based on Jung's type theory, is a self-report, forced-choice inventory (Myers & McCaulley, 1985). The MBTI classifies respondents along four bipolar dimensions, briefly described here; individuals are assigned one of two preferences for each of the following dimensions.

1. General attitude toward the world: Is one focused on the outer world of people and things (Extroverted) or the inner world of ideas and internal reactions (Introverted)?
2. Perceptual or information-gathering process: Does one take in information through the five senses (Sensing) and focus on facts and data or through intuition (Intuition) and focus on possibilities and hunches?
3. Evaluation or judging process: Does one process or evaluate information by relying on logic and reason (Thinking) or on personal values and considering the effects on others (Feeling)?
4 Deposition of information: Does one make quick, firm decisions in order to get closure (Judging) or delay decisions to gather further information (Perception)?

Sixteen possible types can be generated based on the various combinations (e.g., ENFP, INTJ, ISFP). It is beyond the scope of this chapter to describe all of the types. Descriptions of each type can be found in the MBTI Manual (Myers & McCaulley, 1985), and in Myers (1980) and Keirsey and Bates (1978). Here, some general comments about the relationship of the types to work situations are briefly described.

As noted in the MBTI Manual, available data on the relationship of types to occupations shows all sixteen types represented in all occupations, but some occupations attract some types more than others. Since the SN preference shows more statistically significant relationships to occupations than the other dimensions, Myers and McCaulley suggest that the SN preference may be the most important in the choice of an occupation.

They further assert that the EI preference may be the most important for selecting a work setting within a particular occupation. "The basic assumption when using the MBTI in career counseling is that one of the most important motivations for career choice is a desire for work that is intrinsically interesting and satisfying and that will permit use of preferred functions and attitudes, with relatively little need for using less-preferred processes" (Myers & McCaulley, 1985, p. 77). Type theory suggests that feeling tired and inadequate in regard to one's work may be a sign of occupational mismatch because it is more fatiguing to use one's less-preferred function. For example, an individual who prefers direct experience (an S type) might find applied occupations (e.g., civil engineering) more motivating and energizing than occupations requiring attention to theory (e.g., nuclear physics) (Myers & McCaulley, 1985).

Several tables are available in the MBTI manual showing the effects of each preference in work situations (pp. 79-82). Table 7.2 is an adapted version of one of these tables.

Uses of the MBTI

Once the client's type is determined, it can be used in a variety of ways, depending on the purpose for assessment. Of course, whatever the purpose, the counselor should discuss the inventory with the client, following the guidelines for test interpretation provided in Chapter 4 of this volume.

The inventory can be used to explore possible reasons for current job dissatisfaction. Bob, for example, an ENFJ, was employed as a sales trainer in a pharmaceutical firm. He enjoyed interacting with the trainees (E), helping trainees solve sales problems (N), and dealing with trainee feelings about the work (F). What he did not like was that the company had developed packaged training programs, and he was required to follow the protocol in an exacting manner. This requirement would be better suited to an S who enjoys following a plan and paying attention to details. Thus, Bob was not allowed to use his creativity or inspirations (i.e., N) in his work.

The inventory can be used to help clients generate occupational alternatives and identify compatible work settings. Appendix D of the MBTI Manual (Myers & McCaulley, 1985), gives a long list of occupations that are attractive to each of the four preferences (EI, SN, TF, JP) and the sixteen types. The client can peruse these tables to identify possible options for further exploration. These tables have not been generated from research data, however, but rather from a data bank of completed inventories that have been sent to the Center for the Application of Type. Thus, clients should be cautioned that the tables provide ideas rather than prescriptions and that occupations tolerate a wide variety of personalities.

TABLE 7.2   The Effects of Preferences in Work Situations*

Extraversion (E)	*Introversion (I)*
Prefer successive interaction with people.	Prefer solitude and time alone for concentration.
Like variety and action.	Like quiet.
Often impatient with slow jobs.	Will work for long periods of time on one project
Interested in the results of the job.	Interested in the ideas of the job
Sensing (S)	*Intuitive (N)*
Like work that requires attention to details.	Dislike details.
Dislike new problems.	Prefer succession of new problems.
Enjoy using skills already learned.	Enjoy learning a new skill.
Seldom inspired.	Follow inspirations.
Make few errors of fact.	Make frequent errors of fact.
Thinking (T)	*Feeling (F)*
Prefer work that requires logical order, especially with ideas and numbers.	Prefer work that provides service, especially to people.
Able to reprimand people.	Dislike reprimanding people.
Firm-minded.	Sympathetic.
Judging (J)	*Perceptive (P)*
Prefer work that permits planning work and following the plan.	Prefer work that requires adapting to changing situations.
Like to get things settled and finished.	Do not mind leaving things open for alteration.

*(Adapted from Myers & McCaulley, 1985).

The inventory can be used in conjunction with interest inventory results. Myers and McCaulley suggest using the MBTI along with the Strong–Campbell Interest Inventory (SCII). They claim that the SCII points to specific occupations, (i.e., respondents can compare their interests with interests of workers in various jobs), whereas the MBTI shows the reasons why particular occupations might be attractive. For example, artistic jobs appeal to Intuitive types because they can use their creativity and inspirations; Social occupations appeal to Feeling types because they require sympathetic responses to people.

The MBTI can be used to help clients identify compatible work environments. A Sensing-Thinking type interested in administrative assistant jobs would ordinarily prefer a situation that involves frequent contact with and interruptions from people, such as a receptionist, if he or she were an Extraverted-Perceptive type. On the other hand, he or she would prefer a position tucked away in an office if he or she were an Introverted-Judging type.

This brief overview of the MBTI cannot do justice to its richness, complexity, and explanatory power in regard to personality style preferences. Considerable study of the many resources available on the MBTI, as well as experience using it, are required for proficiency.

Although the MBTI will undoubtedly continue to be a frequently used personality inventory, some counselors prefer other inventories, and the reader is encouraged to study the following list of additional possibilities. All of those listed were developed to assess normal or well-adjusted individuals.

Gough, H.G. (1975). *Manual for the California Psychological Inventory*. Berkeley, CA: Institute of Personality Assessment and Research.

Guilford, J.S., Zimmerman, W.S., & Guilford, J. P. (1978). *The Guilford-Zimmerman Temperament Survey*. Orange, CA: Sheridan Psychological Services.

Jackson, D.N. (1976). *Manual for the Jackson Personality Inventory*. Goshen, NY: Research Psychologists Press.

Johansson, C.B. (1977). *Manual for the Temperament and Values Inventory*. Minneapolis: Interpretative Scoring Systems, Inc.

Walter, V. (1985). *Personal Career Development Profile*. Champaign, IL: Institute for Personality and Ability Testing.

LIMITATIONS OF PERSONALITY ASSESSMENT

1. Because occupations tolerate a wide variety of personalities, personality inventories cannot yield information that shows the direct relationship of personality to occupations. Counselors should be skeptical about inventories that claim these direct relationships.

2. Some personality inventories, despite their intent to measure well-adjusted, normal individuals, sometimes contain scales that are viewed as negative by clients. Counselors must be sensitive to this possibility in both selection and interpretation of inventories.

LEARNING PERSONALITY ASSESSMENT

1. Make a list of your own personality traits. Then take several personality inventories and have them interpreted by someone who is an expert. Did you make a good self-estimate? Were any of the results of the inventories conflicting?

2. Interview practicing career counselors about their views on the relevance of personality to occupations. If they use personality inventories, ask them to discuss their approaches and interpretations.

3. Study Holland's typology and the MBTI.

4. If you are in a practicum, administer some personality inventories to some of your clients. Ask your supervisor to help you interpret them.

SUMMARY

Because of a diversity of theoretical approaches, there is no consensus about how personality should be defined. Although formal personality assessment is less frequent in career counseling than, for example, interest or value assessment, most career development theories assume that personality plays an important role in career choice and adjustment.

Personality assessment may be used to increase self-awareness, identify preferred work roles, functions, and environments, and identify sources of work dissatisfaction. Two approaches to personality assessment have been described. A theoretical approach has been illustrated using Holland's typology, and a formal assessment approach, based on a standardized personality measure, has been described using the Myers–Briggs Type Indicator.

REFERENCES AND SUGGESTED READING

Allport, G.W. (1937). *Personality, a Psychological Interpretation*. New York: Holt, Rinehart & Winston.

Bordin, E.A. (1990). Psychodynamic model of career choice and satisfaction. In D. Brown, L. Brooks, & Associates. *Career Choice and Development* (2nd ed.), 102–44. San Francisco: Jossey-Bass.

Brown, D., Brooks, L., & Associates (1990). *Career Choice and Development* (2nd ed.). San Francisco: Jossey-Bass.

Cohen, F.J., Montague, P., Nathanson, L.S., & Swerdlik, M.E. (1988). *Psychological Testing*. Mountain View, CA: Mayfield.

Hall, C.S., & Lindzey, G. (1970). *Theories of Personality* (2nd ed.). New York: John Wiley.

Holland, J.L. (1985a). *Making Vocational Choices*. Englewood Cliffs, NJ: Prentice-Hall.

Holland, J.H. (1985b). *Occupation Finders* Odessa, FL: Psychological Assessment Resources.

Holland, J.L. (1985c). *The Self-Directed Search Professional Manual*. Odessa, FL: Psychological Assessment Resources.

Hopkins, K.D., Stanley, J.C., & Hopkins, B.R. (1990). *Education and Psychological Measurement and Evaluation* (7th ed.). Englewood Cliffs, NJ: Prentice-Hall.

Keirsey, D., & Bates, M. (1978). *Please Understand Me*. Del Mar, CA: Prometheus Nemesis Books.

Kunce, J.T., & Cope, C.S. (1987). Personal styles analysis. In N.C. Gysbers & E.J. Moore. *Career Counseling,* 100–30. Englewood Cliffs, NJ: Prentice-Hall.

Mitchell, J.V. (1985). *The Ninth Mental Measurements Yearbook*. Lincoln: University of Nebraska, Buros Institute for Mental Measurement

Myers, I.B. (1980). *Gifts Differing* Palo Alto, CA: Consulting Psychologists Press.

Myers, I.B., & McCaulley, M.H. (1985). *Manual: A Guide to the Development and Use of the Myers–Briggs Type Indicator*. Palo Alto, CA: Consulting Psychologists Press.

Roe, A., & Lunneborg, P.W. (1990). Personality development and career choice. In D. Brown, L. Brooks, & Associates. *Career Choice and Development* (2nd ed.), 68–101. San Francisco: Jossey-Bass.

Super, D.E. (1990). A life-span, life-space approach to career development. In D. Brown, L. Brooks, & Associates. *Career Choice and Development* (2nd ed.), 197–261. San Francisco: Jossey-Bass.

CHAPTER 8

The Genogram as an Assessment Device

The genogram is a graphic representation of the careers of the client's biological and step-grandparents, parents, aunts and uncles, and siblings. It may also include other individuals who have influenced the client's attitudes toward careers, career aspirations, and career choices (Gysbers & Moore, 1987; Okiishi, 1987). It is primarily used as an assessment strategy in career counseling.

USES OF THE GENOGRAM

The genogram has two major uses:

1. Identify models that may have influenced occupational perceptions.
2. Identify sources of self-perceptions as a worker.

BACKGROUND OF GENOGRAM USE

The genogram, like many of the other career counseling techniques discussed, has its origins in therapy—in this case, family therapy. A number of family therapists (e.g., Bowen, 1980) emphasize that the family is the basic source of attitudes and stereotypes about marital and family relationships. As Okiishi (1987) points out, McGoldrick and Gerson (1985) have written an entire volume on the role of the genogram in family assessment. However, Okiishi (1987), Gysbers and Moore (1987) and Dagley (1984) have adapted the genogram for use in career counseling, and much of this discussion will be based on their adaptations.

Okiishi correctly notes that there is considerable theory and empirical documentation to support the premise that the family of origin is a primary variable in the development of attitudes toward ourselves and the way that we perceive ourselves fitting into the world, including the occupational structure. By helping our clients systematically to explore their interactions with key family members and significant others such as foster parents, we can help them develop an awareness of why they view themselves and occupations as they do. If the view that has been developed is extremely limiting (e.g., stereotyping self), these insights can serve as the beginning point for examining, and perhaps changing, these perceptions.

DESCRIPTION OF THE GENOGRAM INSTRUMENT

Preparing the Client

The genogram should be introduced as a way of exploring the sources of the client's attitudes about and perceptions of work and its relationship to other life roles. The following excerpt illustrates how this might take place:

Co: We've been talking for awhile about the fact that you want a career after college that will allow you to have a family too. So far, you've limited yourself to traditional female jobs. I'd like us both to get a little more insight into why you are limiting yourself in this way, and I think it might help to construct an occupational genogram.

Cl: What?

Co: An occupational genogram looks at your career roots, that is the careers of grandparents, parents, and siblings, and tries to get at what attitudes about work were modeled implicitly or explicitly by these important people.

Cl: That sounds like fun, but my family is pretty boring.

Constructing the Genogram

To construct a genogram , begin with a large piece of newsprint and magic markers, making sure that you have enough newsprint to complete the genogram. Lay out five rows as shown in the sample genogram in Figure 8.1. The first row, for grandparents, should include stepgrandparents if they are part of the family. The second row should include aunts and uncles of both father and mother, including step-aunts and -uncles. The third row should include cousins, the fourth row shows the parents and stepparents, and the fifth row shows siblings, including stepsiblings and half-brothers and -sisters.

Figure 8.1 shows a rather traditional family involving no step relationships. As can be seen in the second genogram—Figure 8.2—the genogram can be quite complicated when steprelationships are involved.

As can be noted in both sample genograms (Figures 8.1 and 8.2), each generation is kept on a horizontal plane; squares stand for males; circles stand for females and a grid indicates that the person is deceased. Step-relationships are denoted with an "s". All children are placed on the genogram, including stillbirths. An "x" indicates that a stillbirth has occurred. Finally, all dates and all occupations known by the client are listed. A slash (/) indicates that a divorce has occurred, a dotted line (. . .) indicates cohabitation without marriage, and a horizontal line with a dotted slash (-/-) indicates that a married couple is separated.

EXPLORING THE GENOGRAM

Both Okiishi (1987) and Dagley (1984), as cited in Gysbers and Moore (1987) have suggested key questions to be posed while exploring the implications of the genogram. Okiishi, who focuses on modeling, suggests that the following questions be posed:

1. What roles were modeled by each person?
2. What behaviors, and attitudes were reinforced for males? Females?
3. What was punished for males? Females?
4. Were there models other than family members?

Dagley added the following questions:

1. What were the values in the family?
2. Do the client's values fit with family values?

Sample Genogram 1.

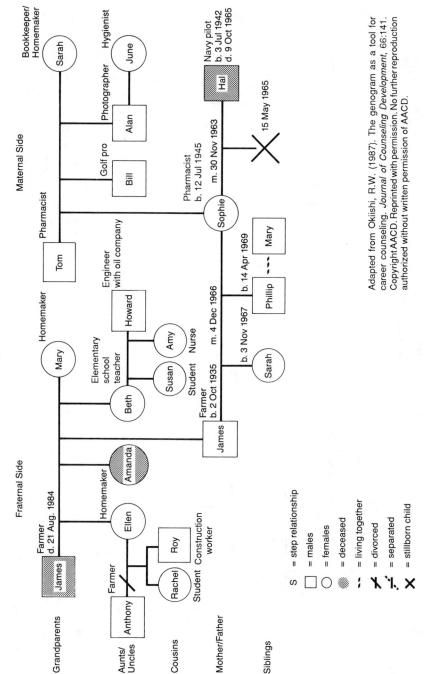

Sample Genogram 2.

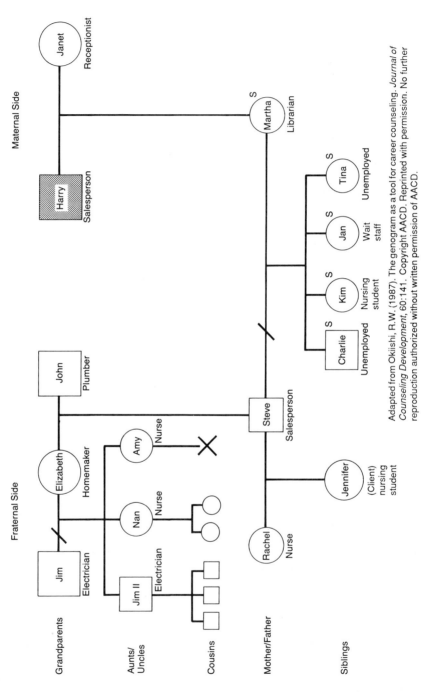

Adapted from Okiishi, R.W. (1987). The genogram as a tool for career counseling. *Journal of Counseling Development*, 60:141. Copyright AACD. Reprinted with permission. No further reproduction authorized without written permission of AACD.

3. Are certain career missions valued (e.g., teaching or business)?
4. Are there generational myths or misperceptions about careers?
5. Are there family traditions, ghosts, or legends that shape attitudes about careers?
6. How does the family address work, family and leisure, and family interrelationships?
7. Have certain boundaries been established that limit career mobility?
8. What are the career patterns that emerge as one looks at the family structure?

To these questions we would add one more: Do any members of the family have unfulfilled goals, aspirations, or fantasies that they are trying to live vicariously through the children or grandchildren?

The following excerpt was taken from the interpretation of a genogram:

Co: The overall picture that emerges is that men fill "men's" careers and women stay pretty much in traditional careers.

Cl: That's about it. Sort of explains why I chose nursing.

Co: Well, three members of your family, including your mother, have been nurses. Can you remember the impressions you had of your mother as a nurse?

Cl: Sure. She liked it, and I know my aunts did too. When we got together for family dinners, the women would talk about their hospitals, along with discussions of kids, recipes, and—well, you know—"women talk." But the overall impression was that nursing is demanding work but very interesting because of the doctors and what goes on in the hospital. I also got the impression that they all thought they were doing something important, even though they complained a lot about the hours and the stress. One time, my mother came home and cried because one of her favorite patients had died that day. I never saw her do that before or after. But after crying, she said that she had done her best, and it was a shame he had to die. She was sad but, I could tell she felt okay about what she had done.

Co: And how did your dad react to your mother as a nurse?

Cl: He was proud of her. He complained when she drew a late shift and couldn't come home and even more when he had to cook his own meals. But I've heard him say he never had to worry about the kids because my mother knew what to do and I don't think the complaining was serious. I can't remember that they ever fought about her working. A part of that was the money, though. We couldn't have gotten along without it.

Co: Your impressions seem very positive, both from your mother's side and your father's side. Let me ask you a related but different kind of question. Do you think you may have limited yourself because of all of this positive "stuff" that was going on around you?

As the foregoing excerpt illustrates, a genogram can help the client determine the sources of his or her perceptions about goals, careers, and other life roles. It can also serve as the basis for changing those ideas. The excerpt continues:

Cl: I suppose that's possible, but I want to find a job that is satisfying, and nursing seems to fit the bill, but as I said when I came in, I don't want to limit myself.

Co: It may be helpful to think of the values your parents held about work, male and female roles, childrearing, money, and so forth, and contrast them with your own values.

Cl: My own values. In some ways, I'm very much like my mother. I love children, and I want to feel like I'm helping others. But I want more than my parents had. We got along financially, but it was a little tough at times. And I wouldn't work all day and then cook my husband's meals. So I guess I am a little different.

Co: Different enough to have higher aspirations, it seems.

Cl: Yes, definitely, and perhaps that means something other than nursing, although just saying that makes me a little sad. I feel like I'm letting someone—my mother—down. That's odd, though. She's never told me she wanted me to be a nurse, although I know it would be okay with her and my aunts.

STRUCTURED GENOGRAM EXERCISE

Another approach to using the genogram is through the use of a structured exercise. A career genogram, such as the one shown in Figure 8.3, should be completed at the outset. Then the client should complete the seven questions shown. This genogram may produce less information than the ones produced in the earlier illustration (Figures 8.1 and 8.2), but this approach to using the genogram does lend itself to classes and large groups.

FIGURE 8.3 Your Career Genogram

Place initials of each relative (living or dead) in the parentheses and identify the current career for each person if known. After you have identified the job title place a U for unsuccessful career history and an S for successful or adjusted. These judgments should be based upon your subjective perceptions of success and need not be based upon factual, first-hand information, Denote females with circles, males with squares.

	Maternal	*You*	*Fraternal*
Grandparents	( ) _____ ( ) _____		( ) _____ ( ) _____
Step grandparents (if appropriate)	( ) _____ ( ) _____		( ) _____ ( ) _____
Aunts and Uncles	( )___( )___( )___ ( )___( )___( )___		( )___( )___( )___ ( )___( )___( )___
Cousins	( )___( )___( )___ ( )___( )___( )___		( )___( )___( )___ ( )___( )___( )___
Parents	( ) _____ ( ) _____		
Stepparents (if appropriate)	( ) _____ ( ) _____		
Siblings	( )___( )___( )___ ( )___( )___( )___		
Step siblings (if appropriate)	( )___( )___( )___ ( )___( )___( )___		

1. Draw *unbroken* lines connecting yourself to persons whom you most *like*.
2. Draw *broken* lines connecting yourself to persons whom you most *dislike*.

(continued)

FIGURE 8.3 Continued

1. What are the job attitudes (e.g., hard work is important; women should do women's work) of people you most like?

   Relative (List most liked first)   *Attitudes*

   A. _____   _____

   B. _____   _____

   C. _____   _____

   D. _____   _____

   E. _____   _____

2. What are the job attitudes of people you least like?

   Relative (List most disliked first)   *Attitudes*

   A. _____   _____

   B. _____   _____

   C. _____   _____

   D. _____   _____

   E. _____   _____

3. List you own job attitudes.

   _____

   _____

   _____

   _____

   _____

4. Are your job attitudes similar/dissimilar to liked /disliked relatives? Identify these areas of similarities/dissimilarities. For example, how do your job attitudes regarding the appropriateness of different careers for your gender compare to those of significant relatives?

   _____

   _____

   _____

   _____

   _____

FIGURE 8.3 Continued

5. Have the job attitudes held by liked/disliked persons restricted their career development? Facilitated it? How?

_____

_____

_____

_____

_____

6. If you have job attitudes similar to liked/disliked relatives, are you restricted by them now? Will you be in the future? How?

_____

_____

_____

_____

_____

7. What stereotypes about careers and yourself have been "transmitted" to you by relatives?

_____

_____

_____

_____

_____

Summary of the Process of Using a Career Genogram

Techniques for a structured activity using a career genogram are as follows:

1. Introduce the technique and explain its purpose.
2. Using newsprint and magic markers, have the client fill in the names of the grandparents, aunts, uncles, cousins, parents, and siblings.
3. Have client insert known dates and occupations.

4. Have client note step relationships, deaths, divorces, and other pertinent facts, including cohabiting couples, separations, and so on.
5. Process, focusing on what has been modeled, family values and traditions, career boundaries that have been established, family perceptions of role relationships among family, leisure, work, and other life roles.
6. Identify stereotypes and self-imposed limitations that may have developed.
7. Draw conclusions about implications for current and future career and life-role planning.

LIMITATIONS OF THE GENOGRAM

There are chiefly five important factors that limit the ability to use a genogram:

1. The genogram is a time-consuming technique. Its cost in time expended must be weighed in terms of likely results.
2. Some clients may not know a lot of family history. If this is the case, a decision must be made about the possibility of making a homework assignment to obtain this information.
3. Discussion of family relationships may evoke feelings and discussions that are unrelated to career counseling. If these are so powerful that they interfere with career counseling, the process may have to be postponed.
4. Much of the data elicited by a genogram can often be obtained more efficiently through usual interview strategies such as asking direct questions about family influences.
5. Effective use of the genogram requires a high level of clinical skill on the part of the counselor.

LEARNING TO USE GENOGRAMS

1. Start by constructing your own career genogram. Write an interpretation. Check with family members about the accuracy of that interpretation. Specifically, check the following with siblings, parents, or both:
   a. What was modeled by parents? Grandparents?

      b. Were people happy in their roles?

      c. What was reinforced? Punished? Were there gender differences?

      d. Were career boundaries established?

2. Construct a genogram for a fellow student or colleague. Interpret without comment from him or her. Then have him or her give you feedback on your interpretation. Repeat this process, but do not share your views until after the "client" has made his or her own interpretation.

3. With a client, first attempt to gain as much information as you can by conducting a family influence investigation simply by asking questions. Then construct a genogram. Which method produced the greatest *amount* of information? Did the genogram produce any new information? Which method did you prefer? Which method did the client prefer? Which was most effective?

SUMMARY

Genograms were first used by marriage and family therapists to gain insight into perceptions and attitudes about family roles. More recently, they have been adopted for use in career counseling because of their potential for helping clients gain some understanding of their perceptions of themselves as workers and their perceptions of how their careers relate to their other life roles. The actual construction of the genogram is relatively simple, although somewhat time-consuming. However, the process of helping the client to "make sense" out of the data generated by the genogram requires a great deal of skill, including the ability to help clients deal with emotions that may be generated by the consideration of family interactions.

REFERENCES AND SUGGESTED READINGS

Bowen, M. *(1978)*. *Family Therapy in Clinical Practice*. New York: Jason Armstrong.

Dagley, J. (1984). *A Vocational Genogram. (Mimeographed.)* Athens, GA: School of Education, University of Georgia.

Gysbers, N.C., & Moore, E.C. (1987). *Career Counseling: Skills and Techniques for Practitioners.* Englewood Cliffs, NJ: Prentice-Hall.

Okiishi, R.W. (1987). The genogram as a tool in career counseling. *Journal of Counseling and Development* 66: 139–43.

McGoldrick, M., & Gerson, R. (1985). *Genograms in Family Assessment*. New York: Morton.

CHAPTER 9

Assessing Interrole Relationships

A role is a life function that involves a socially defined set of activities. Assessment of relationships, in this context, means determining the nature of the interrelationships among the life roles such as worker, student, family or close personal relationships, leisurite, spiritual/religious, and community member. The general objective of this assessment is to determine which roles are complementary, which are compensatory, and which are conflicting. Specifically in career counseling, the objectives of interrole assessment are to (1) determine roles that either now or may sometime in the future interfere with the work role, (2) identify roles that may compensate for the negative effects of work when individuals are "stuck" in unfavorable work roles, and (3) determine roles that are now or may become complementary (at least two roles enhanced).

USES OF INTERROLE RELATIONSHIPS ASSESSMENTS

Assessments of interrole relationships have three main uses:

1. In career planning, interrole assessment is used as a stimulus to increase awareness of work as one role in a constellation of life roles.
2. In career-adjustment counseling, interrole assessment is used as a means of helping clients avoid career changes that will negatively

influence other life roles and/or to identify potentially compensatory roles for persons "stuck" in unrewarding careers.

3. In life-enrichment planning, interrole assessment is used as a
means of identifying potentially complementary roles.

BACKGROUND: LIFE-ROLE RELATIONSHIPS

McDaniels (1978), Hansen and Keierleber (1978), Loesch and Wheeler
(1982), and Ulrich and Dunne (1986) to name a few, have argued that life
roles are interrelated. Goode (1960), Slater, (1963), and Coser (1974) have
posited that, because human beings have limited energy, an increase in
the number of roles occupied has a negative impact upon the individual.
Conversely, Sieber (1974) and Marks (1977) have argued that as number
of roles occupied increases, personal well being increases. Research
regarding physical and mental health variables has generally supported
the latter point of view (Barnett & Baruch, 1985; Thoits, 1983; Verbrugge,
1987). However, at least two studies (Barnett & Baruch, 1985; Baruch &
Barnett, 1986), while generally supportive of the so-called expansion
position, have supported the idea that the quality of life roles filled, rather
than the number of roles filled, is the important determinant of stress and
psychological well being, at least for middle aged women.

ASSESSMENT OF INTERROLE RELATIONSHIPS

The Assessment Process

Many of the previous chapters in this book have focused partially or
totally on assessment of various aspects of human functioning, including
cognitive clarity, values, interest, personality variables, and on some
specific techniques for conducting assessment (e.g., the genogram). The
assessment of person–work-role congruence is important because difficulty within the work role (intrarole incongruence) can lead to interrole
relationship problems (e.g., family role functioning negatively affected).

Interrole interaction can be assessed very straightforwardly by asking
clients to (1) list the life roles in which they are involved, (2) estimate the
amount of time spent in each role, (3) rank order the roles using their
values (Chapter 6) as the basis for the ranking, and (4) identify conflicting,
compensatory, and complementary roles. The following is an illustration
of this process with a college student.

Roles	Hours (112 possible)	Rank	Conflicting	Compensatory	Complementary
A. Student	40	3	A,D,B,E		
B. Worker	20	7			
C. Child	5	1			
D. Leisure	20	5			
E. Citizen (volunteer)	5	6			
F. Spiritual/religion	4	4		F and A,B	
G. Interaction with significant other	18	2			G and A,D

In this particular situation, a young woman's role as student conflicted with her roles of leisurite, worker, and citizen because she felt "guilty" about taking time away from school to spend time on these roles. On the other hand, her relationship with a young man was viewed as complementary with her student role because both roles were enhanced, because they often studied together. They also spent time together in leisure activities. Although this client rated herself as only moderately religious, she felt that her worship activities had a calming effect on her life that reduced the stress resulting from school and work.

A second method of assessing interrole interaction is to ask clients to use geometric figures such as circles to depict role relationships. The following exercise illustrates this process:

1. Have clients begin by drawing circles that represent the roles in their lives (e.g., worker, student, close personal relationships, leisurite, religious, community member, parent, and household maintenance). *Tell them to let time dictate the size of the circle—that is, the more time spent, the bigger the circle.* Label the circles.

2. Once circles are drawn, have clients indicate the relationships among their roles by connecting them as follows:

   conflicting roles ///// _____
   compensatory roles _____>
   complementary roles < >

3. Have clients repeat the exercise listed in No. 1. However, this time instruct them to let their values dictate the size of the circles. The role most valued should be depicted by the largest circle and the one least valued by the smallest circle.

4. Ask: "Are the problems in the role relationships observed in No. 1 the result of values conflicts? Role overload? Too many roles? Too little time? If values conflicts are at the center of the problem, can you identify which values are in conflict?"

5. Have clients consider the information produced in Nos. 3 and 4. Then have them depict role relationships that are ideal, where values are in harmony and role overload is minimized. *Have them draw these relationships, using circles as they did before.* The circle sizes should be dictated by balance between time demands and values.

6. Help clients identify strategies that will help them get from where they are now (No.1) to where they want to be.

The circle-drawing exercise is aimed at helping adults examine the interrelationships of roles that have been assumed. By rewording the directions, it can be converted to a life-planning exercise, as follows:

1. Make a list of life roles (e.g., worker, student, close personal relationship, leisurite, religious, community member, parent, and household maintenance).

2. Think about your life in the future. From the list of life roles (see No. 1), select those you expect to fill at the ages of twenty-five, thirty-five, forty-five, and fifty-five.

3. Using your personal values as a guide, draw circles that portray the relative importance of these roles at each stage of your life.

4. Now, consider time as a variable, and draw circles that depict how you would realistically expect to spend your time at each stage of your life.

5. As you project your life at twenty-five, thirty-five, forty-five, and fifty-five, are there conflicts between your values (as illustrated in No. 2) and the time demands that will be placed upon you as you progress through life? What is the nature of the conflicts?

6. Can you see potentially positive (complementary or compensatory) relationships that might exist among the various life roles that you might assume? Identify these.

7. Considering the life plan you have in mind at this time, can you see the need for alterations? New directions? Identify these.

Processing Assessment Information

In the interrole assessment exercise just described, the interrole assessment data can lead directly to problem identification and goal setting. As can be seen in that exercise, interrole assessment can, and probably should, be tied to the assessment and clarification of values, just as the other assessment procedures discussed in this book have some natural interrelationships (e.g., interest and values; values and personality). The danger in discussing interrole assessment as a separate strategy is that these natural links to other areas of assessment will he overlooked. Therefore, one question that the client must answer as interrole assessment data are discussed is: "How does what I have learned here confirm or fail to confirm what I have learned from other assessment data?"

Perhaps the most important questions to be answered by interrole assessment, at least for adult clients, are:

1. What roles conflict with work?
2. What roles can be strengthened to compensate for a negative work experience?
3. What roles are potentially complementary with work that, if altered or changed, might actually enhance both the work role and the complementary role? (E.g., work and leisure; work and family; work and citizen.)

A CASE

The case that follows illustrates the importance of interrole relationships, how these interrelationships may be assessed, and how the assessment can lead to interventions.

The client was unhappy in his job because he felt that he was unappreciated, and as a result, he was unmotivated. He had been passed over for two promotions, which had resulted in severe criticism from his wife, who also worked and was quite successful. She believed that he needed to spend less time fishing and playing golf, two hobbies that he believed kept him from "going insane."

Performance appraisal reports from the client's supervisor emphasized that while the client's work was minimally satisfactory, he showed a lack of initiative and often failed to meet his sales quota. He countered his supervisor's report with the perception that he has been assigned an unproductive territory. However, other sales representatives had experienced great success in his territory, and his failure to meet his quota did not appear to be caused by a change in the demand for his product.

The client's self-assessments were that he is friendly, hardworking, and diligent, but is unappreciated by both his supervisor and his wife. He described himself as a soap opera character who is destined never to "make it" by the program writers. The client's history suggested that he usually failed to win approval from his parents, who had high expectations for his performance. He listed his main values as (1) intimacy, (2) cooperation, (3) personal tranquility, (4) family relationships, (5) acceptance by peers, and (6) personal fulfillment.

After keeping a record for three weeks of how his waking hours were spent, the client reported the following time allocations: selling—35 percent; golf, fishing, leisure—30 percent; community service—10 percent—household chores—10 percent ; family concerns, (e.g.., taking wife to dinner, PTA)— 5 percent; miscellaneous—10 percent. These percentages translated into 110 hours per week, as follows : job—38; leisure—33; community—11; household—11; family—6; miscellaneous—11.

The counselor and client concluded that (1) there were some perceptual differences between the client and people in his environment (e.g., supervisor and spouse) that needed to be addressed, (2) interrole relationships needed to be considered, with the objective being to bring them more into harmony, and (3) both the work and other life roles needed to reflect his values, which meant that a change in the work role was necessary.

It was decided that the initial strategy would be to involve the client's wife in the counseling process in an attempt to develop a marital support system that could be used as a springboard to his changing to a more satisfactory career. Both the client's wife and the client were taught countering techniques (see Chapter 2) as one means of disrupting some of the client's habitual thoughts about people's expectations ("They expect more than I can deliver.") Marital communication was stressed, and open (controlled) conflict was encouraged because the client typically solved his problems by going fishing or playing golf. Both spouses were asked to relabel their negative interactions as efforts to keep the marriage together. Once the marital relationship was improved, the client entered a training program and became a rehabilitation counselor.

LIMITATIONS OF INTERROLE ASSESSMENTS

Interrole assessments have two limitations worth noting here:

1. Effective interrole assessment is often dependent on other aspects of the assessment process (e.g., values) and thus should not be considered as an independent process.
2. Because interrole assessment is dependent upon client self-

report, the client's cognitive clarity will determine the value of the data generated. It is therefore incumbent upon the counselor to adequately assess cognitive clarity prior to engaging in interrole assessment.

LEARNING THE INTERROLE ASSESSMENT PROCEDURE

1. Complete the circle exercise for your current situation. Then have a friend or a member of your class complete the exercise. Can you identify conflicting, compensatory, and complementary roles in either your assessment or that of a friend? Will these roles shift over time? If yes, discuss the implications for career planning.
2. Review the chapters on assessing interests, values, and personality. It has been suggested that determining values is an important prerequisite to interrole assessment. Where does the assessment of interest and personality fit into the assessment process for interrole relationships?
3. Review one or two of the self-help career planning books available, such as the latest edition (1990) of Richard Bolles' *What Color Is Your Parachute?* Identify the author's approaches to interrole assessment and role adjustment.
4. Once Nos. 1–3 have been completed, conduct an interrole assessment with a client. Get feedback from your supervisor.

SUMMARY

The work role interacts with a number of other roles across the life span. Career planning and adjustment counseling should consider the nature of the these interactions and attempt to "fit" the career into the life space by the most compatible means possible. When clients are stuck in jobs that offer little reward, are highly stressful, or are incompatible in other ways, career counseling may turn to enhancing other life roles as a means of compensating for the deficits in the career role.

REFERENCES AND SUGGESTED READINGS

Barnett, R.C., & Baruch, G.K. (1985). Women's involvement in multiple roles and psychological distress. *Journal of Personality and Social Psychology* 49:135–45.

Baruch, G.K., & Barnett, R. (1986). Role quality, multiple role involvement, and psychological well-being in midlife women. *Journal of Personality and Social Psychology* 51: 578–85.

Bolles, R.N. (1990) *What Color Is Your Parachute?* Palo Alto, CA: Ten Speed Press

Coser, L. (1974). *Greedy Institutions*. New York: Free Press.

Goode, W.J. (1960). A theory of strain. *American Sociological Review* 25: 483–96.

Hansen, L.S., & Keierleber, D.L. (1978). Born free: A collaborative consultation model for career development and sex role stereotyping. *Personal Guidance Journal* 56: 395–99.

Loesch, L.C., & Wheeler, P.T. (1982). *Principles of Leisure Counseling*. Minneapolis: Educational Media Corporation.

Marks, S.R. (1977). Multiple roles and role strain: Some notes on human energy, time and commitment. *American Sociological Review* 41: 921–36.

McDaniels, C. (1978). The practice of career guidance and counseling. *INFORM* 7: 1–2, 7–8.

Sieber, S.D. (1974). Toward a theory of role accumulation. *American Sociological Review* 39: 567–78.

Slater, P. (1963). On social regression. *American Sociological Review* 28: 339–64.

Super, D.E. (1980). A life span, life-space approach to career development. *Journal of Vocational Behavior* 16: 282–98.

Thoits, P.A. (1983). Multiple identities and psychological well-being: A reformulation and test of the social isolation hypotheses. *American Sociological Review* 48: 174–87.

Ulrich, D.N., Dunne, H.P., Jr. (1986). *To Love and Work: A Systemic Interlocking of Family, Workplace and Career* New York: Bruner/Mazel.

Verbrugge, L.M. (1987). Role burdens and physical health of men and women. In F. Crosby (ed.). *Modern Women: Managing the Dual Role*, 186–224. New Haven, CT: Yale University Press.

PART III

Special Issues

CHAPTER 10

Ethnicity and Race in Career Counseling

This chapter is concerned with career counseling with persons who are members of one of the four recognized racial or ethnic minority groups in the United States: Asian-Americans, Native Americans, African-Americans, and Hispanics. Whereas the term *racial, ethnic,* and *minority* are used interchangeably to make the discussion less cumbersome, they should be distinguished, although there is admittedly a great deal of overlap in their meaning.

The term *race* implies biological roots and can be defined as "a subgroup of peoples possessing a definite combination of physical characteristics, of genetic origin, the combination of which to varying degrees distinguishes the subgroup from other subgroups of [humankind]" (Krogman, 1945, p. 49). Physical characteristics such as skin color, head form, facial features, stature, and so on are among those factors that distinguish among races (Atkinson, Morten, & Sue, 1983).

Ethnicity has to do with a group's shared history and culture. Ethnic differences involve issues of language, customs, religion, and the like. Smith (1983) makes the important point that research on race differences

149

often confounds race and ethnicity; that is, racial groups are compared, and any differences are implicitly assumed to be explained by physiological differences rather than people's beliefs, life circumstances, or ethnic or cultural values. (The same kind of error, of course, has also been made in research on sex differences.)

The term *minority* is frequently used to refer to nonwhite racial and ethnic groups in the United States. (Atkinson, et al, 1983); it has a special meaning that goes beyond race and ethnicity. More specifically, a minority group is made up of people who are "singled out from others in the society in which they live for differential and unequal treatment, and who therefore regard themselves as objects of collective discrimination" (Wirth, 1945, p. 347). In essence, this definition incorporates the concept of oppression, that state in which a "person is deprived of human rights or dignity and is (or feels) powerless to do anything about it" (Atkinson, et al, 1983, p. 7). The one common denominator among these groups is "their lack of power when compared to the dominant, white male majority" (Kitano & Matsushima, 1981, p. 165).

BACKGROUND OF CAREER COUNSELING FEATURING RACIAL, ETHNIC, AND OTHER MINORITIES

Since the mid-1960s, counseling practice has been severely criticized as inadequate for American racial and ethnic groups. Numerous studies have documented that American ethnic minorities underutilize counseling services and are more likely than white clients to terminate after one session. One study showed that 50 percent of Asian-Americans, Chicanos, and blacks, versus 30 percent of Anglos, terminated after one session (Sue, S. 1977). Numerous explanations for underutilization of services have been offered. Some authors speculate that the cultural values of some minority groups impose sanctions against seeking help. However, perhaps a better explanation focuses on barriers in the mental health system, such as culturally insensitive services (e.g., counseling approaches based on white, Western values), geographic inconvenience, lack of child-care facilities, prohibitive fees, and so on. Various suggestions have been made for ways to make the system more responsive, and some community mental health centers have implemented programs that have successfully increased the use of services by minorities (see Padilla, Ruiz, & Alvarez, 1983). Of more relevance to this chapter is the considerable attention given to urging counselors, particularly white counselors, to incorporate a cross-cultural perspective in their work with racial and ethnic minorities.

The need to adopt a cross-cultural perspective in counseling with racial minorities is perhaps the central most important task of all counselors, including career counselors. Because such a perspective is much more than a set of specific skills, this chapter devotes more attention to theoretic, conceptual, and knowledge issues than to specific techniques, as earlier chapters do. Some techniques are suggested, but many of them have already been detailed in previous chapters; the point is made that these techniques either need special emphasis or should be used in a more culturally sensitive manner.

This chapter is organized into two sections. The first provides a brief overview of the career status of ethnic minorities and the criticisms of career development theory and counseling approaches. The second section describes the bases of a cross-cultural perspective using the framework of attitudes, knowledge, and skills. Because most of the literature on cross-cultural counseling is focused on white counselor–minority client situations, that is the focus of this chapter.

CAREER STATUS OF AMERICAN RACIAL AND ETHNIC MINORITIES AND THE INADEQUACY OF CAREER DEVELOPMENT THEORY AND COUNSELING

Stereotypes abound regarding occupations suitable for ethnic minorities: The Native American high steelworker, the Hispanic migrant worker, the black skycap, the Asian-American scientist (Smith, 1983). Myths also surround these groups regarding variables related to their career and educational status. Smith (1975) notes, for example, that the literature on the career behavior of blacks paints a portrait of vocationally handicapped individuals (e.g., they lack positive work models, are uncommitted to careers, are alienated from work, are vocationally immature, possess negative self-images, have restricted interests, and low career expectations, and are more focused on job security than on self-fulfillment). Putting aside the issue of whether these characteristics are indeed "handicaps" or simply reflect research based on "culturally disadvantaged" assumptions and a white value system, it seems safe to say these characteristics will describe some ethnic minority individuals (as well as some whites) some of the time and others none of the time. What is true is that when ethnic minorities are viewed in the aggregate, their occupational and material status differs substantially from that of whites. To cite just a few examples:

- The unemployment rate for minority youth is approximately two and one-half times that of whites (Wetzel, 1987).
- Minorities are concentrated in a limited range of occupations.

Black and Hispanic males are overrepresented in low- and moderate-status realistic jobs and are underrepresented in all other categories (Arbona, 1989). Black women are concentrated in social jobs, and along with Hispanic women, are overrepresented in low- and moderate-level realistic jobs (Arbona, 1989). At professional levels, blacks pursue and express greater interest in social occupations (Doughtie et al., 1976; Hager & Elton, 1971; Kimball, Sedlacek, & Brooks, 1973). Asian-Americans disproportionately pursue scientific, mathematics, and technology-oriented fields whereas other ethnic groups are underrepresented in these areas (Leong, 1985; Smith, 1980; 1983).

- Hispanics have lower incomes, less education, higher rates of unemployment, and are more likely to be in menial occupations than are whites (Ruiz & Padilla, 1983). In 1984, of Hispanic families, 25 percent compared with 11 percent of non-Hispanic families had incomes below the poverty level (Arbona, 1990).
- Over 50 percent of Native American school children do not complete high school; the average income of Native Americans is 75 percent below the national average (Atkinson et al., 1983).

These indices of oppression (Griffith, 1980)—higher unemployment rates, lower incomes, and the concentration in a limited range of occupations, usually of lower status and pay—are strong indicators that the career development of racial minorities is different from that of white Americans. As Vontress (1981) observes, minorities in the United States experience three recurrent problems: economic deprivation, educational deficiencies, and negative self-concepts. Given this situation, it is not surprising that career development theory and counseling in general has been denounced as inadequate in regard to ethnic minorities.

The major complaints about career development theories are, briefly, that they reflect a white middle-class perspective: (1) they do not account for the effects of race and social class on career development and choice; (2) they exaggerate the role of personality; (3) they neglect the restraining influences of sociocultural, environmental, and economic forces on individual choice; and (4) they assume that all people have an array of choices open to them from which they can "freely" choose (e.g., Brooks, 1990; Osipow, 1975; Smith, 1983; Williams, 1972). Career counseling guided by theory, then, is likely to be focused on intrapsychic rather than extrapsychic variables (i.e., client problems and solutions are thought to reside within the individual rather than in societal processes).

The attack on counseling practice reflects two recurrent themes: (1) similar to career development theory, counseling approaches are based on Western, white, middle-class cultural values; and (2) white counselors, in particular, fail to offer services that are culturally relevant to ethnic minorities. In regard to counseling approaches, several cultural assumptions have been noted by a number of authors (e.g., Katz, 1985; Smith, 1985; D.W. Sue, 1981; Sue & Sue, 1977). For example, Western counseling approaches focus on the individual. People are thought to be responsible for their lot in life, autonomy and independence are highly valued, and problems are intrapsychically based and rooted in family and childhood. Further, communication processes involve verbal or "talk" therapy using standard English. The client is expected to be self-disclosing about intimate personal details and to engage in intensive self-exploration. Goals are long-term and typically focused on insight, individual behavior change, and adaptation to society's values. Appointments are held in the counselor's office. Outside of the strict adherence to the fifty-minute hour, the general structure is ambiguous, to "allow" client self-exploration. Clear distinctions are made between physical and mental well-being, and explanations of problems emphasize cause-and-effect relationships. D.W. Sue (1981) has described these characteristics as barriers to effective cross-cultural counseling and has summarized them in three categories: (1) language variables, (2) class-bound values, and (3) culture-bound values (see Table 10.1).

TABLE 10.1 Generic Characteristics of Counseling

Language	Middle-class	Culture
Standard English	Standard English	Standard English
Verbal communication	Verbal communication	Verbal communication
	Adherence to time schedules (50-minute session)	Individual-centered
		Verbal/emotional/behavioral expressiveness
	Long-range goals	Client–counselor communication
	Ambiguity	Openness and intimacy
		Cause–effect orientation
		Clear distinction between physical and mental well-being

Source: Sue, D.W., and Sue, S. (1977). Barriers to effective cross-cultural counseling. *Journal of Counseling Psychology* 24: 420–29. Copyright © American Psychological Association. Reprinted with permission.

These underlying assumptions of Western, white counseling approaches direct the counselor to negate the influence of extrapsychic effects (e.g., racism) on individual behavior or problems, to set goals that may be culturally inappropriate (e.g., independence from family for Asian-Americans), to view some behaviors as pathological (e.g., militancy in reaction to racism) rather than healthy esteem-building responses, to use interventions and strategies that require processes that violate the client's culture (e.g., assertiveness for Native Americans), and so on. Further, the predominance of white cultural values in the United States encourages Americans, including counselors, to view American minorities as pathological, genetically deficient, and culturally deprived, rather than culturally different. As is seen later in this chapter, the values underlying common counseling approaches are in stark contrast to some of the cultural values of Native Americans, Asian-Americans, and so on.

The second primary attack on counseling—cultural insensitivity—has focused on the need for counselors to modify their approaches in working with ethnic groups. In an influential position paper, D.W. Sue et al. (1982) outlined the characteristics of the culturally skilled counselor in terms of beliefs and attitudes, knowledge, and skills. In regard to attitudes, culturally skilled counselors are those who are aware of themselves as cultural beings, avoid ethnocentric biases, value and respect cultural differences, recognize and are comfortable with cultural differences between the counselor and client, and are sensitive to those circumstances in which minority clients might need to be referred to someone of their own race or culture. In regard to knowledge, the culturally skilled counselor has an understanding of the sociopolitical system in the United States in terms of how it treats minorities (e.g., the role that cultural racism plays in identity development), has specific knowledge about the history, experiences, cultural values, and life-styles of various ethnic groups, possesses an understanding of the culture- and class-bound values of various counseling approaches, and is aware of institutional barriers that prevent ethnic minorities from seeking mental health services. Skills of the culturally skilled counselor include the ability to generate a wide variety of verbal and nonverbal responses and to offer institutional interventions on behalf of clients when appropriate (e.g., outreach, consultation, and advocacy).

This framework of attitudes, knowledge, and skills provides the organization for the remainder of this chapter, and each of these areas is explored in greater detail.

ATTITUDE, KNOWLEDGE, AND SKILL BASES OF COUNSELING WITH AMERICAN RACIAL AND ETHNIC MINORITIES

Attitude Bases

Perhaps the first step necessary for white counselors to develop attitudes and beliefs facilitative for cross-cultural counseling is that they become aware that they are cultural beings. The predominance of the white culture in the United States is one factor that makes this difficult to achieve. As Katz (1985) notes, the omnipresent existence of the white culture is usually unrecognized and acts as an "invisible veil" that prevents us from seeing it as a cultural system. Some focused reading would be a good beginning. Katz's article, which identifies the values of the white culture (e.g., rugged individualism, competition, mastery and control over nature, success through working hard, etc.), and Ibrahim's (1985) discussion of world views (i.e., different assumptions groups hold about human nature, human relationships, people and nature, time orientation, and activity orientation) are highly recommended.

Confronting and acknowledging one's attitudes toward minorities are also necessary. Counselors commonly like to think of themselves as liberals, so recognition of racist attitudes and/or discomfort in interacting with other racial groups challenges their professional self-concepts. Nevertheless, it seems highly unlikely that white counselors who grew up in this country have escaped racial prejudice. Moving to the point of developing positive attitudes, respecting, valuing, and being comfortable with cultural diversity would seemingly require direct experience with racial and ethnic minorities, and some suggestions are made in that regard at the end of this chapter.

As is the case in many psychologicial processes, the attitude bases of cross-cultural counseling can be presumed to follow a developmental process. Specific proposals along these lines have been proposed by Carney and Kahn (1984) and Helms (1984). As a way of helping white readers assess their attitudes, Helms's model of white racial consciousness is described here. It should be noted that Helms developed this model to predict interactions between various combinations of racial pairings of clients and counselors, so it will serve as a useful departure point for a later discussion of cross-racial counseling. Although Helms's model uses the example of whites' attitudes toward blacks, she suggests that generalizations to other cross-racial combinations may be appropriate.

White Racial Consciousness Model

The *Contact* stage of white racial consciousness is entered when a person realizes blacks exist. The person may be curious about blacks, but is usually naive about their characteristics. He or she is unaware of himself or herself as a racial being. An awareness of society's pressures regarding cross-racial interactions stimulates the person either to withdraw from interacting with blacks or to approach blacks to satisfy their curiosity.

The *Disintegration* stage is entered when a person becomes a victim of ramifications of interacting with blacks (e.g., negative reactions from whites and/or blacks). The person is forced to acknowledge his or her whiteness and feels guilty or depressed about racism. He or she feels a conflict between denying blacks their humanity and violating white norms of mistreatment of blacks. Possible resolutions to this dilemma are (1) overidentifying with blacks, (2) becoming paternalistic toward blacks, or (3) retreating into the white culture.

The *Reintegration* stage is entered when a person chooses the first two solutions to the Disintegration stage and experiences rejection from whites and/or blacks. The person becomes hostile toward blacks and positive toward whites. He or she tends to stereotype blacks, minimize cross-racial similarities, and feel anger and fear.

The *Pseudo-independent* stage is entered if the person uses the Reintegration stage to accept his or her whiteness and "understand the social/political implications of being [w]hite in a racist society" (Helms, 1984, p. 156). There is an intellectual acceptance and curiosity about blacks. Cross-racial interactions may be possible but are limited to blacks who are similar or "special" in some way.

The *Autonomy* stage is entered when the person has been able to supplement his or her intellectual understanding with affective understanding. Racial differences and similarities are accepted. The person actively seeks opportunities to be involved in cross-racial interactions with a mixture of appreciation and respect. He or she values cultural diversity and feels secure in his or her own racial identity.

Because whites are the dominant race in this country, they are free to avoid situations that might challenge their racial attitudes (Helms, 1984). Consequently, they may remain fixated at a particular stage. Helms hypothosizes that each stage will have differential effects on counseling. For example, white counselors in the Contact stage may minimize or ignore racial issues. The Disintegration counselor, feeling pain and anxiety about cross-racial issues, may interact with an ethnically dissimilar client with considerable discomfort, and the client is likely to terminate. The Reintegration counselor who feels negatively about blacks but who, through training, believes bias is unacceptable, will try to hide these feelings. The Pseudo-independent counselor will convey an intellectual understanding of ethnic clients' problems but will have trouble empathizing with their situation. Autonomous counselors, comfortable with racial diversity and their own racial identity, can convey appropriate empathy and recognize the racial and cultural aspects of a client's situation (Helms, 1984).

One point that should be underscored about Helms's model—a point made earlier—is the necessity for white counselors to have direct experience in interacting with blacks in order to progress through the stages. Thus, a purely intellectual approach to this task (e.g., reading about racial differences) is insufficient. Rather, an appreciation and acceptance of cultural diversity would seem to require an experiential component that stimulates affective reactions and forces whites to face and resolve the inevitable emotional conflicts.

KNOWLEDGE BASES

At a minimum, the cross-culturally skilled counselor must be familiar with the cultural beliefs and values of the ethnic client. Also important, however, is an understanding of the range of responses to oppression of persons of different races and ethnic origins, as well as recognition of ways of coping with the conflict between mainstream American values and those of one's ethnic heritage. Of these complex topics, only a few examples of the cultural values and beliefs of the four American racial or ethnic minority groups are provided here, and one must remember that considerable diversity exists within each racial or ethnic group. Responses to oppression and value conflict are discussed through presentation of models of acculturation and racial identity development.

Cultural Values and Beliefs of American Racial and Ethnic Minorities.

The *Asian-Pacific American* is frequently referred to as the "model minority" because many individual members are well-educated and highly achieving (Sue & Sue, 1985). D.W. Sue (1975), however, objects that labeling Asian-Americans as a "model," and holding one minority up as an example, serves the sociopolitical purpose of pitting one group against another and perpetuates the myth that all minority group members can succeed in American democratic society if they work hard enough. Leong (1985) and Fukuyama (1990) add that the "model" label encourages the idea that Asian-Americans need no special attention. Sue and Sue (1985) point out that Asian-Americans show a bimodal distribution of education and success; that, there is one highly educated and successful group and another with low formal education and success. For example, 40 percent of Chinese-Americans earn less than $4000 per year. D.W. Sue (1975) further dispels the myth that Asian Americans have suffered no inordinate discrimination by reviewing the history of Chinese and Japanese in the United States. For example, he notes the harassment of the Chinese in California after the completion of the Union-Central Pacific Railroad in 1869 and recalls the incarceration of 110,000 Japanese-Americans into internment camps during World War II.

There are, of course, many diverse Asian-American groups— Chinese, Japanese, Korean, Vietnamese, Filipino, Samoan, Indian, Pakistani, Bangladeshi—each with its own history, language, and customs. In addition, there is great diversity in terms of acculturation , generational status (fourth- and fifth-generation Chinese- and Japanese-Americans versus recent Vietnamese immigrants), and so on. Generalizing about their commonalities is risky at best. The following discussion, based primarily on D.W. Sue (1975), is most relevant to Chinese- and Japanese-Americans.

According to Sue, roles in the Asian family are rigidly defined by age, sex, and generational status. Elders are revered and respected; fathers are heads of the family, with unquestioned authority; sons' obligations to the family take precedence over roles as husband and father; females are subservient to males. Asian-Americans are thought to emphasize a practical, applied approach to life, preferring structure and concrete situations over ambiguous ones, owing perhaps to highly structured family roles and clear expectations regarding these roles (D.W. Sue, 1975). Leong (1985) speculates that intolerance of ambiguity may be related to Asian-Americans' occupational segregation into scientific and technical fields.

Asians' primary allegiance is to the family; the individual is submerged for the welfare of the family. Thus individuality and autonomy are discouraged, modesty is encouraged, and conformity and obedience are expected. One Japanese-American counselor, for example, stated that he finds himself trying to integrate individuals back into the family rather than trying to help them separate (Henton, 1985). Because behavior of the individual reflects on the whole family, individuals who "shame" themselves and "lose face" shame the whole family. Actions that are contrary to the family are labeled selfish and inconsiderate, and members are kept in line with guilt and family obligation. Problems are to be kept within the family, because public admission of problems brings family shame and harms the welfare and reputation of the family.

The premium placed on family harmony and rigid roles means that family conflict must be minimized so that one role will not interfere with another. Members must avoid offending others (both in and outside the family), and there are strong sanctions against expressing any feelings that might disrupt the system. Thus, the restraint of strong feelings is a must, and aggressiveness, assertiveness, and independence are frowned upon. Confrontation is considered impolite (Wood & Mallinckrodt, 1990); communication styles are thought to be nonverbal, nonassertive, and passive. According to Sue and Sue (1985), however, recent research suggests that nonassertiveness may be situation specific (i.e., assertive with friends and members of one's own race and more passive with authority figures).

Although the subjugation of blacks to slavery in America is well known, its far-reaching and continuing effects are often unappreciated. In Smith's words:

> The history of black people is both the bond that welds them together and sets them apart from other Americans. Black Americans. . . have experienced a cultural press different from that experienced by many minority groups in America. Few ethnic or racial minorities in American society have been so thoroughly blocked from having a constructive identity group formation, have been pressed to trust whites more so than themselves, have had a value system imposed on them that so totally and forcefully undermined their self-esteem and their very existence. (1981, p. 143).

Certainly an understanding of blacks requires a knowledge of the effects of slavery as well as their African-American heritage. Slavery profoundly affected blacks' relationships to one another as well as to whites. Smith (1981) notes two coping strategies used by blacks to survive: (1) identification with the white master (aggressor) and (2) self-debasement. Adoption of the master's values meant that blacks themselves placed higher value on those among them who were more similar to whites in skin color, facial features, and hair texture. Deference, of course, was necessary, and children, especially males, were taught to behave in a nonaggressive and cooperative manner with whites. The Black Pride movement has done much to develop positive self-identity in blacks—to value their differences from the white majority—but the remnants of slavery, whites' explanations of the status of blacks as a result of genetic inferiority and/or social pathology, and the pervasiveness of racism in American society have profound effects on blacks' psychological, economic, and career development, and, of course, their attitudes toward and relationships with whites.

In recent years, blacks have begun to reclaim the African-American heritage that was taken away from them by slavery. According to Shipp (1983), the "key to helping black clients lies in understanding black behavior as it integrates with the African ethos" (p. 109). There is cooperation among and between individuals, collective responsibility of the individual to the group, interdependence, and commonality of individuals. "Even black Americans who are estranged from African traditions and customs exhibit parallel customs and traditions (extended family, elasticity of time, religious emphasis, respect for old age, etc.)" (p. 109). White, Parham, and Parham (1980) also note the considerable emphasis the African-American culture places on cooperation and group cohesiveness. Behaviors are "valued in terms of what they contribute to the group as a collective" (p.58). Indeed, the communal nature of the black experience has led several authors to suggest that greater emphasis be placed on group approaches to counseling blacks (e.g., Lee, 1982; Shipp, 1983; Toldson & Pasteur, 1976). Smith (1981) believes that raising self-esteem may occur more quickly in groups because group interaction that compels members to examine their own behavior.

Mind–body (cognitive–affective) are viewed as different functions and both are highly valued. In comparison with the American white culture, which places a higher value on cognitive-intellectual functions, African-Americans believe that the experiencing of and openness to a range of emotions is necessary for growth. Thus, feelings are not suppressed, and African-American culture is known for its expressiveness. For example, the Call–Response is a feature in black churches; that is, congregations respond to the preacher's call with cries such as "Amen" (White et al., 1980). Being expressive and open with whites is another matter, however, and black clients "may subject white counselors to a series of tests to find out if they are prejudiced against minorities" (Smith, 1981, p. 168).

African-Americans are more present- than future-time oriented; time is conceived of in a broad sweep rather than minutes on a clock. Rather than try to control and master nature, African-Americans believe there is a natural order with which one should flow rather than seek to control. Death is viewed as another stage of life to welcome as a place to live "in peace with dignity, harmony, and equality." (White et al, 1980, p. 61).

Another cultural heritage of blacks is the extended family kinship system (Smith, 1981). The family is used to work out problems, and going outside is viewed as a violation of family ethics. Although the mother may play a prominent role in problem solving (she is revered and viewed as both strong and loving), the earlier myth of the black matriarchy has been dispelled.

Verbal and nonverbal communication patterns are typically different from those of whites in several ways. Standard English involves grammatical elaboration with little reliance on nonverbal cues. Black language, on the other hand, uses nonstandard English with considerable reliance on nonverbal aspects of communication. Further, blacks do not find it necessary to engage in eye contact while talking with another person, and

and some have pointed out that while whites tend to look at a person when listening, blacks are more likely to look at someone while talking and look away while listening. As Smith (1981) notes, white counselors can erroneously interpret lack of eye contact as sullenness, fear, or lack of interest. Further, blacks often engage in little self-disclosure in counseling, which can also be misinterpreted. Smith claims such behavior may be due to a fear of white counselors' negative evaluation of their speech (i .e., "black language"), although most writers explain that black clients' nonverbal, passive behavior in counseling as stemming from mistrust of white counselors.

Even though there are numerous *Hispanic-American* subgroups in the United States (Cuban, Latino, Mexican, Puerto Rican, South American, Central American), they have in common a history of Spanish colonialism in Latin America (Arbona, 1990). Thus, they share a similar heritage in terms of tradition, values, and language although there are also vast intracultural differences (Ruiz & Padilla, 1983). Many speak Spanish only, although some are bilingual. Many are Roman Catholic, although increasing numbers are converting to Protestantism (Casas & Atkinson, 1981). Hispanics in rural areas may live in large, extended families and, as might be expected, there is a strong family orientation. A high value may be placed on cooperation with and obligation to the family. An individual Hispanic may place himself or herself second to the family, which can be erroneously misinterpreted as having a negative self-image. (Garcia & Ybarra-Garcia, 1988). Some believe that intimate details of one's life should be shared only with the family or close friends.

Although the common belief is that there are rigid sex roles, with males being dominant (*machismo*), Ruiz (1981) asserts that these are distortions. He reminds us that the word *macho* in Spanish means "male" and is used by Hispanics as a "flattering term to denote masculinity" (p. 191). Casas and Atkinson (1981) note that younger versus first-generation Mexican-Americans are rejecting traditional sex roles in the family.

Hispanics may have a strong preference for personal contact and individual attention (*personalismo*) in dealing with the power structure. In contrast to Asian-Americans, Hispanics may prefer informal, personal approaches to other people and the use of first names rather than impersonal and formal titles. Hispanics are usually thought to be very present-time oriented (*mañana*) and fatalistic, but Ruiz and Padilla (1983) assert that these are stereotypes. The traditional emphasis placed on group cooperation versus individual achievement may be more characteristic of first-generation Hispanics. Some evidence suggests that Mexican-Americans, for example, become more competitive with greater acculturation (Casas & Atkinson, 1981).

The plight of the *Native American* at the hand of a white-imposed solution to the "Indian problem" is another negative mark in the history of the United States. Native Americans are probably "the poorest of the Poor" (Atkinson et al., 1983, p. 45). Their population has decreased considerably over the years, unemployment is nearly 40 percent, and their average annual income is 75 percent below the national average. Further, there is much understandable resentment among Native Americans about the way the federal government has handled the "Indian problem," not the least of which has been the effort to impose the white culture.

A full understanding of the Native American culture is difficult because there are over 400 recognized tribes (and a few dozen unrecognized ones), each with a unique culture. Generalizations can be made, however, about some values that many Native Americans may hold in common. According to Lewis and Ho (1983), sharing is a deeply ingrained value among Native Americans, thus "accumulation of material goods for social status is alien to the Native American" (p. 66). To illustrate the pervasiveness of the value of sharing, Trimble (1976) cites the case of the Native American child who asked his grandmother to fix him a different kind of school lunch in the future. It seems that his non-Native American teacher had forced him to eat an entire lunch that was intended to be shared with the other children.

Although Native Americans are thought to be oblivious to time, Lewis and Ho assert that they are quite time-conscious—it is just that their time has to do with natural phenomena: mornings, nights, months (in terms of moons). Trimble (1976) notes, however, that in many tribes there is no word for time that is equivalent to the English meaning.

Family ties are usually strong and include extended family members. There is much respect for and deference toward elders; grandmothers frequently raise children, and counselors may need to win their confidence to be effective with Native American clients (Attneave, 1985).

Additional values that Trimble (1976) discusses, using Anglos as the comparison group, are that Native Americans: (1) are present- versus future-oriented, (2) respect age versus youth, (3) exhibit cooperation versus competition, and (4) feel in harmony with nature rather than desiring conquest over nature. Native Americans are schooled in nature and taught to endure all natural happenings including good and evil; maturity is achieved through facing suffering. Because no distinction is made among culture, religion, and medicine, any illness is viewed as disharmony with other forces; only traditional healers can be expected to cure any disease (Richardson, 1981).

Interference with another's affairs is strongly opposed, and personal matters are usually handled within the family or extended family system. Youngman and Sandongei (1983) report that Native Americans are also noted for their tribal loyalty, reticence, humility, avoidance of personal glory and gain, abiding love for their own land, and strong spiritual beliefs.

In recent years, many Native Americans have moved to urban areas, in part because of the U.S. government's employment relocation and educational and career development programs, and in part as a response to hope that life might be better in urban areas. Over 50 percent of Native Americans now reside in urban areas (Trimble, 1976). As a result, some experience extreme conflict in values. They may feel torn, for example, between achieving status in the white culture through achievement and competition and maintaining a connection with their cultural heritage, which values cooperation, sharing, and working for the purpose of immediate pleasure rather than working for retirement (Richardson, 1981).

Native Americans may view counselors as meddlesome, perhaps partly because of the intrusion of uninvited missionaries on reservations over the years. They may be reluctant to discuss their problems with a white counselor, believing that the counselors cannot understand their views of the world. Thus, they might behave in an acquiescent or compliant manner, showing no visible signs of disagreement with what the counselor might suggest or do. Further, their culture may discourage assertiveness, and they may favor hinting or teasing rather than making direct requests or suggestions (La Fromboise, 1982). Because Native Americans show respect by not staring directly at others, they may refrain from making direct eye contact with the counselor.

One crucial career decision faced by Native American youth raised on a reservation is whether to out-migrate or remain on the reservation. The latter choice offers fewer career options, of course. But out-migrating means the youngster is faced with the need to make choices with very limited knowledge of the world of work in the larger society (Smith, 1983; Spencer, Windham, & Peterson, 1975). Further,, the cultural sanctions against speaking of one's accomplishments act as a barrier to career development and advancement.

Racial Identity and Acculturation

What is clear from the preceding discussion is that members of American racial and ethnic minority groups may hold values that are clearly at odds with the dominant white culture in the United States. The necessity of living in two worlds creates tremendous conflicts and identity confusion. Only those who are confined solely to interacting with their own kind (e.g., living in a Chinatown or on a reservation) might escape this conflict, and even then it is doubtful that it can be avoided entirely. Issues that further complicate the process of adapting to two cultures are society's oppression and racism. To understand this process and to account for individual differences within minority groups, models of acculturation and racial identity have been proposed.

Acculturation may be defined as the "steps by which ethnic minorities ascertain world views and cultural or social values of the dominant group and adapt their cultural patterns" (Dillard, 1985, p. 115). Level of acculturation can be expected to be related, among other things, to the kinds of problems clients bring to counseling, their willingness to seek counseling, and their response to working with a white or ethnically dissimilar counselor. In fact, Ruiz and Casas (1981) propose that, for Hispanics, the client's degree of acculturation will determine the extent to which counselors should use culturally relevant methods.

Sue and Sue (1971) propose a conceptual scheme of three different ways that Asian-Americans respond to the conflict between Asian values and the Western, white culture. Though this schema is somewhat controversial, it can serve as a good introduction to other models. The Traditionalist remains loyal to his or her ethnic group, adhering closely to Asian family values and standards. The Marginal attempts to become Westernized and rejects traditional Asian values. This person may reject anything Asian, feel ashamed of Asian heritage, and experience racial self-hatred and, thus, an identity crisis. This person is "marginal" because he or she cannot completely rid himself or herself of the culture and therefore stands between two different cultural conditions. The Asian-American attempts to reconcile aspects of his or her heritage with a new identity and typically rebels against parental authority. Unlike Marginals, however, Asian-Americans are quite sensitive to the forces of American society that have limited them and created problems, such as poverty and racism, and they may become militant in their concern for civil rights.

Acculturation schemas have also been proposed for Mexican-Americans (e.g., Cuellar et al., 1980; Szapocznik et al., 1978). For example, Cueller, Harris, & Jasso (1980) created a scale that classifies Mexican-Americans into one of five levels: (1) very Mexican, (2) Mexican-oriented bicultural, (3) "true" bicultural, (4) Anglo-oriented bicultural, or (5) very Anglicized. As Ponterotto (1987) notes, Mexican-Americans at "lower" levels of acculturation (who frequently speak only Spanish) will desire culturally sensitive counseling, whereas those at "higher" levels may respond well to more Westernized approaches and may have no strong preference for ethnicity of the counselor.

In regard to blacks, several models of racial identity development have been proposed. The most well known model by Cross (1971) has been refined and made operational by Helms (1984) and Parham (1989) and studied in relation to self-esteem (Parham & Helms, 1985a), counselor preference (Carter & Helms, 1987; Parham & Helms, 1981), and self-actualization (Parham & Helms, 1985b). The model proposes that blacks move through four psychological stages, experiencing a conversion from "Negro to black."

In the Preencounter stage, the person views the world from a white frame of reference, thinks and acts in ways that devalue his or her blackness, and is generally pro-white and anti-black. In the Encounter stage, individuals experience many events that are jolting to their "non-racial" identity (such as being denied a job because of skin color). These encounters cause them to realize that their present view of the world is inaccurate, and they begin to develop a black identity. In the Immersion-Emersion stage, people begin to immerse themselves in total blackness and withdraw from interactions with other ethnic groups. The attitude is pro-black, anti-white. Finally, in the Internalization stage, the individual achieves a sense of security in blackness, and the tension and defensiveness of the Immersion stage is replaced by calmness. There is a decline in strong anti-white feelings, adoption of a nonracist perspective, and a willingness to interact with people from other ethnic groups (Cross, 1971; 1978; Helms, 1984; Parham, 1989).

Parham (1989) has extended Cross's model and described how racial identity stages might be manifested throughout the life cycle (late adolescence/early adulthood, middle adulthood, late adulthood). One would expect black clients at different stages of racial consciousness to vary considerably in their attitudes toward several aspects of counseling, such as willingness to seek help, preferred ethnicity of the counselor, trust in white counselors, willingness to self-disclose, and so on. One could also speculate, with Brooks (1990), about the relationship between the stages and perceptions of career alternatives that are desirable. Preencounter blacks who perceive their own characteristics as negative (low self-esteem) and idealize whites might perceive their career options as restricted to those requiring a low level of abilities or to those that fit social stereotypes regarding appropriate choices of blacks. Immersion-stage blacks, focused on racial discrimination, might prefer options that avoid whites and "prove that they have not 'sold out' to the white world" (Helms, 1984, p. 155). As Helms has described, affective issues, counselor–client strategies, and counseling outcomes can be expected to differ depending on the racial identity stage of both the counselor and the client. To illustrate, in black dyads with both the counselor and the client at the Preencounter stage, both will feel anger about being assigned to a black person, both will use strategies to avoid and deny racial issues, the client will terminate with little progress, and the counselor will "push" the client out of counseling. In a racially mixed dyad with a white counselor in the Reintegration stage (see earlier discussion of white racial consciousness) and a black client in the Internalization stage, the counselor feels pain and/or anxiety, uneasiness and incongruence, and interacts with a very reserved manner. The client senses the counselor's discomfort and prematurely terminates.

In those dyads with a progressive relationship (the counselor's stage is more advanced than the client's), the counselor should be able to help move the client toward a healthier state. Parallel relationships (the counselor and the client are at the same stage) may produce a counseling impasse. As Helms explains, "The counselor cannot move the client further than the counselor has come" (1984, p. 159).

Finally, it should be noted that Atkinson et al. (1983) have developed a minority identity model similar to Cross's that is applicable to all American racial groups.

SKILL (TECHNIQUE) BASES

Several caveats need to precede any discussion of specific techniques. First, many of the suggestions are based on the idea that racial or ethnic minorities bring with them a specific cultural background that requires counselors to modify their approaches. It is important, however, to avoid overgeneralizing (e.g., all black Americans are interested in social occupations) and to remember that racial minorities are no more homogeneous than are American whites. For example, even though first-generation Asian-Americans or recent immigrants may be uncomfortable with self-disclosure, this may not be the case with those who have assumed a bicultural identity. Second, the suggested techniques are limited to one-to-one counseling situations. This is a severe limitation because group approaches are the treatment of choice for some problems with some minorities. Further, many of the problems that ethnic clients bring to counseling are externally caused, either directly or indirectly (Pedersen et al., 1981) and effective, long-term solutions require political action—steps that counselors and clients are often unwilling or unable to take. We do maintain, however, that advocacy interventions (e.g., intervening with social service agencies) that require counselors to take direct action and operate away from their offices are necessary at times, although a detailed discussion of these types of strategies is beyond the scope of this chapter.

Because general counseling issues, such as establishing rapport, goal setting, and so forth, are of utmost importance in cross-cultural counseling, more emphasis is placed on these areas than on career counseling techniques.

GENERAL COUNSELING ISSUES

Establishing Rapport

Establishing a working relationship with an ethnic client may be the most important as well as the most challenging task for the white counselor. Many ethnic minorities enter counseling with considerable mistrust of white counselors, as well as negative expectations regarding the usefulness of counseling in resolving problems. Issues of differences in language, socioeconomic status, and racial and ethnic background create additional barriers. Special efforts will often be needed to establish trust and counselor credibility, as well as to create positive expectations about counseling. A number of suggestions for counselors follow.

1. Openly acknowledge and invite the client's reactions to the ethnic dissimilarity between the client and yourself in the first counseling session. This suggestion has been made by many authors (e.g., Jones & Seagull, 1983; Smith, 1981), and at least one study shows that counselors who were willing to discuss race fared better (Krebs, 1971). Failure to call attention to this quite obvious situation can easily be perceived by the client as counselor discomfort or anxiety and interfere with establishing trust. Further, dealing forthrightly with racial dissimilarity lets the client know that you are not hesitant to discuss the client's reaction to you. For example, you might say:

Co: I'm wondering about your feelings about talking with someone from a different culture. Quite understandably, some clients have some concerns about working with a white counselor, and I'm wondering if that's the case for you.

Client responses to this inquiry can be expected to vary considerably, so it is impossible to provide specific suggestions for each situation. In general, too much discomfort on the client's (or your) part may necessitate a referral to another counselor of similar ethnicity to the client. Also, if a client indicates no particular concerns during the first session, for example, because he or she has none at the time, or because sufficient trust has not yet been established for the client to acknowledge such concerns openly, or because the client's culture discourages expression of negative feelings that might offend others (e.g., Asian-American), and so on, you should convey to the client the importance of discussing any issues that may occur in the future. Further, you will want to be alert to the possibility that such "lack of concern" may be related to the client's stage of racial identity or acculturation. For example, black clients in the Immersion stage may keep their angry feelings about being assigned to a white counselor to themselves and simply not return for the next session. Clearly, you should be prepared to discuss potential problems and, if possible, how they might be overcome (Tucker et al., 1981).

2 Be sensitive to cultural differences in nonverbal communication, such as personal space, eye contact, and conversation conventions (D.W. Sue, 1981). Some Hispanic subcultures, for example, are more comfortable with shorter personal space than are many whites. Mexican-American clients may feel rejected if a white counselor moves his or her chair further away. Looking directly at a person who is speaking is a sign of disrespect for Vietnamese; eye-to-eye gazing is a sign of aggressiveness for Navajos. Blacks tend to look at the other person while talking and away while listening— the opposite of patterns for whites. You must be careful not to misinterpret lack of eye contact as rudeness, inattentiveness, or shyness. In regard to conversation conventions, when to speak and when to yield varies among cultures. For example, in the Asian culture, silence is a sign of respect and does not necessarily signal a floor-yielding response. Further, counselors who urge Asians to "get to the point" may be interpreted as rude or immature (D.W. Sue, 1981). Christensen (1983) emphasizes the importance of calling clients by their right name. Puerto Ricans, for example, are given two last names, one from the father and one from the mother. Both are equally important, so to use just one name in calling the client would be offensive. Christensen also urges a counselor to make special efforts to pronounce the Hispanic client's name correctly because the "person's name is the person," seemingly a good suggestion in any counseling situation.

3. Consider how credibility can be attained with the client. Sue and Zane (1987) believe that one of the most important ways that counselors can use their knowledge of the culture of the client is to help themselves understand ways to enhance their credibility with the client; that is, the client's belief in the counselor. For example, some authors suggest that blacks will be more likely to trust and give credibility to white counselors who are willing to be self-disclosing and thus show they are "human beings." According to Vontress (1981), trust is more important for blacks

than understanding. He further asserts that being understood will be threatening to blacks because it raises fears regarding engulfment and loss of autonomy. A comment that indicates your knowledge of the client's culture might enhance credibility. If that is not possible, your acknowledgment that race may be relevant in the client's problems or expression of interest in learning more about the client's culture can be assuring. A study by Pomales, Claiborn, & La Fromboise (1986), for example, showed that the culturally sensitive counselor (i.e., one who indicated a willingness to discuss the effects of race on the client's problem) was rated as more credible than the culture-blind counselor. Trimble (1981), however, warns that counselors can become so fascinated by and preoccupied with cultural differences that they completely ignore the client's problem. With traditional Asians, credibility can be enhanced by establishing the authority of the counselor through, for example, explicitly structuring the counseling (see following) or indicating a willingness to get involved in the client's problem by taking direct action.

Sue and Zane (1987) also assert that credibility can be enhanced and skepticism decreased through "gift giving"; that is, something the counselor does that enables the client immediately to feel a direct benefit from counseling. The "gift" should demonstrate the relationship between counseling and problem resolution. Examples of gifts are crisis intervention, which focuses on helping clients develop cognitive clarity, and normalizing the client's problem (i.e., assuring clients that their thoughts, feelings, and behaviors are common)—particularly important in those cultures in which individuals do not discuss problems outside the family. Other examples of gift giving are reassurance, hope, goal setting (see following), anxiety reduction, depression relief, and providing a coping perspective.

4. "The more similar two people are, the better they should be able to communicate" (Stewart, 1981, p. 102). Smith (1985) suggests that counselors try to find some common reference point with clients to enhance assumed similarity, much like two strangers getting acquainted who discover they have a friend in common. Overzealousness in calling attention to points of similarity should be curbed, however, to avoid the client's perception that you are making phony attempts to identify with him or her.

5. Emphasize the confidential nature of the relationship. Though confidentiality is presumably important to all clients, it deserves

special emphasis with ethnic clients from cultures with sanctions against talking about problems outside the family.

6. Language barriers can be a serious deterrent to establishing rapport with a minority client. If neither the client nor you are bilingual, an interpreter will be needed, or the client should be referred. If the client lacks facility with standard English, and you are monolingual, it is a good idea to frequently restate the client's utterances to prevent misinterpretation. Do not be reluctant to indicate a failure of comprehension and ask for clarification.

7. Be patient with clients who say little and reveal minimal information about themselves. Many ethnic minorities are suspicious of white counselors and will be unwilling to be self-disclosing until some basis for trust has been established. This reluctance may be particularly true for blacks and Native Americans. Self-disclosure for traditional Asians involves shame and loss of face and is not necessarily resistance. A confrontive and emotionally intense approach at the onset of counseling might increase that client's shame (Sue, 1975), as might questions that seem to seek very personal information.

GOAL SETTING

As discussed in Chapter 13, developing explicit goals for counseling is essential. Of particular importance to the subject at hand is that the goals be culturally relevant and congruent. For example, urging traditional Asians or Hispanics to "cut the apron strings" in order to pursue a career may be offensive. On the other hand, clients may want to pursue career goals that will remove them from their subculture. Intermediate goals would then to be to assist clients with the necessary intermediate adjustments, such as removing guilt for leaving others behind. According to Vontress (1981), "fear of achievement. . . is pervasive among disadvantaged minorities" (p. 104). They fear the envy and rejection that may come from their ethnic peers. Though goals should generally be culturally congruent, Sue and Zane (1987) appropriately caution us that at times culturally incongruent goals will be necessary; for example, the client may need to learn new behaviors such as assertiveness in order to engage in effective job interviewing.

STRUCTURING THE COUNSELING

The need to explicitly structure the counseling has been repeatedly emphasized in this book. More attention than usual to this aspect of counseling may be needed with many ethnic minority clients who have little knowledge about counseling, may be suspicious of outsiders in general and white counselors in particular, and may be from a culture that encourages structured situations (Vontress, 1981). Trimble and La Fromboise state, for example, that "many Native American clients simply do not know what is expected of then'; the notion of what constitutes good client behavior may never have occurred to them" (1985, p. 131). Providing structure might also enhance the counselor's credibility because it conveys the message that the counselor knows what he or she is doing. Explaining the role of the counselor (what and how) and the expected role of the client is a good beginning. Also needed, however, is an explanation of why the counselor is doing certain things. Sue (1981) gives the example of a Chicano career counseling client who was uncomfortable with the questions the counselor was asking about her interests and past experiences. Once the counselor explained the career counseling process (e.g., assessment of likes, dislikes, skills, job experience, goals, and fit with possible jobs), the client relaxed and eagerly participated.

A good place to start in establishing structure is to ask the client about his or her expectations, for example: "What do you expect to happen when we meet together?" The counselor, of course, needs to be prepared to modify his or her approach if necessary, for example, be more action oriented, directive, or play an advocacy role. Ruiz and Padilla (1983) suggest that some Hispanics may anticipate an active approach that leads to concrete solutions. Before the client leaves the first session, there should be some explicit initial agreement about how the counselor and client will work together.

ASSESSMENT AND DIAGNOSIS

In any counseling situation, the counselor must diagnose and assess the client's problems in order to provide appropriate interventions. Several special issues arise in cross-cultural counseling, however. Because language can be a barrier, it is necessary to determine the client's readability level in standard English if tests and inventories are to be used. Cultural barriers can also be an issue for those who have remained physically and psychologically isolated from the cultural mainstream of American life

(Vontress, 1981). Whether a formal assessment device developed and normed in the United States, such as an interest or personality inventory, will be valid and useful will depend in part on a client's acculturation status and/or the degree to which his or her cultural values are similar to those in mainstream America. Lonner (1985) notes, for example, that mainstream America "values competition, quick intelligence, independence, achievement, and other characteristics that correlate with success as defined by a free enterprise system" (p. 604). Tests of intelligence, achievement, and abilities reflect these values. He notes that psychological measurements are based on assumptions that may not be valid for some groups, such as assumptions that people can rank stimuli along a linear continuum and that they can engage in self-assessment using evaluative and reflective processes. Further, many of these measures do not provide specific norms for various ethnic groups, and to the degree that race and ethnic origin may produce inaccurate test scores—admittedly a controversial and unresolved issue—the results must be interpreted cautiously.

Finally, the accuracy of scores from certain ethnic groups may be reduced by "response sets" (Lonner, 1985). For example, the tendency to agree rather than disagree—the acquiescent response set—might be expected from some Native and Asian-Americans; thus, scores on inventories with a true–false format may be invalid. Answering inventories in a "socially desirable" way may be more indigenous to one culture than another but might also reflect lack of rapport with and trust in the counselor. Some inventories, of course, have special scales to detect response sets (such as a "lie" scale), but they are based on the culture of the norm group used in scoring and interpreting the inventory. Lest the reader conclude that there are few instances where a standardized inventory might be useful with ethnic minority clients, the following should be noted: (1) the inventories can generally be used quite effectively with ethnic clients who are truly bicultural; (2) some inventories do have versions in other languages (e.g., the Spanish version of the SDS); and (3) counselors can assess the degree to which response sets might have influenced scores by discussing this issue with client. Extreme response sets would, of course, invalidate the scores but could also provide important clues about the client's personality, approach to life (Lonner, 1985), or cultural values.

An alternative to formal assessment is an informal approach, although the extent to which informal approaches provide more objective measures is questionable as they are more susceptible to lack of rapport and trust in the counseling relationship, as well as counselor stereotypes and cultural blind spots. For example, a Native American's humility or an Asian-American's modesty about skills and accomplishments might lead the counselor to believe that the client has limited abilities and interests.

In another realm, assessment for purposes of conceptualizing the sources of the client's problem is a particularly thorny issue. Counselors with little awareness of the ethnic client's culture, interpersonal styles, and ways of interacting with whites can easily misinterpret the client's problems or interpret them in ways that lead to interventions that would be culturally insensitive (e.g., encouraging traditional Asians to confront parents about conflicting occupational goals).

A final assessment issue of importance is the level of acculturation or racial identity of the client. Acculturation or racial identity status can be expected to affect (1) the client's general response to being assigned a white counselor, (2) the kinds of problems the client brings to counseling, and (3) the degree to which counseling should be modified to be culturally relevant. Acculturation can be assessed informally or through measures (see the previous section on racial identity) designed for this purpose. Some general guidelines for assessment follow:

1. Delay hypotheses about client problems, because important critical information may not be forthcoming until later.

2. Be alert to internalized oppression (i.e., clients have taken on or internalized society's negative views of their ethnic group) as a source of low self-esteem or views of self as deficient. Help the client distinguish between intrapsychic and extrapsychic sources of stress (Smith, 1981, 1985). Intrapsychic problems are those that arise independent of the client's ethnic membership. For, example, the need to obtain a job is an issue faced by most adults, and anxiety about this situation may not be related to one's ethnic minority status. Extrapsychic problems are those that originate in societal or environmental conditions. A poor self-concept or limited occupational opportunities due to race are examples of extrapsychic sources of stress.

3. Important areas to assess in regard to career choice are range of perceived options, perceived structure of opportunity, influence of others such as parents and extended family, self-estimates of ability, and locus of control. Assessment issues related to job adjustment include the degree to which the client understands and/or adheres to white standards in the workplace (e.g., punctuality).

RESISTANCE

Resistance, covered in Chapter 12, can be an especially difficult issue in cross-cultural counseling. On the one hand, many writers have urged the ethnically dissimilar counselor to be careful about labeling certain culturally relevant client behaviors as resistance, such as low self-disclosure of Native Americans or late arrivals for appointments by blacks. On the other hand, counselors can be so overwhelmed by differences between themselves and the client (Vontress, 1981), or be so concerned about being culturally biased, that they ignore signs of resistance that would be obvious in other counseling relationships. Vontress cites the example of Hispanic-heritage clients who present themselves as lacking fluency in English when in actuality they are quite adept. Similarly, black clients may be appear to be shy, withdrawn, and nonverbal, or alternatively quite agreeable. Nonverbal clients may be quite verbal in other situations but are "playing it cool" until they are convinced the counselor is of good will. Vontress suggests that a counselor should be willing to verbalize to a black client any cues that the client is appeasing the counselor.

There are no simple solutions to distinguishing resistance from culturally sanctioned behaviors or from merely cautious behavior as a coping response to a racist society. Perhaps the best advice is that counselors be alert to the usual signs of resistance as covered in Chapter 12 (e.g., overcompliance and cooperativeness, late arrivals, low self-disclosure), develop hypotheses about how these behaviors might be related to the specific culture or coping devices of the ethnic client, and at the same time remain alert to any behaviors or actions of their own that might be contributing (e.g., inadequate stucturing).

CAREER COUNSELING ISSUES

"Career planning [is] an unaffordable luxury for minorities, who were, and to a great extent still are, concerned with survival" (Jackson, 1982, p. 15). In part because of this situation, many authors suggest that counselors take on other roles, such as advocacy, consultation, outreach, and psychoeducational programming. Still, minority clients do show up occasionally at career counselors' doors, and counselors must be prepared to use techniques that will effectively address client needs.

Increasing Clients' Occupational Information

Several methods to increase client occupational awareness are discussed in Chapter 15. Emphasis is placed there on the effectiveness of exposing clients to successful role models. For many racial and ethnic minorities this approach needs even greater attention. Minorities raised in culturally isolated situations (e.g., Native Americans on the reservation) may have quite limited ideas about their occupational alternatives because of lack of exposure to Native American workers. Spencer, Windham, and Peterson (1975) found that 60 percent of their sample of high school students from the Choctaw nation limited their aspirations to those jobs found on the reservation (e.g., teacher, automobile mechanic, and secretary). Exposure to ethnically similar occupational role models is important for expanding visions, raising expectations for achievement, and increasing general self-efficacy (Bandura, 1977). Such exposure can best be accomplished by arranging face-to-face meetings, and vocational biographies can also be helpful. Dean (1984) suggests that career exploration sites be developed, particularly with black entrepreneurs. In addition, McDavis and Parker (1981) propose that culturally relevant materials be developed, such as scrapbooks of articles about successful minorities, audiotaped interviews, and slide/tape presentations. Dean notes the need for meaningful, systematic job tryouts, not just field experiences. In many instances, it would also be effective to present career information to those who will have considerable influence on the client's decision, such as parents (Campbell, 1975).

The Client with Limited Career Interests

The client with few interests is discussed in Chapter 12, and several suggestions are made for helping clients expand their stated interests. Some clients with limited interests may be restricting themselves because of low self-estimates of ability and/or lack of information about the world of work in general, as a result of limited life experiences and opportunities. Suggestions for dealing with these issues, as noted in Chapter 12, include reattribution training, and skill identification through assessment of achievements.

In regard to minority clients, it is likely that an additional constraint may underlie their small range of perceived options. More specifically, the opportunity structure is or is perceived by them to be extremely restricted for their ethnic group. Research showing that blacks and Hispanics have higher educational and occupational aspirations but lower expectations than whites for achieving their aspirations supports the idea that these groups "may be aware that they will encounter barriers (economic, educational, discriminatory) in the process of pursuing their educational goals" (Arbona, 1990, p. 305). Certainly, the reality is that oppression and racism have interfered with the career development of minority group members, and those who have encountered that situation may feel discouraged or defeated. For others without direct experience with occupational discrimination, the opportunity structure can act as a nonconscious barrier when the only models they have are those in low-paying menial jobs. Exposing clients to successful role models would seem especially important to help them increase their expectations.

One way to discover if clients are limiting themselves to beliefs about what occupations are ethnically appropriate or possible, is to administer an occupational card sort (see Chapter 5) and then ask whether they believe any of the occupations in the card sort are unavailable to them because of their race or ethnicity. Alternatively, as Griffith (1980) proposed, the counselor might simply ask clients how they view the role of race in their options. Another assessment technique would be to administer a measure of perceived opportunity for attainment (Howell, Frese, & Sollie, 1984). What these techniques might reveal is that clients think they have no control over the environment; that is, they have an external locus of control (Leong, 1985; Sue, 1981). Though counselors would certainly not want to negate the client's feelings, they also need to help the client assess the reality of his or her beliefs (see the section in Chapter 12 on realistic aspirations) and perhaps develop skills to cope with issues he or she may face in employment, such as racism. Many clients will never seek career counseling, therefore counselors concerned about this issue may want to be proactive in setting up programs in schools or community agencies, as suggested by Smith (1980). Dean (1984), for example, recommends Tucker's (1973) "action counseling" with black youth with an external locus of control—a seven-step process that helps young people achieve short-term goals and teaches them that they can have control over their immediate environment. Several authors suggest that group approaches would be effective with blacks because of their communal heritage. An approach used by Lee (1982) in a career program for black youth relies heavily on popular black music. Dean also suggests using genealogy to encourage black young people to see their academic potential in a project wherein they conduct oral interviews with family members (parents, aunts, uncles, grandparents) with particular emphasis on family members' views about their aspirations and how they were thwarted or facilitated. This process, according to Dean, will teach students that certain environmental constraints can be overcome.

LIMITATIONS OF CROSS-CULTURAL CAREER COUNSELING

1. Despite efforts of counselors to develop the attitudes, knowledge, and skills of a cross-culturally skilled counselor, cross-ethnic counseling dyads may be unsuccessful.
2. Our knowledge about the necessary and sufficient conditions for successful cross-cultural counseling is still limited.

LEARNING TO BE A CROSS-CULTURALLY SKILLED COUNSELOR

Five techniques are helpful in enhancing a counselor's cross-cultural counseling skills:

1. Obtain knowledge about the history and cultural values of the ethnic client especially to gain an understanding of ways particular groups have been and are oppressed by American society. Extensive reading about the four major American ethnic minority groups is a must. Autobiographies can be extremely useful in gaining an understanding of oppression and racial identity development (e.g., Malcolm X, 1964). When faced with a client of an unfamiliar culture, acknowledge your ignorance and ask the client to teach you about his or her culture. Between sessions, do some reading on your own.

2. Intellectual knowledge about cultures is insufficient. Experiential or affective understanding is a must. As Alderfer (1982) puts it, "we whites seem to have an almost endless array of tactics to avoid facing the emotions in ourselves in relation to the subject of race. I believe it is very difficult, if not impossible, for white people to learn about race without having our emotions aroused" (p. 182). Start by getting in touch with your own oppression—all individuals are oppressed in some way; and "feeling" your own experience is an important exercise in empathy building. Several authors suggest that white counselor's need to place themselves deliberately in situations where they will experience what it is to feel different and where they will learn the culture, lifestyle, and language of the minority group. Such situations include attending ethnic social functions and taking every possible opportunity to interact with minorities (McDavis & Parker, 1981). Vontress (1981), believes that counselors should live on location for several days or weeks, such as in a predominately black neighborhood.

3. Assess your white racial consciousness using Helms's (1984) model. Ask yourself how your current level will affect your work with ethnic minority clients. Arrange experiences for yourself that will facilitate your movement through the stages.

4. Seek out opportunities to work with ethnic clients and to have a member of an ethnic minority as a supervisor, if possible.

5. If you experience prejudicial attitudes, deal with them by seeking supportive consultation.

SUMMARY

Counseling and career development theory have been criticized as inadequate with regard to American racial and ethnic minority groups. Career development theory minimizes the constraining forces of American society as factors that greatly influence career development and choice. Instead, the emphasis is on intrapsychic explanations and, in line with Western, white, middle-class values, the person is viewed as able to make free choices that will bring occupational success and satisfaction.

Counseling approaches are also embedded in the white culture and similarly reflect values that are alien to American racial and ethnic groups. Premiums placed on individual autonomy, independence, separation from family, self-disclosure, and self-exploration, for example, can lead white counselors to provide culturally irrelevant and insensitive services.

Counseling ethnic clients should be based on a cross-cultural perspective. Such a framework requires that counselors become aware of the white culture-bound assumptions underlying counseling approaches, move beyond an unconscious ethnocentric bias and lack of awareness as a racial being to an intellectual and affective appreciation and respect for cultural diversity, attain knowledge about the culture of their clients and an understanding of the effects of oppression (e.g., racism) on the psychological and career development of ethnic minorities (e.g., acculturation and racial-identity processes), and develop a larger, more flexible repertoire of skills that are culturally relevant and effective.

REFERENCES AND SUGGESTED READING

Alderfer, C.P. (1982). Problems of changing white males' behavior and beliefs concerning race relations. In P. Goodman (ed.). *Change in Organizations* 122–65. San Francisco: Jossey-Bass.

Arbona, C. (1989). Hispanic employment and the Holland typology of work. *Career Development Quarterly* 37: 257–68.

Arbona, C. (1990). Career counseling research and Hispanics: A review of the literature. *The Counseling Psychologist* 18: 300–23.

Atkinson, D.R., Morten, G., & Sue, D.W. (1983). *Counseling American Minorities*. Dubuque, IA: Wm. C. Brown.

Attneave, C.L. (1985). Practical counseling with American Indian and Alaska Native clients. In P. Pedersen (ed.) (1985). *Handbook of Cross-cultural Counseling and Therapy* 135–40. Westport, CT: Greenwood Press.

Bandura, A. (1977). *Social Learning Theory*. Englewood Cliffs, NJ: Prentice-Hall.

Brooks, L. (1990). Recent developments in theory building. In D. Brown, L. Brooks, & Associates, *Career Choice and Development* 364–94. San Francisco: Jossey-Bass.

Campbell, R.E. (1975). Special groups and career behavior: Implications for guidance. In J. Picou, & R.E. Campbell (eds.). *Career Behavior of Special Groups* 424–44. Columbus, OH: Merrill.

Carney, C.G., & Kahn, K.B. (1984). Building competencies for effective cross-cultural counseling: A developmental view. *The Counseling Psychologist* 12(1): 111–19.

Carter, R.T., & Helms, J.E. (1987). Relationship of black value orientations to racial identity attitudes. *Measurement and Evaluation in Counseling and Development* 19: 185–95.

Casas, J.M., & Atkinson, D.R. (1981). The Mexican American in higher education: An example of subtle stereotyping. *Personnel and Guidance Journal* 59: 473–76.

Christensen, E.W. (1983). Counseling Puerto Ricans: Some cultural considerations. In D.R. Atkinson, G. Morten, & D.W. Sue. *Counseling American Minorities* 204–12. Dubuque, IA: Wm. C. Brown.

Cross, W.E. (1971). The Negro to Black conversion experiences: Towards a psychology of Black liberation. *Black World* 20(9): 13–27.

Cross, W.E. (1978). The Cross and Thomas models of psychological Nigrescence. *Journal of Black Psychology* 5: 13–19.

Cuellar, J., Harris, L.C., & Jasso, R. (1980). An acculturation scale for Mexican American normal and clinical populations. *Hispanic Journal of Behavioral Sciences* 2: 199–217.

Dean, S.A. (1984). External locus of control and career counseling for black youth. *Journal of Non-White Concerns in Personnel and Guidance* 12: 110–16.

Dillard, J.M. (1985). *Multicultural Counseling*. Chicago: Nelson-Hall.

Doughtie, E.B., Chang, W-N, Alston, H.L., Wakefield, J.A., Jr., and Yom, B.L. (1976). Black-white differences on the Vocational Preferences Inventory. *Journal of Vocational Behavior* 8: 41-44.

Fukuyama, M.A. (1990) Career Development and Asian-Americans: A response to the Gallup Survey. Paper presented at the National Conference of the National Career Development Association, Scottsdale, AZ (January)

Garcia, F., Jr., & Ybarra-Garcia, M. (1988). Strategies for Counseling Hispanics: Effects of racial and cultural stereotypes. (Revised). ERIC reports, ED # 300-687., U.S. Department of Education.

Gottfredson, L.S. (1978). Providing black youth more access to enterprising work. *Vocational Guidance Quarterly* 27: 114–23.

Griffith, A.R. (1980). Justification for a black career development. *Counselor Education and Supervision* 19: 301–09.

Hager, P.C., & Elton, C.F. (1971). The vocational interests of black males. *Journal of Vocational Behavior* 1: 153–58.

Helms, J.E. (1984). Toward a theoretical explanation of the effects of race on counseling: A black and white model. *The Counseling Psychologist* 12(4): 153–65.

Henton, W. A. (1985). Toward counseling the Japanese in America: A cross-cultural primer. *Journal of Counseling and Development* 63: 500–03.

Howell, F.M., Frese, W., & Sollie. R. (1984). The measurement of perceived opportunity for occupational attainment. *Journal of Occupational Behavior* 25: 325–43

Ibrahim, F.A. (1985). Effective cross-cultural counseling and psychotherapy: A framework. *The Counseling Psychologist* 13: 625–38.

Jackson, S.M (1982). *Career Planning for Minority Women*. Washington, DC: Women's Educational Equity Act Program, U.S. Department of Education.

Jones, A., & Seagull, A.A. (1983). Dimensions of the relationship between the Black client and the White therapist: A theoretical overview. In D.R. Atkinson, G. Morten, & D.W. Sue, *Counseling American Minorities* 156–66. Dubuque, IA: Wm. C. Brown.

Katz, J.H. (1985). The sociopolitical nature of counseling. *The Counseling Psychologist* 13: 615–24.

Kimball, R.L., Sedlacek, W.E., & Brooks, G.C. (1973). Black and white vocational interests on Holland's Self-Directed Search (SDS). *The Journal of Negro Education* 42: 1–4.

Kitano, H.H.L., & Matsushima, N. (1981). Counseling Asian Americans. In P.D. Pedersen, et al. (eds.). *Counseling Across Cultures* 163–30. Honolulu: University Press of Hawaii.

Krebs, R.C. (1971). Some effects of a white institution on black psychiatric outpatients. *American Journal of Orthopsychiatry* 41: 589–96.

Krogman, W.M. (1945). The concept of race. In R. Linton (ed.), *The Science of Man in World Crisis* 38–62. New York: Columbia University Press.

La Fromboise, T.D. (1982). *Assertion Training with American Indians: Cultural Behavioral Issues for Trainers*. Las Cruces, NM: ERIC Clearinghouse on Rural Education and Small Schools.

Lee, C.C. (1982). The school counselor and the black child: Critical roles and functions. *Journal of Non-White Concerns in Personnel and Guidance* 10: 94–101.

Leong, F.T.L. (1985). Career development of Asian Americans. *Journal of College Student Personnel* 26: 539–46.

Lewis, R.G., & Ho, M.K. (1983). Social work with Native Americans. In D. R. Atkinson, G. Morten, & D.W. Sue. *Counseling American Minorities* 65–72. Dubuque, IA: Wm. C. Brown.

Lonner, W.J. (1 985). Issues in testing and assessment in cross-cultural counseling. *The Counseling Psychologist* 13: 599–614.

McDavis, R.J., & Parker, W.M. (1981). Strategies for helping ethnic minorities with career development. *Journal of Non-White Concerns in Personnel and Guidance* 9:130–136.

Malcolm X. (1964). *Autobiography of Malcolm X*. New York: Golden Press.

Osipow, S.H. (1975). The relevance of theories of career development to special groups: Problems, needed data, and implications. In J.S. Picou, & R.E. Campbell (eds.). *Career Behavior of Special Groups* 9–22. Columbus, OH: Merrill.

Padilla, A.M., Ruiz, R.A., & Alvarez, R. (1983). Community mental health services for Spanish-speaking/surnamed population. In D. R. Atkinson, G. Morten, & D.W. Sue. *Counseling American Minorities* 181–203. Dubuque, IA: Wm. C. Brown.

Parham, T.A. (1989). Cycles of psychological nigrescence. The *Counseling Psychologist* 17: 187–226.

Parham, T.A., & Helms, J.E. (1981). The influence of Black students' racial identity attitudes on preference for counselor's race. *Journal of Counseling Psychology* 28: 250–57.

Parham, T.A., & Helms, J.E. (1985a). Relation of racial identity attitudes to self-actualization and affective states of Black students. *Journal of Counseling Psychology* 32: 431–40.

Parham, T.A., & Helms, J.E. (1985b). Attitudes of racial identity and self-esteem of Black students: An exploratory investigation. *Journal of College Student Personnel* 26: 143–46.

Pedersen, P.D., Draguns, J.G., Lonner, W.J., & Trimble, J.E. (1981). *Counseling Across Cultures*. Honolulu, University Press of Hawaii.

Pomales, J., Claiborn, C.D., & La Fromboise, T.D. (1980). Effects of black students' racial identity on perceptions of white counselors varying in cultural sensitivity. *Journal of Counseling Psychology* 33: 57–61.

Ponterotto, J.G. (1987). Counseling Mexican Americans: A multimodal approach. *Journal of Counseling and Development* 65: 308-312.

Richardson, E.H. (1981). Cultural and historical perspectives in counseling American Indians. In D.W. Sue. *Counseling the Culturally Different* 216–55. New York: John Wiley.

Ruiz, R.A. (1981). Cultural and historical perspectives in counseling Hispanics. In D.W. Sue. *Counseling the Culturally Different* 186–215. New York: John Wiley.

Ruiz, R.A., & Casas, M.M. (1981). Culturally relevant and behavioristic counseling for Chicano college students. In P.D. Pedersen et al. *Counseling Across Cultures* 181–202. Honolulu: University Press of Hawaii.

Ruiz, R.A., & Padilla, A.M. (1983). Counseling Latinos. In D.R. Atkinson, G. Morten, & D.W. Sue, *Counseling American Minorities* 213–31. Dubuque, IA: Wm. C. Brown.

Shipp, P.L. (1983). Counseling blacks: A group approach. *Personnel and Guidance Journal* 62: 108–11.

Smith, E.J. (1975). Profile of the black individual in vocational literature. *Journal of Vocational Behavior* 6: 41–59.

Smith, E.J. (1980). Career development of minorities in nontraditional fields. *Journal of Non-White Concerns in Personnel and Guidance* 8: 141–56.

Smith, E.J. (1981). Cultural and historical perspectives in counseling Blacks. In D.W. Sue (1981). *Counseling the Culturally Different*, 141–85. New York: John Wiley.

Smith, E.J. (1983). Issues in racial minorities' career behavior. In W.B. Walsh, & S.H., Osipow (eds.): *Handbook of Vocational Psychology*. Vol 1: 161–222. Hillsdale, NJ: Lawrence Erlbaum.

Smith, E.J. (1985). Ethnic minorities: Life stress, social support, and mental health issues. *The Counseling Psychologist*, 13 (4): 537–80.

Spencer, B.G., Windham, G.O., Peterson, J.H., Jr. (1975). Occupational orientations of an American Indian group. In J.S. Picou, & R. E. Campbell (eds.), *Career Behavior of Special Groups* 199–223. Columbus, OH: Merill.

Stewart, E.C. (1981). Cultural sensitivities in counseling. In P. Pedersen et al (eds.), *Counseling Across Cultures*, 61–86. Honolulu, HI: The University Press of Hawaii.

Sue, D.W. (1975). Asian-Americans: Social-psychological forces affecting their life styles. In J.S., Picou, & R.E. Campbell (eds.). *Career Behavior of Special Groups,* 97–121. Columbus, OH: Merrill.

Sue, D.W. (1981). *Counseling the Culturally Different.* New York: John Wiley.

Sue, D.W., Bernier, J.E., Feinberg, L., Pedersen, P., Smith, E.J., Vasquez-Nuttall, E. (1982). Position paper: Cross-cultural counseling competencies. *The Counseling Psychologist* 10(2): 45–52.

Sue, D.W., & Sue, D. (1985). Asian-Americans and Pacific Islanders. In P. Pedersen (ed.). *Handbook of Cross-cultural Counseling and Therapy,* 141–46. Westport, CT: Greenwood Press.

Sue, D.W., & Sue, S. (1977). Barriers to effective cross-cultural counseling. *Journal of Counseling Psychology* 24: 420–29.

Sue, S. (1977). Community mental health services to minority groups: Some pessimism, some optimism. *American Psychologist* 32: 616–24.

Sue, S., & Sue, D.W. (1971). Chinese-American personality and mental health. *Amerasia Journal* 1: 36–49.

Sue, S., & Zane, N. (1987). The role of culture and cultural techniques in psychotherapy: A critique and reformulation. *American Psychologist* 42: 37–45

Suinn, R.M., Rickard-Figueroa, K., Lew, S., & Vigil, P. (1987). The Suinn-Lew Asian Self-Identity Acculturation Scale: An initial report. *Educational and Psychological Measurement* 47: 401–07.

Szapocznik, J., Scopetta, M.H, Kurtines, W., & Arnalde, M.A. (1978). Theory and measurement of acculturation. *Interamercian Journal of Psychology* 12: 113–20.

Toldson, I.L., & Pasteur, A.B. (1976). Therapeutic dimensions of the Black aesthetic. *Journal of Non-White Concerns in Personnel and Guidance* 4: 105–17.

Trimble, J.E. (1976). Value differences among American Indians: Concerns for the concerned counselor. In P. Pedersen, W.L. Conner, & J.G. Draguns (eds.). *Counseling Across Cultures,* 65–81. Honolulu: The University Press of Hawaii.

Trimble, J.E., & La Fromboise, T. (1985). American Indians and the counseling process: Culture, adaptation, and style. In P. Pedersen (ed.). *Handbook of Cross-cultural Counseling and Therapy,* 127–33. Westport, CT: Greenwood Press.

Tucker, S.J. (1973). Action counseling: An accountability procedure for counseling the oppressed. *Journal of Non-White Concerns in Personnel and Guidance* 2: 34–41.

Tucker, C.M., Chemault, S.A., & Mulkerne, D.J.. (1981). Barriers to effective counseling with blacks and therapeutic strategies for overcoming them. *Journal of Non-White Concerns in Personnel and Guidance,* 68–76.

Vontress, C.E. (1981). Racial and ethnic barriers in counseling. In P. Pedersen, et al. (eds.). *Counseling Across Cultures,* 87–107. Honolulu:University Press of Hawaii.

Wetzel, J.R. (1987). *American Youth: A Statistical Snapshot.* Washington, DC: William T. Grant Foundation Commission on Youth and America's Future.

White, J.L., Parham, W.D., & Parham, T.A. (1980). Black psychology: The Afro-American tradition as a unifying force for traditional psychology. In R.L. Jones (ed.). *Black Psychology* (2nd ed.), 56–66. New York: Harper & Row.

Williams, W.S. (1972). Black economic and cultural development. In R.L. Jones (ed.). *Black Psychology,* 233–45. New York: Harper & Row.

Wirth, L. (1945). The problem of minority groups. In R. Linton (ed.). *The Science of Man in the World Crisis*. New York: Columbia University Press.

Wood, P.S., & Mallinckrodt, B. (1990). Culturally sensitive assertiveness training for ethnic minority clients. *Professional Psychology: Research and Practice* 21: 5–11.

Youngman, G., & Sandongei, M. (1983). Counseling the American Indian child. In D.R. Atkinson, G. Morten, & D.W. Sue. *Counseling American Minorities* 73–80. Dubuque, IA: Wm. C. Brown.

11

Gender As An Issue in Counseling

Because of the gender role socialization process experienced by males and females, gender is inevitably an issue in all types of counseling, particularly career counseling. However, the fact that boys and girls are oriented differently to the world generally, and to careers specifically, is not the only reason why career counselors must concern themselves with the gender of their clients. The nature of the roles for and between men and women are changing rapidly and shifting in directions that make it imperative that some traditional perceptions of gender role be discarded and replaced with a set of pragmatic expectations about the roles males and females will fill. One of the primary objectives of this chapter is to heighten the reader's awareness of the need to develop gender-aware career counseling strategies. Another purpose is to put forth some strategies that may be useful in conducting gender-aware career counseling.

DEFINITIONS USED IN DISCUSSIONS OF GENDER

Mintz and O'Neil (1990) reviewed the literature regarding gender roles, sex, and the process of counseling and conclude that the field has suffered from "definitional confusion and ambiguity" (p. 381). Earlier, Hansen (1984) reached a similar conclusion in a discussion of the interrelationship of gender and career counseling. In order to avoid confusion, the works of Hansen, Mintz and O'Neil, and Bem (1977) were drawn upon to establish the set of definitions used in this discussion.

Sex	The biological basis that identifies people as male or female
Role	A life function that involves a socially defined set of activities.
Gender role in socialization	The process by which society transmits expectations of males and females. This transmission is based upon a culturally shared set of assumptions about sex differences in abilities, aptitudes, and so forth.
Gender identity	A secure sense of one's maleness or femaleness (not to be confused with sexual preference or one's notions about masculinity or femininity).
Gender (sex) role in identity	The extent to which an individual identifies with society's beliefs and expectations of males and females.
Gender role conflict	Detrimental consequences of gender roles (e.g., the stress that occurs for individuals when people devalue them for pursuing occupations that are nontraditional for their gender).
Gender role in stereotyping	Beliefs or expectations concerning the *appropriateness* of activities for men and women based upon fallacious assumptions.

BACKGROUND

During the past twenty years there has been an increasing interest in the career development of women, as societal changes such as the feminist movement affected our society. The result has been volumes of material such as special issues of journals (see Brooks & Haring-Hidore, 1988), new theories of career development focusing on women and the influence of gender on career choice and development (e.g., Astin, 1984; Gottfredson, 1981), and a vast amount of research focusing on the career counseling and development of women (e.g.,Betz & Fitzgerald, 1987) and sexism in career counseling and counseling materials, including interest inventories and occupational information (e.g., Birk, Tanney, & Cooper, 1979; Diamond, 1975; Tittle & Zytowski, 1978; Thomas & Stewart, 1971). Within the past ten years, a small but growing number of authors have begun to focus on the gender-related problems of men, usually contrasting these with those of women (Berger & Wright, 1980; DiBenedetto & Tittle, 1990; Skovholt & Morgan, 1981). One comparison that is frequently made is that men and women approach the career planning process with different perspectives (e.g., women may perceive an interrelationship between family and career while men may view these roles as independent (Coombs, 1979; DiBenedetto & Tittle, 1990)).

Paralleling this work on the relationship of gender to career choice and development has been a focus in the counseling and psychotherapy literature on the need to avoid sexist assumptions when working with clients. As might be expected, early research and writing emphasized sexist counseling as a women's issue. For example, an early and still frequently cited study found that mental health professionals described healthy behavior for women in gender stereotypic ways, such as submissive, subjective, excitable in minor crises, disliking math and science, and so on. (Broverman et al., 1970). The results showing equally stereotypic depictions of men (e.g., independent, unemotional) were virtually ignored.

Similarly, early studies on sexism in career counseling also focused on women clients. Thomas & Stewart (1971), for example, asked high school counselors to evaluate a female client with deviate (engineering) and conforming (home economics) career goals. Counselors rated the deviate goals as more inappropriate and the "deviant" client as more in need of further counseling. Thomas and Stewart interpreted their results as indicating sex bias in counselors, although Betz and Fitzgerald (1987) offer an alternative explanation. Almost ten years later, Robertson and Fitzgerald (1990) studied bias in career-related counseling for men. In this study, marriage and family therapists reacted to two versions of a videotape. One version showed a white male client who assumed major responsibilities for domestic affairs while his wife was the breadwinner.

In a second videotape, the same client depicted himself in the more traditional role of breadwinner. In both tapes, the client presented himself as satisfied with his marital arrangement and discussed his psychological problems, which were identical in both videotapes. The therapists associated nontraditional gender roles with more severe pathology and were more likely to attribute the client's depression to the nontraditionality in his life.

Certainly, counselors must guard against tendencies to draw conclusions on the basis of sex-role stereotyping. Moreover, counselors need to recognize the pervasiveness of gendered phenomena in all aspects of clients' lives. As Brown (1990) states, "There are few other variables that are as persistently present in the lives of humans and that cross all bounds of race, class, and place" (p. 13). Gender membership profoundly affects identity development, life goals, interpersonal behavior, and problem incidence (e.g., rape for women; emotional restrictiveness in men), as well as career-related issues such as occupational choice and advancement and integration of occupational with other life roles. Clearly, in regard to career choice and development, gender affects not only how we view ourselves and our options, but also how others, including employers and colleagues, perceive and interact with us and affect our choices and career success and mobility.

Given this situation, counselors need to adopt what has recently been proposed as gender-aware or gender-sensitive counseling (Carter, 1989; Good, Gilbert, & Scher, 1990). In this approach, gender is not just a backdrop to be nonconsciously taken for granted; rather, gender phenomena are consciously integrated into the entire counseling process from problem conceptualization to termination. More pertinent to this book is the idea of gender-aware career counseling—an approach that relies to a large degree upon the work of the American Psychological Association's task force (APA, 1985) on sex bias in psychotherapy, feminist therapy (e.g., Gilbert, 1987), and articles by Good et al. (1990) and Brown (1990). It also draws on Hansen's (1984) conceptualization of career counseling, as well as our own thinking.

Gender-aware career counseling is an approach that goes beyond nonsexist counseling (i.e., equal treatment of women and men) and incorporates an understanding of the pervasive effects of gender and sexism on the client in general and on counseling strategies and goals in particular. Both sexist assumptions (i.e., one sex is superior to the other) and heterosexist assumptions (i.e., heterosexual relationships are superior to homosexual relationships; Morin & Charles, 1983) are avoided. During the process of gender-aware career counseling, the counselor considers the social and political context in conceptualizing client problems, including actively examining taken-for-granted assumptions about what is gender usual or "normal" (Brown, 1990); attempts to alter gender-related injustices; emphasizes the collaborative nature of the counselor-client relationship in seeking to empower the client; and perhaps above all, respects clients' rights to make congruent career choices "despite the gender scripts they may have previously learned, currently experience, or fear in the future" (Good, et al., 1990, p. 377). The gender-aware career counselor is fully cognizant of the developmental issues that shape gender role identity, understands how gender role identity can result in self-limiting stereotypes and play a role in client difficulties, and has developed a set of strategies for overcoming the problems associated with gender role socialization and gender role conflict Additionally, gender-aware career counselors are aware of the work-setting forces that limit the career development of males and females and are able to prepare their clients to cope with and overcome these forces.

GENDER-AWARE CAREER COUNSELING (GACC)

Relationship Between Gender and Career Choice and Development

As noted in the definition, GACC attempts to establish a collaborative liaison with the client. As Mintz and O'Neil (1990) note, two factors must be considered in this process:

1. Counseling may be antithetical to the male role and thus, in order to reduce threats to self-esteem, male clients may attempt to "one-up" or compete with the counselor. The one- up situation may be characterized by dominant statements such as "I already knew that" or other combative statements.

2. Women may wish to assume a more passive, subordinate role and may accept interpretations of data such as interest inventory profiles too readily. One result of this is that in the career counseling, counselors may also accept the results of these instruments too readily and fall to consider their relationship to gender role.

In order to establish a collaborative atmosphere, the following structuring statement and strategies are recommended:

1. Make it clear to the client that he or she can reject or accept suggestions growing out of data or those made by counselor.

2. Emphasize responsibility for client decision making.
3. Use words like "cooperation" and "collaboration" in structuring counseling.
4. Be aware of your own gender role identity and *avoid* falling into traditional gender role interactions. If the client's interaction style tends to elicit traditional gender role behaviors, use this information as important assessment data about the client.

Assessment

Brown (1990) has stressed that gender is a neglected issue in both standard and clinical assessment, and she has developed a set of guidelines for enhancing the clinical assessment interview. The guidelines are divided into pre-assessment and assessment-process strategies and can be summarized as follows:

Pre-Assessment Strategies

1. Counselors familiarize themselves with theory and research on the relationship between gender and career choice and development. Specific knowledge to be gained from this reading includes (a) how gender interacts with other demographic variables such as race/ethnicity, class, and age, and influences career choice and development; (b) what types of critical incidents and experiences affect the career choice and development of males and females, such as role models, encouragement/ discouragement from others; (c) differences and similarities between men and women regarding career choices and career patterns; and (d) the nature of discriminatory patterns that exist in the work place. A list of resources is included at the end of this chapter.

2. Counselors examine their own implicit and explicit assumptions and expectations regarding gender. Such an examination includes (a) seeking feedback in counseling, and (b) exploration of perceived costs and benefits of compliance with and deviance from gender stereotype behavior expected from self and others. One way for counselors to begin to examine their own unexamined gendered beliefs would be to fantasize spending a day or more as the other sex.

The Assessment Process

Six guidelines for enhancing the assessment interview follow:

1. Actively determine the meaning attached by the client to his or her gender as it relates to career. For example, with a female client who states she wants to be successful, you might inquire: "What are your ideas about the meaning of career success or failure as a woman?"

2. Determine clients' perceptions of their gender as it relates to the life span. You could inquire, for example, about the roles clients expect to assume over their lifetime, and then question any gender-based assumptions or beliefs that are expressed.

3. Actively assess compliance and/or noncompliance with culturally prescribed gender roles. Is adherence to traditional roles in their efforts toward upward mobility causing any problems in functioning in males, such as health problems or aversive competetiveness with others? What rewards or punishments has the client received for compliance or noncompliance?

4. Monitor your own gender-related responses during the counseling interaction, such as feelings about gender role compliance and noncompliance. It has been suggested, for example, that male counselors are more uncomfortable with clients who have cross-gender characteristics (i.e., feminine men and masculine women) whereas female counselors are more apt to respond negatively to clients with exaggerated gender role behaviors (i.e., hyperfeminine women, hypermasculine men).

5. Actively develop hypotheses about the nature of the gender interaction during the counseling process.

6. Evaluate diagnoses and problem conceptualization for gender-stereotyped conclusions. For example, identify the unexamined gender role based assumptions in the following two cases.

Case 1: C came for career counseling, expressing much distress that he had been passed over twice for promotions in his company. He stated the importance to him of increasing his salary and moving to a higher level of management. The counselor identified the goal as one of helping C discover ways to improve his work performance and to establish more effective relationships with his colleagues and supervisors. If the counselor had first examined C's beliefs about gender role expectations, she might have discovered that C was operating on a "should" rather than a "want," and that he would have welcomed the counselor's support in reconsidering his stated goal of climbing the corporate ladder.

Case 2: R, a married full-time graduate student with a part-time job, entered career counseling with a concern about whether she was in the right field. Among her concerns was whether she should continue to pursue a field that demanded a high level of professional commitment. Both her husband and her husband's parents wanted her to quit graduate school so that she could more adequately attend to matters at home, especially keeping the house in better order. She expressed much distress about the situation because she wanted to continue her education, but she was upset that she could not handle her duties at home more effectively. The counselor decided that R would be unable to attend to her career concerns without first resolving her distress with her husband and his parents. Thus, he proceeded to help her develop time-management skills so that she could more effectively perform "her" household chores. In this case, the counselor failed to explore R's feelings about the gender role based demands of the husband and thus reinforced the client's self-degradation.

INTERVENTIONS

Although it is true, as Hansen (1984) points out, that considerable attention has been given to developing career counseling interventions for women, it is probably true that few of these are unique to women. It is certainly the case that many interventions have been developed assuming that they could work equally well for men and women without regard to gender-role issues. However, there are some interventions that may be useful for dealing with certain gender -related career choice and development issues such as self-limiting stereotypes and family and career issues. One result of self-limiting stereotypes is a restriction of the range of occupations explored, and as Brooks (1988) points out, while this is a particular problem for women it also restricts career exploration for men. Similarly, family and career planning has long been viewed as primarily an issue for women, but the breakdown in traditional family roles will certainly make this an issue for men as well (Hansen, 1984). Therefore, interventions are discussed that relate specifically to these issues. This discussion begins with an outline of a specific strategy that can be used to expand career horizons. This is followed by an outline of some career–family-planning strategies that are particularly relevant to young people but could be adapted for adults.

Expanding Career Horizons

One way to help clients challenge old ideas and develop new ones is to examine their self-limiting stereotypes in a systematic manner. Here is one way to do that:

1. Ask the client to sort the following occupations into three piles: Would consider, Not sure, Would not consider.

elementary school teacher

teacher's aide

cosmetologist

retail salesperson

nurse's aide

lawyer

pharmacist

physician

editor

clothes designer

auto mechanic

landscape architect's helper

accountant

small appliance repairer

economist

laboratory technician

secretary

social worker

librarian

flight attendant

secondary school teacher

stockbroker

psychologist

dancer

bank loan officer

engineer

dentist

electrician

truck driver

2. Take the cards from each stack and separate them into three categories: Stereotypically male, Stereotypically female, Androgynous. Have the client discuss the positive and negative features of the occupations in each stack.

3. As the client discusses each career, listen for statements that suggest clients have (a) little confidence that they can either complete the training for, or perform the work involved in the career, (b) misperceptions regarding the opportunities in the career related to their own gender, and (c) concerns about the social support of others if they enter a particular career.

4. You may wish to assess the client's confidence (self-efficacy) regarding completing the preparation for and/or the ability to function in a job by asking him or her to rate his or her abilities

to function on a 1 to 10 scale, with 1 being very low self-confidence and 10 being extremely high. Look for discrepancies between demonstrated ability and self-confidence.

5. Using one of the values assessment devices listed in Chapter 6, look at values as they relate to careers chosen and rejected. Are there discrepancies?

6. Help the client examine his or her personal assumptions about careers in the following way:

   a. Show how careers that have been eliminated because of gender stereotyping are compatible with values.

   b. Provide information about the numbers of males and females in an occupation to combat perceptions of limited opportunities for members of the client's gender.

   c. Point out discrepancies between demonstrated ability and confidence levels.

   d. Link the client to same-gender role models who have been successful in potentially rewarding but unchosen careers. Occupational information that discusses the entry of men and women into the career fields under consideration may also be useful.

   e. Help clients develop assertiveness skills so they can effectively represent and defend their choices to potential detractors.

   f. Use guided fantasy to have the client actually experience success in careers that have been eliminated on the basis of self-limiting stereotyping (see Chapter 19).

   g. Urge clients "to try on" careers not considered because of stereotyping by engaging them in life-style planning that places the career in the context of family, leisure, and geographic location.

   h. Dispute fallacious self-limiting statements such as "I cannot be an engineer because I cannot do math."

A second technique that will help clients examine the relationships of gender-role based assumptions to career concerns is to conduct a sex-role analysis. This method focuses on the costs and benefits of pursuing traditional versus nontraditional occupational roles (Fitzgerald, 1986; Rawlings & Carter, 1977). Table 11.1 presents an abbreviated version of this technique with a male and female, both of whom have high ability and a strong interest in mathematics. Fitzgerald (1986) suggests this structured technique can be very effective in either a group or workshop or with an individual client. She further suggests that more traditional clients may feel threatened with this explicitly structured technique and recommends that sex- role analysis can simply be brought to the attention of those kinds of clients when appropriate during a counseling session.

TABLE 11.1 Comparative Analysis of Costs and Benefits of Homemaker, Traditional, and Nontraditional Career Roles

	Benefits	Costs
Full-time Homemaker		
Female client	Autonomy; freedom from competition and risk taking; development of nurturance, warmth, etc.	Emotional and financial dependency; low self-esteem and self-confidence
Male client	Autonomy; freedom from competition and risk taking; development of nurturance, warmth, etc.	Emotional and financial dependency; low self-esteem and self-confidence; devaluation by others
High School Math Teacher		
Female client	Economic security; schedule matches children's; contribute to young people	Low income; home–career conflict; relatively low status role
Male client	Economic security; schedule matches children's; contribute to young people	Low income; low status role
Engineer		
Female client	Economic freedom and security; recognition; self-respect and esteem; power and authority	Possible subordinate to men, sex discrimination; pressure to achieve and compete; home/career conflict; devaluation by others
Male client	Economic freedom and security; recognition; self-respect and esteem; power and authority	Competitive stress; less time to spend with family

Source: Adapted from Fitzgerald, L.F. (1986). Career counseling women: Principles, procedures, and problems. In Z.B. Liebowitz and H.D. Lea (eds.). *Adult Career Development: Concepts, Issues, and Practices*, (116–31). Washington DC: National Career Development Association.

Career–Family Planning

As noted earlier in this chapter, counselors must avoid heterosexist assumptions in their counseling. They should also refrain from assuming that all clients will wish to pursue traditional roles of spouse and parent. Both of these cautions are particularly important in the area of life–with or without career planning, which for many, but not all clients, includes a heterosexual marriage, and children. Thus, whereas career–family planning in the traditional sense may be extremely useful with some clients, such automatic assumptions with some clients (e.g., gay men and lesbians, who may not have acknowledged their life style to the counselor, heterosexual men and women who are not interested in marriage or children) can quickly lead to loss of counselor credibility. Thus, before launching into an examination of career–family planning, counselors should conduct an interrole assessment of the client's image of future roles. For example, the counselor might say:

> Co: In exploring career options, I believe it is important to consider your picture of the future in terms of roles you expect to fill and how your career might or might not be affected by these roles. Frequently, these future pictures can be very helpful in identifying some career strategies you might want to consider. I'd like you to think about ten years in the future and perhaps fifteen or twenty. What do you envision for yourself in the areas of work and intimate relationships? What roles do you think you would fill? What roles would you want to avoid? (See Chapter 9 for a discussion of other strategies.)

Some clients may be too reticent to respond to this inquiry and if so, counselors should respect their right to silence. Others, however, will be quite forthcoming with clear visions and well-defined expectations. With clients who include heterosexual marriage and children in their future picture, the following procedure can be helpful. Some may envision marriage but reject and feel ambivalent about children, and counselors should refrain from being yet another cultural agent who explicitly or implicitly pressures clients to have children. Still others may acknowledge they are gay or lesbian and may wish to explore how their life style may affect career choice, mobility, and advancement. Alternatively, they may wish to engage in career–family planning because many of the decisions they will face may in fact be quite similar to those of clients who expect heterosexual marriages (e.g., integrating work with home roles; timing of children in relation to career goals).

1. Ask client to list age at which he or she expects (hopes) to get married.
2. Have client project his or her age when first child would be born (if a child is planned), second child, and so on.
3. Ask client to forecast points on his or her career path at age of marriage, first child, second child, and so on.
4. Have client project spouse's career at the time of marriage, first child, second child, and so on.
5. Look for discrepancies between career projections for client and spouse. Are the expectations for women more limited than those for men?
6. Determine if future family projections are limiting current choices.
7. Develop alternative family-career "futures":
   a. What if spouse does not work?
   b. What if child rearing and household chores are shared equally?
   c. What if two careers are necessary to support the expected life style?
   d. What if spouse dies? Divorce occurs?
   e. What if client gets "hooked" on career and neglects the family?
   f. What if marriage and/or children does not occur?
8. Determine if alternative futures alter current perceptions regarding career choice.

Life-Role Planning.

Zunker (1986) has suggested a series of strategies that may be useful in promoting life-role career planning:

1. Begin by having client draw a life line, marking the present with an *X* and projecting important future dates including graduation(s), first jobs, marriage (if desired), promotions, retirement, and death.
2. Client should identify current life roles (e.g., student, worker, spouse, child, leisurite) and identify the negative and positive aspects of each. Then, one by one, client should strip roles and discuss the positive and negative effect associated with giving up that role.
3. Once the client has stripped all roles, ask him or her how he or she would plan his or her life. Zunker (1986) calls this "fantasy time" because people, stripped of all life roles, are free to plan a new life.

4. As life planning begins, client should focus on typical and special days. What are the characteristics of each? What values are manifested by the client? How many of each kind of day will there be?

5. Reassemble roles. Individuals should consider their needs and values in this process.

6. Have clients write a news release focusing upon their accomplishments and roles in the future. Clients can also be asked to write their obituary with these same focuses.

7. Once reassembly of roles is completed, analysis should occur. How are new roles the same as old roles? Different? Are they more or less ambitious?

8. Future goal setting should now begin. As a result of the fantasies clients have experienced in the process, they should begin to establish short- and long-term life goals.

LIMITATIONS OF GENDER-AWARE CAREER COUNSELING

There is always the danger that some clients will be offended because of efforts to expand their career horizons, particularly if confrontive techniques are employed. As Gottfredson (1981) and Brooks (1988) note, it is not the counselor's role to actively engage in dissuading their clients to change their career choices. However, as Brooks also indicates, if the counselor engages in a process that helps clients "remove some obstacles, ambiguities, and ambivalence" (p. 237) about career choice using supportive strategies that are based on respect for individual choice, this is acceptable. Obviously the line between "dissuading clients" and providing supportive interventions so that they may broaden their horizons and thus change their minds is a fine one.

BECOMING SENSITIVE TO GENDER ISSUES

Several suggestions have already been put forth regarding becoming sensitive to gender issues in career counseling, including becoming familiar with the research literature in this area. Here are three more:

1. Compile a list of stereotypical statements about careers and women. Conduct the same activity for men.

List for Women	*List for men*
A. Women don't have the strength for longshoring	A. Men don't have the finger dexterity to sew
B. _____	B. _____
C. _____	C. _____
D. _____	D. _____
E. _____	E. _____
F. _____	F. _____

Do you know.....

1. Do you now or have you ever subscribed to any of these stereotypes? Discuss those you once held or those you now hold with a member of the other sex. Ask the client how he or she would feel if they perceived you holding that stereotype in a counseling session in which he or she was the client.

2. Develop a mind-set that stereotypes either men or women and conduct a practice interview in which you actively employ this mind-set. Observe how it directs your responses to your client. Then conduct a session with an androgynous mind-set, that is, one as free from gender stereotyping as possible. Contrast the two interviews.

3. In role play, try in a subtle way to manipulate a client into accepting a traditional career choice.

SUMMARY

Gender profoundly affects all aspects of one's life, including career choice and advancement. Though early work on gender-role perceptions and sexism in counseling were viewed as solely a women's concern, counselors must acknowledge that these are issues of concern to men as well.

In considering gender as an issue in career counseling, this chapter advocated the adoption of gender-aware career counseling. This approach views gender as an integral aspect of all stages of career counseling.

Even though the techniques employed in providing career counseling to males and females are essentially the same, the mind-set of the counselor regarding the role of gender in career choice and development can be a powerful influence in the counseling process. By examining one's own gender-related perceptions and becoming familiar with the literature related to gender as a variable in career choice and development, inappropriate counseling behavior can be avoided.

The techniques described can help clients expand career horizons (gender card sort; sex role analysis) and engage in planning for life, family, and career roles.

REFERENCES AND SUGGESTED READINGS

American Psychological Association. (1985). Report of the task force on sex bias and sex-role stereotyping in psychotherapeutic practice. *American Psychologist* 30: 1169–75.

Astin, H.S. (1984). The meaning of work in women's lives: A sociopsychological model of career choice and work behavior. *The Counseling Psychologist* 12: 117–26.

Bem, S.L. (1977). Beyond androgyny: Some presumptuous prescriptions for a liberated sexual identity. In C.G. Carney & S.L. McMahon (eds.), *Exploring Contemporary Male/Female Roles: A Facilitator's Guide,* 209–29. San Diego: University Associates.

Berger, M., & Wright, L. (1980). Divided allegiance: Men, work, and family life. In T.M. Skovholt, P.G. Schauble, & R. Davis (eds). *Counseling Men,* 157–63. Monterey, CA: Brooks/Cole.

Betz, N.E., & Fitzgerald, L.F. (1987). *The Career Psychology of Women.* Orlando, FL: Academic Press.

Birk, J.M., Tanney, M.F., & Cooper, J.F. (1979). A case of blurred vision: Stereotyping in career information illustrations. *Journal of Vocational Behavior* 15: 247–57.

Brooks, L. (1988). Encouraging women's motivation for non-traditional career and lifestyle options: A model for assessment and intervention. *Journal of Career Development* 4: 223–41.

Brooks, L. & Haring-Hidore, M. (1988). Career interventions with women. *Journal of Career Development* 14,(4): (entire issue).

Broverman, I.K., Broverman, D.M., Clarkson, F.E., Rosenkrantz, P.S., & Vogel, S.R. (1970). Sex-role stereotypes and clinical judgments of mental health. *Journal of Consulting and Clinical Psychology* 34: 1–7.

Brown, L.S. (1990). Taking account of gender in the clinical assessment interview. *Professional Psychology: Research and Practice,* 21: 12–17.

Carter, B. (1989). Gender sensitive therapy: Moving from theory to practice. *Family Therapy Networker* 13: 57–60.

Coombs, L.C. (1979). The measurement of commitment to work. *Journal of Population* 2: 203–23.

Diamond, E.E. (ed.) (1975). *Issues of sex bias and sex fairness in career interest measurement.* Washington, DC: National Institute of Education.

DiBenedetto, B., & Tittle, C.K. (1990). Gender and adult roles: Role commitment of women and men in a job family trade-off context. *Journal of Counseling Psychology* 37: 41–8.

Fitzgerald, L.F. (1986). Career counseling women: Principles, procedures, and problems. In Z.B. Leibowitz & H.D. Lea (eds.) *Adult Career Development: Concepts, Issues and Practices*, 116–31. Washington, DC: National Career Development Association.

Fitzgerald, L.F., & Crites, J.O. (1980). Toward a career psychology of women: What do we know? What do we need to know? *Journal of Counseling Psychology* 27:44–62.

Fitzgerald, L.F. (1980). Nontraditional occupations: Not for women only. *Journal of Counseling Psychology* 27: 252–59.

Fretz, R.B. (1981). Evaluating the effectiveness of career interventions. *Journal of Counseling Psychology Monograph* 28: 77–90..

Gilbert, L.H. (1987). Dual-career families in perspective. *The Counseling Psychologist* 15: (1): (entire issue).

Good, G.E., Gilbert, L.A., & Scher, M. (1990). Gender aware therapy: A synthesis of feminist therapy and knowledge about gender. *Journal of Counseling and Development* 68: 376–80.

Gottfredson, L.S.. (1981). Circumscription and compromise: A developmental theory of occupational aspirations. *Journal of Counseling Psychology Monograph* 28: 545–79.

Hansen, L.S. (1984). Interrelationships of gender and career. In N.C. Gysbers and Associates, *Designing Careers*, 216–47. San Francisco: Jossey-Bass.

Mintz, L.B., & O'Neill, J.M. (1990). Gender roles, sex, and the process of psychotherapy: Many questions and few answers. *Journal of Counseling and Development* 68: 381–87.

Morin, S.F., & Charles, K.A. (1983). Heterosexual bias in psychotherapy. In J. Murray and P.R. Abramson (eds.),*Bias in Psychotherapy*, 309–38. New York: Praeger.

Osipow, S.H. (1982). Research in career counseling: An analysis of issues and problems. *The Counseling Psychologist* 28: 77–90.

Rawlings, E.I., & Carter, D.K. (eds.) (1977) *Psychotherapy for Women*. Springfield, IL: Charles C. Thomas.

Robertson, J., & Fitzgerald, L.F. (1990). The (mis) treatment of men: Effects of client gender role and life-style on diagnosis and attribution of pathology. *Journal of Counseling Psychology*, 37: 3-9.

Scher, M. (ed.) (1981). Counseling males. *Personal and Guidance Journal* 60 (4): (entire issue).

Skovholt, T., & Morgan, T. (1981). Career development: An outline of issues for men *Personnel and Guidance Journal* 60: 231–37.

Skovholt, T., Schauble, P., and Davis, J. (eds.) (1980). *Counseling Men*. Monterey, CA: Brooks/Cole.

Thomas, A.H., & Stewart, N.R. (1971). Counselor response to female clients with deviate and conforming career goals. *Journal of Counseling Psychology* 18: 352–57.

Tittle, C.K., & Zytowski, D.G. (eds.) (1978). *Sex-fair Interest Measurement: Research and Implications*. Washington, DC: National Institute of Education.

Voydanoff, P. (ed.) (1984). *Work and Family: Changing Roles of Men and Women*. Palo Alto, CA: Mayfield

Zunker, V.G. (1986). *Career Counseling: Applied Concepts of Life Planning*. (2nd ed.). Monterey, CA: Brooks/Cole.

CHAPTER 12

Dealing with Problem Clients

Perhaps the majority of individuals who seek career counseling readily engage in the process and continue through to termination, posing no undue difficulty for the counselor. Some clients, however, bring special problems, and the counselor is faced with the challenge of how to help these clients proceed. Experienced counselors could no doubt identify a large number of problem cases, but only those thought to be the most common are discussed in this chapter.

Recognizing problem clients is relatively easy; selecting and implementing effective interventions is more of a challenge. Kinds of problem clients that are discussed are clients who (1) have few or no interests, (2) express unrealistic aspirations, (3) have too many options, and (4) are resistant.

CLIENTS WITH TOO FEW INTERESTS

The client with few or no readily identifiable interests is perhaps the most common "problem" career client. This client names at best one or two interests without enthusiasm and then, much to the counselor's dismay, has a low, flat profile on an interest inventory (i.e., low scores on all occupational areas).

In the majority of cases, the client with few interests lacks information, either about self, occupations, or the world of work; as Isaacson (1985) states it, "Ignorance is the cause of many problems" (p.126). There are several sub-groups of clients who can be expected to suffer from a lack of information about careers: adolescents with little life experience;

women with little or no paid work experience outside the home; and racial and ethnic minorities who have not been involved in the culture of mainstream America (e.g., Native Americans who have grown up on a reservation; Chinese or black Americans who have grown up in a ghetto). These same subgroups may also lack self-awareness, probably due to lack of involvement in the kinds of activities that stimulate self-reflection and feedback from others, such as participation in social activities or interaction with diverse groups of people. The suggestion for working with this group that lacks information about self, occupations, and the world of work involves a broad-based, multistrategic approach aimed at engaging the client in intensive self-exploration and providing direct experiences in work-related activities.

Ignorance is not the only explanation for "few interests," however. Some clients can be expected to have more severe psychological problems, such as a confused or disorganized sense of identity. These clients lack cognitive clarity and usually need personal counseling. Other clients may be depressed. This possibility can be evaluated by determining whether the client expresses a similar lack of interest in other aspects of life. Severe depression may prohibit progress in career counseling and necessitate personal counseling, although one can usually proceed if the client is moderately or mildly depressed. However, if the primary cause of the depression is work-related (e.g., the client was recently fired), then career counseling is probably the treatment of choice.

Another subset of clients with few interests may be suffering from low self-esteem. They may view themselves as having few if any abilities, and though they may have some ideas about interests, they are unable to seriously consider them or express them to others because the related career options seem beyond their reach. The recommended treatment for these clients is reattribution training, which is discussed later in this chapter under the topic of clients with unrealistic aspirations.

Still other clients express few interests because of perceived or real environmental constraints, such as a limited opportunity structure for their gender, class, racial, or ethnic group, internalized restrictive opinions of significant others, and so on. Approaches to helping clients with environmental restraints regarding gender, class, and race and with barriers posed by significant others is beyond the scope of this chapter, but it should be noted that the Balance-Sheet approach to decision-making (see Chapter 17), coupled with role playing (Chapter 16) and other similar techniques, can be effective.

In some instances, it is necessary to resolve the underlying problem (e.g., confused identity or clinical depression) before career counseling can proceed. In general, however, unless the problem is so severe that no progress can be made, it is best in the early stage of counseling (i.e., assessment of interests, values, etc.) to proceed with some special techniques to help clients generate a list of tentative interests and to engage them in general self-exploration. As Yost and Corbishley (1987) note, the aim at this early stage is to heighten clients' enthusiasm, and wandering off to other issues may be discouraging. Yost and Corbishley suggest that an intervention targeted at the underlying problem, if indeed it is necessary, will be more powerful later in the process when the client is considering specific options. It should also be noted that focusing on underlying issues, such as low self-esteem, will be viewed by some clients (e.g., some Native American or Asian- American clients) as irrelevant and unnecessarily probing into their personal life. Still, in some cases, it will be necessary to do so, and discussing this possibility early in the process (e.g., in the first interview) can prepare the client for the need to "stray" a bit from the initial presenting problem.

Techniques

Effective counseling with the low information / low self-aware client can be expected to extend over considerable time, so it is important that the counselor initiate a discussion about the extended nature of the counseling and elicit the client's commitment and involvement. The counselor also needs to be extremely clear about the expected outcome of any assigned task in order to prevent client discouragement (e.g., "the purpose of volunteer work is to directly experience one's likes and dislikes").

The first task of the counselor is to loosen the client's cognitive restraints. One way to approach this task is to convey the importance of refraining from evaluation; that is, clients are encouraged to brainstorm, to "dream," to assume there are no limitations imposed by other people or by time, lack of finances, education, abilities, gender, class, race, ethnicity, or age. Any ideas, no matter how trivial or impossible they may seem, are important. Evaluation and decision making will come later. In short, the cognitive set is to be "all things are possible."

Along with the effort to loosen the client's cognitive set, the counselor will need to explain the rationale for the overall strategy of diverse and intensive exploration. For example, the counselor might explain the strategy in the following manner:

> Co: What I'm going to be suggesting to you is that you become involved in an intensive self- and occupational exploration process. I'll be giving you several exercises to complete in between our sessions. All of them will be designed to help you learn more about yourself, the world

of work, and eventually how you might fit into that world. The main idea here is that you are lacking in information, and it's my job to help you find ways to obtain that information. Sometimes the purpose of my suggestions may be unclear to you and, if so, you need to let me know. For example, I may suggest that you get involved in some clubs or other organized activities. That may seem far removed from finding career options. The idea, though, is that since you seem to lack information about what you like, dislike, and value, experiences such as these can provide the direct exposure you need to be able to determine what is important to you, how you interact with others, and so on. At this point, anything you can learn about yourself will be helpful. Later, when you've had multiple exploration opportunities, we can piece all information together into some possible options.

Once the counselor has helped the client to approach the process with an evaluation-free mind-set and has elicited his or her commitment to broad-based exploration, the counseling can begin. In general, the goals are to stimulate self-exploration, begin to identify some likes and dislikes, and obtain direct experience in work-related activities. Though some discrete techniques are suggested here, how they should be sequenced or whether they should be concurrent will depend on the counselor's assessment of the client's situation.

Self-Exploration
The counselor instructs clients to keep a log of their activities for a week, noting how they spend their time, money, and energy. These activities can be analyzed for what they reveal about the clients (Yost & Corbishley, 1987). Yost and Corbishley also suggest that clients think about the various places they have lived and what they liked and disliked about each. Younger people can be asked about their likes and dislikes regarding school in general, subjects, part-time jobs, or duties at home. These inquiries should be preceded by an explanation that the overall purpose is to work toward a summary of the clients' characteristics: that is, a better self-understanding.

For some clients, personality assessment can help to give them a way of thinking about themselves. Even a simple checklist of adjectives can be useful, as might a standardized personality inventory (see Chapter 7). Clients also can be encouraged to obtain feedback from family and friends regarding how they are viewed. Isolated clients, such as those living alone, can be urged to join organized activities such as clubs or social groups. Reading assignments might also be made. Published autobiographies can be examined for how the main character is similar to and different from the client. Terkel's *Working* (1972), which describes people in a variety of occupations, can be assigned with instructions to read those sections that are of most and least interest and to take notes on what is appealing and unappealing about each person's work and life style (Yost & Corbishley, 1987). Terkel's *The Great Divide* (1989) might be used in a similar manner with mature clients.

Identifying Likes, Dislikes and Interests.

One technique suggested by Yost and Corbishley (1987) for clients with few interests begins with instructing clients that their task is to generate a list of thirty to fifty occupations. The client is told that evaluation of the occupations should be avoided at this point; the aim is merely to form a list. Several suggestions can be made for generating the list: identify jobs performed by relatives, neighbors, friends, or people in newspapers, magazines, and TV. The alphabet exercise in Table 5.1 (Chapter 5) could be modified by having the client list one occupation for each letter of the alphabet. After the list is compiled, clients select the ten least aversive and discuss what is attractive about each. Clients are then instructed to do minimal research by reading about each one of the ten in the *Occupational Outlook Handbook* (U.S. Department of Labor, 1988–89) or the *Dictionary of Occupational Titles* (U.S. Department of Labor, 1977) and to add one new occupation for each one rejected. If the client eliminates all of the occupations, the counselor inquires about rationales to determine if they are valid; for example, is the client making erroneous assumptions? Is the client limited by the opinions of significant others?

Experience in Work-Related Activities

Exposing the client to the world of work can be accomplished in a variety of ways as discussed in Chapter 15, such as encouraging the client to pursue volunteer work, shadow a worker, or obtain a part-time job. Clients who have had no paid or volunteer work experience can profit from almost any work experience because it can provide a direct opportunity for self-reflection. Holland's (1985) typology can be an effective tool in organizing and selecting work experiences; that is, clients are taught Holland's system, and then experiences are selected that represent most, and in some cases all, of the six personality types. Clients can also profit from interviewing workers they know well—for example, family members and friends. They should be instructed to focus particularly on what the person likes and dislikes as well as the duties of the job.

In discussing their findings, emphasis is placed on how the person interviewed is similar and dissimilar to the client.

UNREALISTIC OR SELF-LIMITING ASPIRATIONS

Another challenging client is the one with unrealistic aspirations. The aspirations may be too high or too low, but in any case, there is an ability/ interest discrepancy. Clients who judge their abilities as very low may be unable or reluctant to identify occupational interests. In extreme cases, these clients simply cannot imagine being able to perform in any job. A more common situation is when clients can identify some occupations of interest but discard them too quickly as out of reach. This problem is more often observed in women than in men and in lower rather than in higher socioeconomic classes.

The flip side of the foregoing situation—that is, clients who underestimate their abilities—are those who overestimate their talents and/or underestimate the odds of entering and succeeding in a field. Youngsters who have a dream of "making it" in the performing arts or in professional athletics often cannot and will not consider other alternatives until lack of success throws them into turmoil.

Though realistic choices have long been a goal of career counseling, an adequate, objective definition of *realism* is elusive. Clearly, counselors should be cautious about making hasty judgments about the realism of a client's goals lest they allow their own subjective views to influence the client. One school counselor tells the story of a "low ability" ninth grader who came to him with the aspiration of becoming a physician. He gently suggested that the student consider other alternatives, but the student persisted. The student graduated from high school in the upper third of his class, went on to medical school, and did his internship at a highly prestigious teaching hospital. The counselor's perception of low ability was based upon an aptitude test that accounts for only about half of the factors that contribute to achievement. For some groups, such as minority clients, these tests may account for fewer than half of those factors. This example illustrates the possible danger of counselors making predictions for clients. Counselors need to keep in mind that clients have both the "right to fail" and the right to try. In general, counselors should probably err on the side of encouraging rather than discouraging goals and aspirations and thus permit clients to arrive at their own conclusions regarding their strengths and shortcomings.

Gottfredson (1985) provides a definition of realism that includes two dimensions. First is suitability, meaning the odds that individuals will be satisfied in a field, that potential employers will consider them as a candidate, and that employers will find their performance satisfactory. The second dimension is accessibility, or the odds of finding or creating a relevant position with a reasonable amount of time and effort. Accessibility depends on the number of vacancies, the likelihood that the person will become aware of them, and the number of other qualified candidates. Promoting realism in clients would entail, at a minimum, encouraging them to make their own assessments of both suitability and accessibility by gathering relevant, comprehensive occupational information. Gottfredson recommends a rather elaborate exploration system for helping clients go through this process, and some of her suggestions have been incorporated into the techniques that follow.

Salomone and McKenna (1982) have also discussed the problem of realism and suggest that the causes of unrealism can rest with both the client and the counselor. Client causes include (1) inaccurate self-perceptions as a result of limited exposure to the work world, limited awareness of abilities, and the like, and (2) distorted perceptions of the world of work because of inadequate or inaccurate occupational information or unwillingness to consider more than one alternative. Counselor "causes," meaning that the counselor may promote unrealism, can be produced by a variety of factors including counselor inexperience, lack of knowledge about various types of work, limited knowledge of the client's abilities, and reluctance to encourage clients to engage in a realistic self-evaluation.

Techniques

Techniques to help clients explore the match between their abilities and aspirations may differ somewhat depending on whether the client is over- or underestimating personal abilities and opportunities. Many of the techniques that are useful in this endeavor have already been discussed in previous chapters (e.g., assessment of interests, skills, values, gathering occupational information) and are relevant for both types of clients. Before discussing various techniques, it should be noted that the primary aim of any technique is to provide ways for clients to develop realistic estimates of their abilities and opportunities, rather than to actively persuade them in one direction or another (e.g., steering people away from occupations that have been traditional for their gender, class, or racial group). Still, the counselor does assume some responsibility for helping clients identify the consequences of their choices and devise ways to cope with them

During interest assessment, a technique used with many types of career counseling clients, it is important to urge clients to identify as many alternatives as possible for further exploration, no matter how reluctant they are to do so. Some clients tenaciously hold on to one alternative (e.g., professional musician) because to give it up would be to give up the major component of their self-concept. Pickman (1987), for example, has discussed the painful losses of professional dancers faced with the need to find a postperforming career (e.g., losing body image, attractiveness, public recognition, and social support of the dance company). Identifying new alternatives is especially difficult for those who have concentrated their energies and identities in one area from a very early age. For those who are facing the prospect of a career transition after a successful career in the performing arts, it will frequently be necessary to help them first begin to deal with separation and loss issues. For others who have but "dreams," it can be effective to help them identify other, perhaps only slightly appealing, alternatives and at the same time assure them that all alternatives will be examined carefully. This exploration process can bring clients to discard "impractical" alternatives on their own. As Salomone and McKenna (1982) put it, "'dreams die hard,' but they die easier if you kill them yourself" (p. 286).

Skills identification exercises can often provide a boost in confidence for clients with low estimates of ability. For example, the client might be instructed to make a list of all personal activities for a week. The counselor would then help the client identify the skills used in each activity. It can be pointed out to the adolescent who repairs his or her own bicycle that he or she probably has some mechanical aptitude. Adults who care for their aging parents, as well as their preschool children, have time-management skills. Not infrequently, clients will protest that the skills involved in their daily activities are irrelevant to the world of occupations. The counselor needs to urge them to refrain from making these linkages too soon, lest they dismiss their abilities as trivial. This can be done by asking them to delay evaluation and to concentrate on the longer–term task of building a comprehensive self-picture. (See Chapter 16 for additional skills identification exercises.)

Another effective approach to help clients with low self-estimates of ability is derived from attribution theory. In brief, attribution theory posits that humans strive for a causal understanding of their world in order to maximize their control over it. As shown in the following chart, attributions can be classified along two dimensions: internal–external and stable–unstable. Attributions for success that are internal and stable and for failure that are external and unstable are more likely to enhance one's self-efficacy or esteem. For example, attributing successes to effort or ability is more likely to be self-enhancing than attributing them to luck or the ease of the task. Viewing failure as caused by bad luck or difficulty of the task rather than by low ability also preserves one's self-esteem and confidence. Thus the way that people explain their successes and failures to themselves can have a powerful impact on self-esteem. "I won first prize in the science project because there wasn't any real competition" attributes the cause to an external rather than internal source. "I won because I'm good in science" is clearly more esteem-enhancing. "I sold the most cars this month because I got lucky—I just happened to get the buying customers when they walked through the door", is an example of an external attribution; its opposite would be: "I can quickly gain a customer's confidence and then figure out the best strategy to use."

	Internal Attributions	External Attributions
Variable Attributions	Effort	Luck
Stable Attributions	Ability	Task difficulty

A reattribution-training approach involves attempts to shift clients' invalid attributions to more realistic ones (Fösterling, 1980). For example, the obviously bright, talented adult client who painfully recalls poor grades in school and is thus reluctant to act on his wish to return to school for a graduate degree might be persuaded that his low achievement was not the result of inability but rather of his greater interest and involvement in sports; that is, lack of effort was the cause of low marks rather than lack of ability (shift from internal-stable to internal-variable). An adult client who is down on herself because she performed poorly at her one job and was fired could be helped to see that she was "unlucky" in accepting a job with a negative environment (shift from internal-stable to external-variable). The adolescent whose dreams of becoming a professional dancer were squashed by his dance teacher blames his lack of ability (internal-stable) rather than the low odds of becoming a star, that is, the task difficulty (external-stable).

Any of the cognitive restructuring techniques, such as Ellis's "socratic dialogue" (Ellis & Harper, 1975), Beck's hypothesis testing (Beck, 1976), and Meichenbaum's self-talk strategy (Meichenbaum, 1977) can be used in reattribution training. In essence, each technique is devoted to challenging the client to consider all the relevant information that bears on different explanations for the client's successes and failures. Further, counselors could teach attribution theory to clients and give them homework assignments with directions to think about causes for achievements and failures that would make them feel good about themselves.

One example of challenging the client's attributions is illustrated in the following vignette with a college sophomore.

Cl: I'm interested in journalism but the trouble is I can't write [ability attribution].

Co: Could you tell me what information you have used to arrive at the conclusion that you can't write?

Cl: I received very low grades on high school English papers.

Co: You received negative feedback from one or more teachers in the form of grades on papers you wrote?

Cl: Well, just one teacher really.

Co: Any other information you have used to decide that your writing is not one of your strong assets?

Cl: Hmm—just that one teacher I guess.

Co: So your conclusion is based mostly on grades you received from one teacher several years ago.

Cl: Just hearing you say that makes me realize I've put a lot of stock in her opinion. And actually, since I've been in college, I have received some positive feedback on a few papers I've written.

Co: Maybe your view of yourself as a poor writer needs to be reevaluated, then.

Cl: Maybe so.

Co: Let's probe a little deeper. What might account for the difference between the feedback from your high school teacher and that of your professors here?

Cl: I suppose the teacher in high school might have been biased in some way. Also, in Freshman composition class, we learned a lot about writing and wrote a lot of papers. So, I suppose I've profited from that. And I have to admit that I didn't work very hard in high school—I've put a lot more time and effort in the papers I've written in college.

Co: I think you've made three important points. One is that you know more about writing now than you did in high school. Two is that as a result of instruction and experience, you've probably increased your writing skills. Three, you've put more effort into your writing. It seems to me that perhaps you've confused lack of training and lack of effort with lack of ability.

Cl: I'm not quite sure what you mean.

Co   A few minutes ago you said "I can't write," which says you don't think you have the ability. But you've also just acknowledged that you didn't work very hard in high school. So perhaps your poor grades in high school have to do with lack of effort rather than lack of ability.

Cl: Hmm—I see what you mean. Maybe I need to rethink my view of myself. I do write better now, I see that. Maybe I have more ability than I thought, but writing is hard work!

Co: But hard work doesn't equal no ability, right? And let me put it this way. Suppose you would receive a great amount of money—say $100,000—to write a paper. Could you write a good one?

Cl: You bet!

A technique to promote realism that can be especially effective with clients with unrealistically high aspirations is occupational exploration (Gottfredson, 1985; Salomone & McKenna, 1982). As discussed in Chapter 15, gathering occupational information is an integral part of career counseling. In the case of the client with unrealistically high aspirations, however, special emphasis should be placed on assessing suitability and accessibility. Further, the counselor must first persuade these clients that further information is needed. The counselor can begin by asking clients to discuss what they know about the occupation or field in question, particularly emphasizing their knowledge about the ability and training requirements for entering the field and performing successfully. In most instances, it is also important to inquire about the source of their knowledge. Great-Uncle Murray's information—that it is practically impossible to get into medical school—may be quite outdated.

The counselor can then introduce the idea of the importance of gathering accurate information by noting that the decision to be made is a very important one and that in order to make the best one possible, the field should be explored in depth. Mention can also be made of the highly competitive nature of the field (if appropriate) and the importance of attaining a full understanding of the requirements, so that the client can work on some ways to gain a competitive edge. Further, even though some clients may be reluctant to do so, they should be urged to identify one or two backups with the explanation that everyone needs a contingency plan. Gottfredson (1985) suggests sending the client off for exploration with specific worksheets and, for each occupation explored, creating two lists: one list (see Table 12.1) for the essential requirements for the occupation (e.g., training, ability), the client's estimate of the odds for meeting them (good, fair, poor, don't know), and the client's justification for his or her "odds" estimate, and the second list (see Table

12.2) for the client's indication of advantages and likes in one column and disadvantages and dislikes in another. A third worksheet can then be used to compare the occupations explored in terms of most advantageous and least advantageous, culminating in identifying the "best bets."

TABLE 12.1 Worksheet I: Occupational Exploration

Alternatives	Training, Ability and Other Requirements	My Odds of Meeting Requirements				Rationale for "Odds" Rating
		Poor	Good	Excellent	Don't Know	
1. _____	_____	____	____	____	____	_____
2. _____	_____	____	____	____	____	_____
3. _____	_____	____	____	____	____	_____

TABLE 12.2 Worksheet II: Occupational Exploration

Alternatives	Advantages and Likes	Disadvantages and Dislikes
1. _____	_____	_____
2. _____	_____	_____
3. _____	_____	_____

Source: Adaopted from Gottfredson, L.S. (1985). Using an Occupational Aptitude Patterns (OAP) Map to promote reality-based vocational exploration. Paper presented at the August meeting of the APA.

The next step is to help clients develop ways to improve their competitive edge for their "best bet" alternative; that is, ways to increase their odds of entering and performing well. Lower ability students might study more than other people to attain the necessary GPA, fine-tune their interpersonal skills, or gain experience in the field. This process provides the client with a realistic picture of the demands of the alternative he or she wishes to consider, of the odds that the goals can be achieved , and an understanding of the special efforts he or she may need to make to become competitive. In other words, the client knows what he or she is up against, and if the client still wishes to pursue what might seem like a risky goal to the counselor, at least he or she has both eyes open.

Finally, group counseling can offer an experience that is both supportive and confrontive for clients with unrealistic aspirations (Salomone & McKenna, 1982). The U.S. Olympic Committee, for example, recently sponsored a series of career exploration workshops for former Olympic stars, a group that typically has great difficulty letting go of former successes and finding new alternatives.

MULTIPOTENTIALED CLIENTS

The multi-interested and multitalented client is a unique challenge. Some may envy these clients, but the multipotentialed individuals themselves, confronted with "overchoice," may long for the removal of the yoke of indecision. As Charlie Brown put it, "There is no heavier burden than a great potential" (Blackburn & Erickson, 1986).

What is a multipotentialed client? Pask-McCartney and Salomone (1988) subscribe to Frederickson's definition of a *multipotentialed client* as one who "when provided with appropriate environments, can select and develop [a] number of competencies to a high level" (1972, p. 60). As Pask-McCartney and Salomone point out, this definition expands the view of the multipotentialed clients beyond those who have been identified by others (such as schools) as gifted and talented to include those "who [have] exhibit[ed] potential (i.e., aptitudes, talents, abilities) and have related interests. Their career indecision may result from a self-perception of multiple talents and related interests" (pp. 233–34). The authors view gifted and talented students as just one subset of multipotentialed individuals.

How does a counselor identify the truly multipotentialed client? Pask-McCartney and Salomone have two suggestions:

1. First, some but not all multipotentialed people are highly creative. Counselors can observe whether a client exhibits the following characteristics during an initial or early interview: cognitive complexity and flexibility, intense curiosity, perfectionist tendencies, openness to a wide variety of experiences, strong interest in mastering problems, and ability to "assimilate a multitude of

environmental stimuli" (p. 235). In addition, performance records would indicate aptitude in a wide variety of activities.

2. Another indication of a multipotentialed client would be a flat but high-interest inventory profile; that is, on the SCII (for example) the client would have high scores on a great number of occupational scales. Pask-McCartney and Salomone suggest that Holland's Vocational Preference Inventory (VPI) can be used to check for differentiated scores on Holland's typology. High scores and low differentiation (i.e., total scores on most of the six types are high and close in number) would provide support for the hypothesis that the client is multipotentialed.

Techniques

A small subset of multipotentialed clients may profit from relatively simple educative responses from the counselor. For example, some clients lack realistic information about themselves and the world of work. These clients are relatively easy to deal with through the standard techniques of interest assessment and occupational information gathering. Values clarification can also be revealing and may help these clients develop long-range plans and select first options.

Another client may simply be suffering from the myth that he or she "must choose one option that will be my life's work." In that instance, the counselor can point out that the average person changes jobs seven or eight times over a lifetime and that a path chosen now does not necessarily eliminate future paths or require that the client forever renounce valued parts of the self. Further, some interests and talents can be pursued through leisure activities, community service, and the family.

Still other multipotentialed clients may not realize that many jobs are actually complex, calling for a variety of talents and interests. Some clients hold stereotyped views of jobs as single-dimensional, not realizing the outlets provided not only for many talents and many interests, but also for creativity and individuality. Some specific examples would help illustrate this point with skeptical clients. For example, an accountant may become a CPA, which requires "people skills," and then become a department head, which entails management ability. Counselors who work in an agency of some kind, or any setting that requires a diversity of job duties, could use themselves and their own work for an example. Counselors could also point out that occupational roles evolve over time, and require new skills and new interests. Though some occupations may use more talents than clients realize, it is also true that the likelihood of finding occupations that use all of the multipotentialed client's abilities and interests is slim, although many jobs can be modified (Frederickson, 1986).

Some multipotentialed clients can be expected to lack cognitive clarity, so the counselor should assess for these issues before proceeding with counseling. For example, gifted individuals may suffer from the idea that "you're a hero or a zero" (Edwards & Kleine, 1986). Other inhibiting cognitions might be related to paralyzing fears of failure, perfectionist thinking, myths of adulthood as a static state, and so on. Cognitive restructuring techniques such as those described in Chapter 3 can be used to alleviate these kinds of problems. Still, none of the educative techniques suggested previously may be helpful, and the counselor may continue to be faced with the seemingly formidable task of helping indecisive, multipotentialed clients narrow their options. Similar to the situation of the client with few interests, considerably more self-exploration will be necessary for the multipotentialed than for other clients, so both the counselor and the client need to be prepared for considerable investment of time and energy.

Pask-McCartney and Salomone emphasize three points in working with the truly multitalented. First, there is a need to establish a special kind of client-counselor relationship; one characterized by a highly facilitative, accepting atmosphere. Second, futures thinking should be encouraged, whereby individuals envision themselves taking several paths, developing in different ways, and working in different environments. Third, there is a need to balance fantasy and reality and freedom and structure, as described in the following discussion.

The initial task in counseling multipotentialed clients is to stimulate a "free spirit," perhaps using the techniques discussed in Chapter 18. Such promotion of freedom and creativity can help set the stage to identify unusual, previously unrecognized options (e.g., cross-disciplinary options such as medical illustrator). Multipotentialed clients who have long been plagued by indecisiveness need to be "unstuck," to release their creative energies and engage in possibility thinking. In addition, such cognitive freedom, accompanied by an accepting, affirming counseling atmosphere, may enable the client to express concerns heretofore unexpressed, such as issues about identity, pressures from others, restrictive self-images, and so on. (Pask-McCartney & Salomone, 1988).

Besides freedom, however, clients also need structured, systematic ways of assessing and evaluating options (Pask-McCartney & Salomone, 1988). For example, each alternative might be examined separately, noting advantages and disadvantages. Counselors can provide feedback and suggest activities to confirm these assessments. Other decision-making aids provided in Chapter 17 also could be used to help clients systematically assess their options. Balancing freedom and structure, then, requires that one initially encourage the client to be creative and to engage in future imaging and then use more structured reality-based assessments.

The outcome of counseling is ideally a decision. However, "some clients choose not to choose, at least for the moment" (Pask-McCartney & Salomone, 1988, p. 239). This decision is desirable for those clients who have not yet crystallized their interests. Delaying the choice may be the best option and may lead to effective exploration and personal development.

RESISTANT CLIENTS

Counseling theories differ in their definition of *resistance*. The term was first used by Freud to mean the client's opposition to bringing unconscious material into awareness. Resistance was thought to serve a defensive purpose (i.e., protect the ego), and identifying the form of the resistance was believed to reveal the client's characteristic reaction to threatening situations. Analysis and interpretation of the resistance, particularly as manifested in the transference relationship, is still a central focus of psychodynamically oriented therapy. Other theorists such as Perls and Rogers also viewed resistance as serving a defensive purpose and indicating that part of the client that did not want to change.

As might be expected, cognitive-behavioral theorists are less likely to use the word *resistance*, although such terms as *noncompliance* and *nonconformity* indicate behavioral manifestations of resistance. However, unlike psychodynamic theorists, behaviorists are more apt to view the source of the resistance as residing in the counselor rather than the client. Counselor errors, such as not providing adequate structuring or establishing a facilitative relationship, are thought to be responsible for the client's noncompliance. In general, when clients do not meet the counselor's expectations, resistance is occurring [Kanfer & Schefft, 1988). Whether this noncompliance is caused by client anxiety or counselor error is something that will need to be determined by the counselor.

The variety of ways that resistance may be manifested in counseling are readily recognized, such as failing to complete homework assignments, arriving consistently late for appointments, failing to pay fees, criticizing the counselor, expressing dissatisfaction with results, making unreasonable demands, displaying pessimistic attitudes, or asking for advice or direction but then responding with "Yes, but. . . ." Often overlooked, especially by beginning counselors, is the idea that many positive or neutral behaviors may also signal the presence of resistance, such as overcompliance with the counselor's suggestions, agreeing with everything the counselor says, being overly cooperative, asking for more time, and even expressing too much interest in the counselor's personal life.

It is important that counselors be alert to resistance but, at the same time, they must refrain from overinterpretation. Moreover, some behaviors of racial and ethnic minorities (e.g., low self-disclosure, tardiness for appointments) may reflect cultural norms rather than resistance. Working to resolve the resistance, like any other problem that impedes the progress of the counseling, requires first that the counselor understand the underlying mechanisms (Kanfer & Schefft, 1988). Counselors need to develop hypotheses regarding the factors responsible for the resistance.

Sources of Resistance

Client anxiety about change is a common source of resistance. Client reluctance to schedule a job interview may represent fear of failing in a new job. Anticipated loss of secondary gain is another source of client resistance (i.e., solving the problem will mean a loss of payoffs). Common secondary gains include money, attention, security, control, gratification of needs, and avoidance of responsibility (Cormier & Cormier, 1985). A young adult may fail to initiate a job search because obtaining paid work means moving out of the parents' house and giving up the luxuries that are provided. Some clients have countersupportive social networks that interfere with their motivation, such as adolescent friends who point out that drug peddling is more profitable than a job in the legitimate labor market. Clients who expect counseling and tests to provide "magic" answers may not complete a homework assignment to generate a list of interests because they are waiting for the results of an interest inventory to provide the answers. Failure to become actively involved in the counseling may signal an overly dependent client but might also indicate a skills deficit or that the counselor has provided insufficient structure for the counseling process or assigned tasks. For example, a client fails to ask for a raise because of a lack of assertiveness skills, or a client does not complete a homework assignment because the counselor did not explain the task clearly. Some client behaviors will be manifestations of true resistance to change or progress, whereas other seemingly noncompliant reactions may signal counselor error.

Techniques

Although slightly different approaches may need to be taken depending on the individual client, the general principle of dealing with resistance or noncompliance is to talk about it directly if it is interfering with progress. Some minor signs can be ignored, however (e.g., the client is anxious about a job interview but is willing to do it, and the counselor believes anxiety will not unduly interfere with performance).

Perhaps one of the most important considerations in dealing with resistance is that the counselor prepare for the possibility of noncompliance from the beginning of counseling. Many clients are ambivalent about seeking help and will often say so in one way or another in the first session, such as inquiring about the counselor's credentials or how long the counseling will take or expressing a lack of enthusiasm for the counselor's recommendations. These responses may be of no significance at all, but the counselor needs to try to find out what the behavior means. Novice counselors are often reluctant to address the client's resistance because of their strong need for clients to like them and to keep coming for counseling. The paradox is that failure to confront client resistance can result in premature termination, the exact behavior the novice fears. As Teyber (1988) states it, clients *act on* their conflicted feelings rather than *talking about them* (e.g., fail to return for counseling rather than discussing their fears of change).

As proposed in Chapters 2 and 3, adequate structuring and goal setting early in counseling can enhance motivation. They can also reduce or prevent resistance (Kanfer & Schefft, 1988). For example, some clients expect the counselor or tests to provide magical answers, and they approach counseling in a dependent manner. Asking these clients in the first session to describe what they expect to happen in counseling provides the counselor with the opportunity to explain the collaborative nature of counseling and the expectation that the client will be actively involved in the process.

An additional area to explore during goal setting would be to inquire about any factors that might interfere with progress toward goals, such as secondary gain. For example, one or more of the following questions might be asked:

> *Co:* What is good about having this problem?
>
> If you resolved this problem, what would you have to give up?
>
> Imagine this problem is resolved. How might your life be worse?
>
> The good thing about having this problem is——————?

Another effective technique that prepares both the counselor and the client for possible resistance would be to call attention to the mixed feelings the client might have about counseling and inquire about ways the client might act on the negative side of the ambivalence. For example:

> *Co:* Sometimes people have mixed feelings about counseling and moving toward their goals. One part wants to make some decisions, and the other part is fearful. One part says "Go" while the other says "Whoa—be careful!". Often clients have difficulty expressing or acknowledging these mixed feelings, so they don't tell the counselor about them. Instead, they sabotage the counseling, and convince themselves that they aren't. If you were going to sabotage the counseling, but didn't want me to know about it, what methods would you use? (Adapted from McMullin, 1986)

Counselors may prevent unnecessary resistance by adequate structuring and goal setting in the first or second session, but noncompliance may occur later in the process. Again, the counselor may be responsible. If a client does not complete homework assignments because of skill deficits, in this instance, the counselor may not have been properly sensitive to the need to spend time on development of skills or to pace the tasks. The client who failed to ask his boss for a raise lacked assertiveness skills. The client who did not schedule any information interviews was uncertain about how to conduct the interview; that is, she needed help with identifying the questions to ask in the interview, as well as practice in conducting the interview. The latter could be provided, of course, during a counseling session through role playing and outside of counseling by practicing with a friend.

Other clients might not complete homework assignments because the task was not clear. It is better to err on the side of too much rather than too little detail; for example, "Keep a log of your daily activities to identify your interests" is too vague; better is "Each day, write down what you did that day in one column, then in column 2, rate your interest in that activity on a 1 to 5 scale, with 1 being very uninterested and 5 being very interested. In column 3, indicate what about that activity was interesting and why." What should also be explained is how the task will contribute to the overall goals, because clients are naturally reluctant to complete tasks that seem meaningless or irrelevant to them.

Of course, all forms of resistance cannot be prevented despite adequate structuring and appropriate goal setting. Rather, insofar as resistance represents clients' characteristic ways of responding to threat and, to the degree that clients become threatened as counseling proceeds, resistance is inevitable, and the counselor's challenge is to find effective ways of dealing with it.

In an especially lucid discussion of resistance, Teyber (1988) identifies three steps that can be taken that are progressively more direct.

First, the counselor tries a permission-giving response to encourage clients to talk about their conflicted feelings. Some examples of these types of response follow.

1. *Co:* You seem reluctant to work on this right now.
2. *Co:* You say you were unable to complete the homework assignment. Could you tell me what got in your way?
3. *Co:* I want to inquire as to how you're feeling about coming here. Last week you missed our appointment, and today you were several minutes late. Is there something about coming here that makes you feel uncomfortable? If so, it would help if we could talk about it.

Some clients, of course, will deny any reluctance or ambivalent feelings. In these cases, counselors then stress that conflicted feelings or discomfort are quite natural and that if something comes up in the future, it would be important to talk about it. Other clients will respond to the above queries with less than honest answers, such as "I've been busy." In some instances lack of time is a legitimate reason, but it is axiomatic that people give time to what is important to them. Thus, the counselor needs to probe further. For example:

Co: Clearly, you're a very busy person, and it is difficult to do everything you want to do. Most of us are able to complete those things that are really important to us, so I'm wondering if there are some other issues in addition to lack of time that are getting in the way.

One client, for example, acknowledged that it was becoming clear to him that his decision was going to be one that would be in opposition to his father's wishes and he was delaying the inevitable confrontation. Another client realized that her interest in a job in another state was connected to her dissatisfaction with her current partner. Further progress on making a decision would mean that she would need to face her conflict about this relationship.

If the permission-giving approach fails to elicit adequate responses from the client, then Teyber (1988) suggests the next step is to address the defense. In essence, addressing the defense is an attempt to find out why the client is avoiding talking about the conflict, rather than exploring the content of the conflict per se. Some examples of addressing the defense follow:

1.*Co:* What would it be like for you to talk about your dissatisfaction with me or the counseling?

2.*Cl:* I don't want to talk about Dad. He's irrelevant.

  Co: What might happen if we talked about Dad?

The third even more direct approach is to interpret the content of the resistance. This requires that the counselor develop hypotheses about the underlying conflict.

3.*Co:* I'm wondering if lack of time is the only reason you've been unable to complete the homework. Based on what happened when we met last, I wonder if you're angry with me because I suggested it was time for you to take some steps toward finding a job so that you could move out of your parents' house and get out on your own.

In summary, there are two general approaches for dealing with resistance. First, noncompliance can often be prevented if the counselor carefully structures counseling in the beginning, establishes clear goals, and paces the counseling properly. Second, resistance that is caused by client characteristics (e.g., anxiety about change, loss of secondary gain) can be addressed with progressively more direct responses that are permission-giving, that address the defense, or that interpret the conflict.

LIMITATIONS OF DEALING WITH PROBLEM CLIENTS

With some problem clients (e.g., clinically depressed, confused identity), long-standing conflicts prevent substantial progress through career counseling. Some will clearly need longer-term personal counseling. Dealing successfully with some problem clients (e.g., very resistant and indecisive clients) requires advanced skills. Novice counselors will need to seek supervision to manage these cases effectively (as well as, in some instances, to manage their own anxiety!)

LEARNING TO DEAL WITH PROBLEM CLIENTS

The five suggestions that follow will help the counselor learn to manage problem clients:

1. Try some of the techniques suggested for "few interest" clients on yourself or with a client.
2. Identify some successes and failures from your own life and formulate your attributions from these experiences. Shift them, if necessary, to those that are esteem enhancing. Listen to people in your environment as they talk about their successes and failures, and try to identify their causal attributions.
3. If you are presently working with clients, be alert to any signs of resistance. Address their resistance directly if appropriate.
4. Review how you have structured the counseling and have set goals with your present clients, and try to anticipate whether noncompliance may become an issue.
5. Consult the references listed on resistance, especially Teyber.

SUMMARY

Problem clients are those who pose special challenges to the counselor. Common problem clients discussed are those with few interests, or too many options, or unrealistic aspirations, or those who are resistant. Many of the techniques discussed in other chapters in this book are frequently helpful, such as intense occupational exploration for unrealistic clients. Several specific techniques have been recommended for each type of problem client.

REFERENCES AND SUGGESTED READINGS

Baldwin, B.A. (1977). Psychodynamic considerations in resistance encountered during behavior therapy. *Journal of the American College Health Association* 25:254–58.

Beck, A.T. (1976). *Cognitive Therapy and the Emotional Disorders*. New York: International Universities Press.

Blackburn, A.C., & Erickson, D.B. (1986). Predictable crises of the gifted student. *Journal of Counseling and Development* 64: 552–55.

Brammer, L.M., Shostrom, E.L., & Abrego, P.J. (1989). *Therapeutic Psychology*. (5th ed.) Englewood Cliffs, NJ: Prentice-Hall.

Cormier, W.H., & Cormier, L.S. (1985). *Interviewing Strategies for Helpers*. Monterey, CA: Brooks/Cole.

Edwards, S.S., & Kleine, P.A. (1986). Multimodel consultation: A model for working with gifted adolescents. *Journal of Counseling and Development* 64: 598–601.

Ellis, A. (1985). *Overcoming Resistance: Rational-emotive Therapy with Difficult Clients*. New York: Springer.

Ellis, A., & Harper, R.A. (1985). *A New Guide to Rational Living*. Hollywood: Wilshire.

Erikson, E.H. (1963). *Childhood and Society* (2nd ed). New York: Norton.

Fösterling, F. (1980). Attributional aspects of cognitive behavior modification: Theoretical approach and suggestions for techniques. *Cognitive Therapy and Research* 14: 27–37.

Frederickson, R.H. (1972). The multipotential as vocational decision-makers. In R.H. Frederickson, & J.W.M. Rothney (eds.). *Recognizing and Assisting Multipotential Youth*. Columbus, OH: Charles Merrill.

Frederickson, R.H. (1986). Preparing gifted and talented students for the world of work. *Journal of Counseling and Development* 64: 556–57.

Gottfredson, L.S. (1985). *Using an Occupational Aptitude Patterns (OAP) Map to promote reality-based vocational exploration*. Paper presented at the August meeting of the American Psychological Association.

Holland, J.L. (1985). *Making Vocational Choices*. Englewood Cliffs, NJ: Prentice-Hall.

Isaacson, L.E. (1985). *Basics of Career Counseling*. Boston: Allyn and Bacon.

Kanfer, F.H., & Schefft, B.K. (1988). *Guiding the Process of Therapeutic Change*. Champaign, IL: Research Press.

Meichenbaum, D. (1977). *Cognitive-Behavior Modification: An Integrative Approach*. New York: Plenum.

McMullin, R.E. (1986). *Handbook of Cognitive Therapy Techniques*. New York: W.W. Norton.

Pask-McCartney, C., & Salomone, P.R. (1988). Difficult cases in career counseling: III. The multipotentialed client. *Career Development Quarterly* 36:231–40.

Pickman, A.J. (1987). Career transitions for dancers: A counselor's perspective. *Journal of Counseling and Development* 66: 200–01.

Salomone, P.R., & McKenna, P. (1982). Difficult career counseling cases: I. Unrealistic vocational aspirations. *Personnel and Guidance Journal* 60: 283–86.

Terkel, S. (1989). *The Great Divide: Second Thoughts on the American Dream*. New York: Avon.

Terkel, S. (1972). *Working*. New York: Pantheon.

Teyber, E. (1988). *Interpersonal Process in Psychotherapy*. Chicago: Dorsey Press.

Yost, E.B., & Corbishley, M.A. (1987). *Career Counseling: A Psychological Approach*. San Francisco: Jossey-Bass.

PART IV

Goal Setting
and Intervention

CHAPTER 13

Goal Setting

A goal is a purpose toward which an endeavor is directed. In the endeavor of career counseling, goals refer to the outcomes that are sought as a result of counseling. Goals provide direction for counseling; in their absence, counseling is a wandering, largely aimless enterprise. Though the general goals of counseling are determined by clients and their stated needs, counselor input is needed to help clients develop clearly defined, specific goals. Thus, goal setting is a collaborative process between client and counselor.

Preliminary goals are usually set in the initial interview, once the counselor has some understanding of why the client has come for counseling. However, the initial goals usually need to be considered tentative and subject to change because it is often impossible to obtain enough information in the first session to set long-term goals. Further, as counseling proceeds and client progress is made, new concerns or previously unrecognized issues arise, and goals may need to be changed or redefined.

USES OF GOAL SETTINGS

Goal setting has three main uses:

1. To provide direction for counseling
2. To provide a basis for selecting counseling strategies and interventions
3. To serve as a basis for evaluating the outcome of counseling

CHARACTERISTICS OF GOALS

Appropriate client goals contain several important characteristics. First, they are specific. "I'd like to do something different with my life" is too vague to guide the counseling process. "I want to find a different job within the next six months" is specific enough to provide some initial ideas about the focus of counseling.

Second, goals should be feasible. A feasible or achievable goal is one for which the client has the necessary time, energy, ability, and resources. Further, a feasible goal is one over which the client has some control; that is, the goal is not dependent on the cooperation of others. For example, "I want to make a decision about a new job next week" is unrealistic for a client at the beginning of the exploration process. "I want to be a tennis pro" is not feasible for someone without the necessary skills. "I want my boss to give me a $10,000 raise" is risky and unwise because the goal depends on an action that must be taken by someone other than the client. On the other hand, "I want to earn more money in my work" may be realistic and feasible, as various options that are more under the control of the client can be explored, such as identifying a different job, improving one's performance at work to meet the criteria for merit raises, and so on.

Though goals must be feasible, counselors must be careful not to over- or underestimate the client's potential (Cormier & Cormier, 1985). A highly motivated individual can reach seemingly unattainable goals. The media inform us almost daily about the "impossible" achievements of very goal-directed individuals, such as the 5-foot 4-inch basketball star, the champion one-legged skier, the ghetto child who grew up to be a millionaire.

Third, goals should be wanted or desired by the client. Goals reflecting "shoulds" or expectations of others ("My fiance wants me to get a more respectable job") interfere with client motivation. At times, however, clients feel they are required to achieve certain goals because of conditions they believe are beyond their control. For example, a divorced male financing his childrens' education believes it imperative that he find a job with a higher income, in spite of his high satisfaction with his present job. In this case, the counselor would urge the client to first explore other options for handling his situation. If none can be found, then setting the goal of finding another job might be appropriate. It might be important, however, to establish the additional goal of resolving any feelings that may interfere with this process, such as anger, resentment, and the like.

Fourth, the client's goals must be compatible with the skills of the counselor if counseling is to continue. Occasionally, an individual seeks out a career counselor when what he or she needs is a another kind of service, such as a job placement agency or a vocational rehabilitation office. In other instances, the person may need assistance that goes beyond the competencies of the counselor, such as couples' counseling when dual-career couples are in conflict about their next career move, or intensive psychotherapy when a personality disorder is deterring adequate job performance. In these instances, of course, a referral will be needed.

IDENTIFYING CLIENT GOALS

Determining Client Outcome Goals

Clients' initial statements about why they have come for career counseling provide one of the most important clues regarding the goal or problem that the client wants to work on. Once the presenting concern has been assessed in some depth, and it has been determined that career counseling is the appropriate intervention (see Chapter 3) the counselor can move to the initial goal-setting process. A primary technique to use to elicit client goals is "interview leads" (Cormier & Cormier, 1985), such as the following:

> What would you like to be the outcome of counseling?
> What do you hope to accomplish as a result of counseling?
> Suppose it's the end of counseling. How would things be different from what they are now?

In many instances, the responses to the foregoing leads will be ones that indicate clear, specific goals, particularly if the counselor and the client have already fully explored the presenting problem. Still, the counselor will usually need to use follow-up probes in order to attain the needed level of specificity. The following vignette illustrates the use of leads and follow-up probes.

Co: You've indicated that you're dissatisfied with your current job. What would you hope to accomplish as a result of coming here for counseling?

Cl: Decide what kind of job I could look for that I would like.

Co: It sounds like you're pretty certain that your current job cannot be satisfactory to you.

Cl: That's right. I don't see how it could be.

Co: Tell me more.

Cl: Well, my wife is on my back a lot because I don't spend enough time with her and the kids. And I guess she's right—I have to work long hours and I'm on the road a great deal. So, maybe the best solution is to find another job that involves less time and travel.

Co: You don't sound very enthusiastic.

Cl: No—I guess I'm not. It's not easy to find a job these days that pays enough but that can be done from 8:00 to 5:00.

Co: The sense I'm getting is that you think you *should* find another job but you're not so sure you *want* to.

Cl: That sounds about right.

Co: Then it seems to me that the goal may not be identifying other job possibilities as much as it is to explore some ways to resolve this dilemma, which may or may not involve finding another job. Perhaps, for example, there are some ways to make some adjustments in the job you have now. Would it make sense to you to set as our initial goal that of exploring some alternative ways for resolving this conflict?

Cl: Hmm—that does make sense.

That vignette illustrates two important points. First, the goals were set collaboratively. Second, the counselor was sensitive to the need to probe beyond the client's initial statement in order to determine whether the goal would meet the characteristic of "want" versus "should."

DETERMINING THE FEASIBILITY OF GOALS

Once the overall goals are established, the feasibility of the goals should be explored with the client. As noted above, the feasibility of the goal is concerned with the realism of the goals in terms of clients' time, energy, and ability, resources, and the degree to which clients have control over the situation. Some interview leads to identify whether the goal is realistic are the following.

Co: How much control do you have over this situation? What would you have to do to reach this goal?

How feasible is it for you to be able to _____ ?

What, if anything, might prevent you from achieving these goals; for example, barriers within your self or from others?

Do you have a time frame in mind, for example, a date by which you feel you need to achieve your goals?

The intent of these leads, of course, is to have the client assess whether the goals are realistic. If the client expresses what appear to the counselor to be unfeasible goals, or ones that cannot be achieved within the expected time frame, then the goals will need to be negotiated or, if agreement cannot be reached, a referral made to another counselor or service. For example, if the client's time frame is unrealistic, it may be possible for the counselor to provide a new perspective on the seeming urgency of the concern. College sophomores are notorious for seeking help with selecting a major the week before they need to officially declare a major. Though Figler (1974) has suggested an approach to use with a client who says: "I only want to give an hour of my time," the following vignette illustrates a successful attempt to persuade the client to relax the time limits.

Cl: I need to declare a major next week and thought I could take one of those tests that would help me.

Co: Hmm—next week. I believe I can help you with that decision, but it usually takes a bit longer than a week.

Cl: It does? Can't I just take one of these tests right away?

Co: Yes, and something like that might provide some clues, but they seldom provide quick, easy answers. I appreciate the sense of urgency you feel, and I'm willing to try to work quickly. But we'll probably need to buy some more time if you're to make the best decision. Let's talk about your understanding of the procedures at this university for declaring a major. For example, is it impossible to change your major once you declare it?

Cl: Hm—I guess not, but if I don't get started on the course work next fall, it might take me longer than four years. One of my friends changed his major during his junior year and now he has to stay an extra semester. I don't want that to happen—I need to get out of here in four years.

Co: So, your goal is to be sure about your major by the time fall semester rolls around. That means that we would have the rest of this spring semester to work on helping you make a decision. Perhaps today we could discuss what might be your best guess right now. You could declare a major next week and then change it next fall if you need to, once we've explored the possibilities a bit more.

Cl: Yes, I suppose so. But will this take all the rest of the semester?

Co: That's difficult to know just yet, as I don't know much

about you yet. Usually, though, it takes a minimum of four
to five meetings together. How does that sound?

Cl: OK, I guess.

Co: You guess?

Cl: I just thought we could do it faster.

Co: You're disappointed that we can't do it in a week.

Cl: Yes, but, well—this is an important decision. And if it
takes some time to make a good decision, then I'm willing
to do that.

Co: OK, let's get started. Tell me what majors you've considered.

ESTABLISHING SUBGOALS

Once the overall outcome goals have been defined, it may be important
to establish a road map to the goals by identifying subgoals. Though
counselors frequently construct such a map in their mind, they sometimes
fail to share their structure with the client. Such an omission can be
discouraging to clients and interfere with their motivation and sense of
control over achieving the desired outcomes (Bandura, 1969). For
example, in a reasonably straightforward career-choice situation, a
counselor's implicit model of the steps involved might be the following:
(1) assessment of client's values, skills, and interests; (2) generation of
occupational alternatives; (3) gathering of occupational information; and
(4) applying a decision-making model. Sharing this plan with clients and
obtaining their agreement to these subgoals can reduce the ambiguity and
increase the likelihood that the client will become engaged in the process.

Not all outcome goals can or need to be broken down into subgoals,
but some do involve a series of tasks that can be hierarchically arranged
according to complexity (least to most difficult), sequencing (this first, that
second), or both (Cormier & Cormier, 1985). For example, one ordinarily
cannot determine what to do about a dissatisfying job until the sources of
the dissatisfaction are determined. Leads such as the following can be
useful in identifying appropriate subgoals:

> What exactly do you need to do to make this happen?
>
> Let's think of the steps you need to take to get from where
> you are now to where you want to be—and arrange them
> in an order from which seem easiest to which seem
> hardest for you.
>
> How could we order these steps to maximize your success
> in reaching your goal?

Can you think of some things you need to do before doing some other things as you make progress toward your goal? (Cormier & Cormier, 1985, p. 241).

Leads such as the foregoing, for example, were used to help a client, who wished to start his own business, establish the following initial subgoals:

1. Determine amount of start-up money needed.
2. Consult with lending institutions to determine the feasibility of borrowing the necessary funds.
3. Determine the willingness of his family to support the financial risk involved, as well as living more frugally.

The following vignette illustrates establishing subgoals. The client is a woman in her forties who has just discovered that her husband has terminal cancer. She has two children, a mentally retarded sixteen-year-old boy who needs constant care and a ten-year-old "normal" girl. The client has been essentially housebound since her son was born, and her only work experience outside the home was as a secretary two years before she was married.

Co: I believe I have a pretty clear picture of your situation. In essence, your ultimate goal is to find a job that will provide adequate income for your family after your husband's death. Let's talk about some steps that you need to take to reach that goal. When you think about the things that will have to be done, what steps come to mind?

Cl: I guess I have to decide to institutionalize my son. There's just no way to continue to care for him at home if I go to work every day.

Co: You're very reluctant to do that but know it's inevitable. What do you need to do to accomplish this?

Cl: Well, basically, I need to find out what the alternatives are in the area so I can decide which is the best place that is affordable.

Co: So making arrangements for your son is the first order of business. What other steps do you see?

Cl: I need to get more information about my husband's finances so I have a better idea about how much money will be coming in. And then, with your help, I need to figure out what my job possibilities might be.

Co: And what time frame do you have in your mind?

Cl: I've been thinking six months. Surely, I can make arrangements for my son by then, hopefully sooner. If I can, then maybe I can find a part time job first, so I can gradually ease into managing a job and my family responsibilities.

ASSESSING COMMITMENT TO GOALS

Clearly stated, specific and feasible goals and subgoals are necessary but nevertheless useless if the client is not motivated to invest the time and energy necessary to pursue them. Thus, it is important to assess the client's commitment to the goals as well as to counseling. In many instances, it is clear from the beginning of the first interview that clients are highly motivated to work on their concerns. In other cases, the counselor detects hesitancy or ambivalence. In either situation, it is important to encourage clients to verbalize their commitment. Some counselors like to take the additional step of constructing a written contract.

Interview leads such as the following can be used to assess client motivation:

> Reaching your goals will take some work. How willing are you to do the do the necessary work?
>
> Can you think of anything that might interfere with your motivation to work on these goals?
>
> We've identified your goals and subgoals. I find it helps to make a written contract that specifies these goals and that we both sign. Your signature says you're willing to work on these goals, and mine says I'll make efforts to help you.

Any hesitancy or resistance on the part of the client in committing to the goals should, of course, be discussed. Openly calling attention to the client's reluctance (e.g., "You seem hesitant") is usually the best approach.

LEARNING TO SET GOALS

Suggestions for *increasing your skills in goal setting* include the following:

1. Identify a goal you wish to achieve. State the goal in specific terms. Then determine the steps or subgoals involved in reaching the goal. Ask yourself: Is this goal achievable? Do I have the necessary time, energy, and resources? Do I *want* it? Is the goal stated specifically enough that I will know when I have achieved the goal? Is the goal under my control? Am I committed to the goal?

2. Read a career counselling case in the *Career Development Quarterly*. Write down the client's goals and subgoals. Ask a supervisor or instructor for feedback.

3. If you are in a practicum or field experience, take a client through the goal- setting process. Obtain feedback from your supervisor.

SUMMARY

Goals are the outcomes that are sought by clients as a result of counseling. Goal setting is a collaborative process between counselor and client that occurs after the client's presenting problem has been thoroughly explored.

Important characteristics of goals are that they are specific, feasible, "wanted," and congruent with the counselor's skills. Once the client's general outcome goals have been determined, it is sometimes necessary to identify subgoals and arrange them in a hierarchy according to complexity or sequence. Eliciting the client's commitment to the goals through a written contract or verbal statement can be useful in assessing the client's motivation.

REFERENCES AND SUGGESTED READING

Bandura, A. (1969). *Principles of Behavior Modification*. New York: Holt, Rinehart & Winston.

Cormier, W.J., & Cormier, L.S. (1985). *Interviewing Strategies for Helpers*. Monterey, CA: Brooks/Cole.

Figler, H.E. (1974). How to counsel students when they offer you only an hour of their time. *Journal of College Placement* Fall: 33–40.

Gysbers, N.C., & Moore, E.J. (1987). *Career Counseling*. Englewood Cliffs, NJ: Prentice-Hall.

CHAPTER 14

Improving Career Time Perspective

Mark L. Savickas

Time perspective means a mental picture of the past, present, and future. Career time perspective interventions increase concern about the future and connect present behavior to future goals. Orienting clients to the future and teaching them how to design their futures develops the planning attitudes and skills needed for career choice and adjustment. Time perspective interventions may be used with all clients who want assistance in the process of making decisions about their futures. Interventions that deal with the personal experience of time work best early during the career counseling process because they address fundamental issues and provide a context for other career interventions.

USES OF CAREER TIME PERSPECTIVE INVENTORIES

There are eight major uses of career time perspective inventories:

1. To induce future orientation
2. To foster optimism about the future
3. To make the future feel real
4. To reinforce positive attitudes toward planning

5. To prompt goal setting

6. To link present behavior to future outcomes

7. To practice planning skills

8. To heighten career awareness

BACKGROUND

It is easy to overlook the fact that career planning requires individuals to know that they have careers. Everyone has a career, but not everyone knows that he or she does. Hughes explains this paradox when he distinguishes between *objective* and *subjective* career. He writes that "a career consists, objectively, of a series of status and clearly defined offices. . . . Subjectively, a career is the moving perspective in which the person sees his [or her] life as a whole and interprets the meaning of his [or her] various attributes, actions, and the things which happen to him [or her]" (Hughes, 1958, p. 63). Thus an individual's objective career is externally observable because it consists of the series of positions occupied during his or her life cycle. In contrast, an individual's subjective career is not externally observable because it consists of thoughts about the vocational past, present, and future. Everyone has an objective career but not everyone conceives a subjective career.

To experience a subjective career, people must be able to remember the past and anticipate the future. People who can only think about the present, for whatever reason, do not have a subjective career. They cannot recognize the links that connect their vocational past, present, and future. Recollecting the past and anticipating the future allows people to recognize their subjective careers. People who can adopt the perspective of three different time dimensions have more vantage points from which to observe their own vocational behavior. The way in which they develop their careers depends on which time perspective (i.e., past, present, or future) they adopt when they make career choices and work. A counselor who knows a client's time orientation— that is, which of the three time dimensions takes precedence in decision making—can better understand that client's career concerns and reactions to career counseling.

Some people orient their career decision making to the future. They make choices based on what will be best in the future rather than what is best today or was best in the past. People who orient themselves to the future worry about what they will do in the future. To reduce their anxiety about the future, they prepare for tomorrow by working hard in school and by making occupational plans. They often seek career counseling as a way of designing their occupational futures. Typical career interventions empower these clients to increase their sense of self-efficacy, use decision-making skills, and form career plans.

Other people orient their career decision making to the past. They are more concerned about family traditions and pursuing proper occupations. When they envision the future, they usually view their prospects as a repetition of the past but with themselves playing roles once played by other people. They typically do not seek career counseling about occupational choice. If they request career counseling, then they usually want assistance in making plans to achieve their "inherited" goals or help in solving problems that block goal attainment.

Still other people orient their career decision making to the present. They are more concerned with survival issues such as securing food and shelter or with distractions that offer quick payoffs and short-term gratification. The future does not interest people who are "stuck in the present". Present-oriented people rarely seek career counseling to discuss their futures. When they do seek career counseling, they want help in finding a job now.

Traditional career counseling interventions work well with future-oriented clients. Unfortunately, these interventions do not work well with clients who are oriented toward the past or present. Career interventions such as interest inventory administration and interpretation lack meaning for these clients because they know that their future will repeat the past or because current situations and immediate demands preoccupy them. For clients who are oriented toward the past or present, meaningful career counseling must start by helping them to envision the future and to believe that they have a place in it. If they cannot learn to foresee the future and use that vision as a context for career planning, then they may conclude that career counseling wastes their time.

Counselors can use time perspective interventions to teach clients that they have a future. Clients who are oriented toward the past can learn that the future need not repeat the past. Clients who are oriented toward the present can learn that they have a future. Clients who are oriented toward the future can learn to make the future more meaningful by populating it with anticipated events.

THE CIRCLES TEST

Description

One particularly effective time perspective intervention builds on Cottle's (1967) Circles Test. When taking the Circles Test, people draw three circles that represent their past, present, and future. Cottle devised the test to assess which time dimension dominates an individual's time perspective and how that individual relates the time dimensions. Circle size indicates the relative primacy of the time dimensions and placement of the circles indicates how the time dimensions relate to each other. In addition to assessing temporal dominance and relatedness, counselors can use the Circles Test to improve the time perspective of individuals or groups. The time perspective intervention based on the Circles Test is divided into three phases that correspond to three aspects of the psychological experience of time: orientation, differentiation, and integration. The following description of each phase includes goals, rationale, and procedures as well as supplementary activities that can be included as part of the intervention or used as follow-up activities.

Operation Phase

Goals

The goals are to induce or increase future orientation, and to foster optimism about the future.

Rationale

People use their conceptions of the past, present, and future as perspectives that can be adopted or dropped. Each perspective contributes something different to life quality.

Thinking about the future raises concern about survival in the future. Work is the response that reduces this anxiety because it aims to improve the future. Being in the present can give rise to play because play is for the nonce, it has no future goal beyond immediate enjoyment. Reflecting on the past gives knowledge about self and the world. A good life requires that people learn from the past, enjoy the present, and prepare for the future. People who can comfortably shift perspectives from present to future and back again are more likely to balance work and play. If people rigidly use one perspective to view everything, then they restrict themselves. For example, people who are stuck in the present play too much, whereas people who are stuck in the future work too much. When it comes to career planning, the appropriate time perspective is a future orientation. An orientation to the past or present impairs decisiveness and realism in career choice and planning.

Procedures

1. Provide clients with a blank sheet of paper. Give them the Circles Test instructions:

   Think of the past, present, and future as being in the shape of circles. Now arrange these circles in any way you want that best shows how you feel about the relationship of the past, the present, and the future. You may use different size circles. When you have finished, label each circle to show which one is the past, which one the present, and which one the future (Cottle, 1967, p. 60).

2. Help clients explore what their circles mean. During this discussion, reinforce any client statements that indicate the future is important or that they are optimistic about the future. Convince clients that effective career choice and planning require an orientation to the future. Encourage clients to make career decisions based on future outcomes, not on present preferences or past habits. Use the following prompts to guide individual self-exploration or group discussion:

Co: What were you thinking about as you drew the circles?

What do their relative sizes mean to you?

Describe a recent choice you have made and identify the time dimension you focused on while making that decision.

Use three words to describe how you feel about your past, your present, and your future.

Define work and play. Compare and contrast them.

How will your (future) adult life be different from that of your parents? How will the world be different from the way it is now?

Supplemental Activities

1. Explicitly discussing clients' attitudes toward career choice can increase their future orientation. One method for doing this is to discuss clients' responses to the Career Maturity Inventory Attitude Scale (Crites, 1978). In particular, teaching clients the rationale for mature responses to items in the orientation and involvement subscales induces a future orientation. The items in these subscales address awareness of the occupational future and inclination to prepare for it. Savickas (in press) describes a three-step cycle for item discussion that can be used to induce or increase a future orientation through nondirective exploration to examine a client's thoughts about an item, directive shaping to develop future orientation, and active learning to reaffirm a future orientation.

2. Help clients generalize what they have learned about future orientation to other areas of concern such as diets or school grades. Weight loss requires a future orientation in present decision making about food choices. Sayings such as "a moment on the lips, a lifetime on the hips" convey the wisdom of a future-oriented approach to eating. Academic achievement also rests on delayed gratification. Students who do not envision a future have little incentive to study now for rewards tomorrow.

Differentiation Phase

Goals

The goals are to make the future feel real, reinforce positive attitudes toward planning, and prompt goal setting.

Rationale

Time differentiation refers to the density and extension of events within a time dimension. The more events that populate a time dimension and the farther these events extend, the more that time dimension seems real to an individual. A person who densely populates the future with anticipated events projected far into the horizon has a cognitive schema ready for career planning. A differentiated future provides a meaningful context for setting personal goals. It also alleviates anxiety about the future because a person can envision her or his place in it. Identifying anticipated events also allows people to plan on and prepare for the events, thus enhancing their adaptability.

Procedures

1. Ask clients to make a list of responses to two questions: "who will you be?" and "what will you do?" (Kastenbaum, 1961).
2. After clients have completed this task, ask them to list ten events that might happen to them in the future (Wallace, 1956).
3. When clients have listed ten events, ask them to indicate the age they would be when each event might occur and to place a mark next to the events over which they have some control.
4. Assist clients to assess the density and extension of their futures. Begin with density by counting the number of responses to the two questions about "what will you be" and "what will you do." Then have clients score extension by identifying which of the ten

events extends farthest into the future. You may also have clients determine the average extension of events by calculating the mean age of anticipated events.

5. Explain to clients why future differentiation is important in career and life planning. Provide clients with feedback about their differentiation, both density and extension. Explore client reactions to this feedback. If clients have adequate differentiation, then proceed to the integration phase of this intervention. If clients' future vista seems undifferentiated, then continue the intervention with the following activity.

6. On a blank sheet of paper, draw a straight line and mark the left end with the word "birth" and the right end with the word "death." Ask clients to view this line as their life. Mark a spot on the line to represent the age at which clients will graduate or have graduated from high school. Then ask clients to indicate on the line their responses to the "what will you be and do" questions and the ten events that they foresee happening to themselves. Then ask them to insert any of the following events that they have omitted and the age at which the event might occur: obtain first full-time job, buy a new car, finish college or training, enjoy life your way, take a long vacation, get married, own first home, move to bigger home, first child born, last child born, last child in grade school, first child gets married, establish self in permanent job, get promoted, think about midcareer change, be hospitalized, a friend dies, become a grandparent, plan for retirement, retire, and move to smaller home.

7. Discuss clients' life lines and identify any implicit assumptions that they seem to hold about the future. Draw brackets on clients' life lines to demarcate the life stages of growth (birth–14), exploration (15–24), early adulthood (25–45), middle adulthood (45–64), and late adulthood (65–death). Teach clients that the lives of most people follow a predictable course through these stages. During each life stage people share similar situations, demands, pressures, concerns, and problems. People who anticipate tasks that they will face have time to prepare to meet them. When they do encounter the tasks, they master them and thereby increase their life success and satisfaction.

8. Once clients envision the future in general, they can dream of a personal future. As noted in a perfume commercial, "dreams are where we design our lives." Tell clients to view their life line as a skeleton that they should flesh out with specific, personal details. Ask them to write an imaginative history of their futures entitled "My Future Autobiography" (Maw, 1982). If time does not

permit the writing of a full autobiography, then counselors can abbreviate the activity by asking clients to focus their personal scenarios on just two points in the future, for example, a day five and a day ten years hence.

9. When clients have written their future autobiographies, counselors can help clients further differentiate these personal scenarios by making them denser and extending them farther into the future. Counselors may also direct clients to examine the goals in their future autobiographies and to restate abstract or ambiguous goals in terms that are more achievable ("I can do it"), believable ("I want to do it"), controllable ("I do not need the help of others to achieve it"), and concrete ("I will objectively know when I have done it").

Supplemental Activities

1. Ask students to write down the important events that they expect will occur during the school year. Given the initial list, help students differentiate and extend their lists. Students who envision more events and who anticipate events farther into the school year will probably earn higher grades and like school more.

2. Helping people learn the course of a typical life enables them to think about the progress of their own lives. Media presentations make good discussion stimuli for this topic. Many popular movies deal with life stages. Counselors may use excerpts from old movies such as *Saturday Night Fever, Down to the Sea in Ships*, and *Peggy Sue Got Married.* Art and music also provide appropriate stimuli. For example, Thomas Cole's paintings that deal with time's passing and its continuity (e.g., *Voyage of Life* series) prompt discussion about life stages, as does Christopher Bertelli's sixteenth-century copper engraving *The Seven Ages of Man.* Emily Lou Harris's *Sally Rose* song cycle may serve the same purpose. A film that presents Marcel Marceau's (1975) mime of Shakespeare's seven ages of people, *Youth, Maturity, Old Age, and Death*, similarly focuses discussion on life stages.

3. Rather than using media excerpts to stimulate guided discussion about life stages, counselors may use resources that directly teach about life stages. For example, an animated movie called *Everybody Rides the Carousel* (Hubley & Hubley, 1975) teaches Erikson's model of the life cycle. Reading and reflecting upon Sheehy's (1976) *Passages: Predictable Crises of Adult Life* also facilitates future differentiation.

4. Teaching about career stages, as opposed to life stages, also can be effective. The Adult Career Concerns Inventory (Super, Thompson, & Lindeman, 1988) operationally defines four major career stages with sixty developmental tasks that most people will encounter as they develop their careers. The tasks are listed in chronological order so individuals can determine how far they have come, where they are, and what comes next. Thus, the inventory provides a superb lesson plan for teaching individuals or groups about careers and the vocational development tasks that they may face in the near and distant future.

Integration Phase

Goals
Goals for the integration phase are to link present behavior to future outcomes, practice planning skills, and heighten career awareness.

Rationale
Orientation makes the future important, and differentiation makes the future meaningful. Time integration makes the future seem controllable. Temporal integration refers to the relatedness of time dimensions. Conceptualizing relations among the past, present, and future provides clients with a cognitive schema that enables them to make plans for achieving their goals. The schema allows people to impose direction on their vocational behavior which, according to Miller-Tiedeman & Tiedeman (1990), is the essence of a subjective career. Enacting contingent plans empowers purposeful action directed toward goal attainment.

Procedures

1. Ask clients to look at their Circles Test while you explain how time dimensions can relate. Remind clients that circle size represents time orientation and that number of events represents time differentiation. Then explain that the relative placement of the circles represents the following four types of time relatedness:
   a. Circles that do not touch indicate *isolation* of time dimensions. This view of time means that people cannot do anything in the present to improve their futures.
   b. Circles that touch but do not overlap indicate *connection* of time dimensions and a linear flow of discrete events. This view of time means that events follow one another yet each

remains distinct and independent. Events can be sequenced but not controlled.

c. Circles that partially overlap indicate *association* of time dimensions. This view of time means that the present has been inherent in the past and the future is inherent in the present. The area where the present and future circles overlap represents the time zone in which people can foretaste their futures and can act to shape future outcomes.

d. Circles that totally overlap indicate the *integration* of time dimensions. When people draw the past and future circles within the present circle, they realize that only the present exists and that, in the present, they remember the past and anticipate the future. This panoramic view of the present envisions the three dimensions that St. Augustine first identified: the present of things past, the present of things present, and the present of things future.

2. Understanding the association of the past and present provides self-knowledge that is important in career decision making. Help clients who drew isolated circles to envision how the past overlaps with the present by identifying past events that continue to influence their present situations, choices, and concerns. One way to show time association is to identify life themes with the technique of functional self-analysis (Haldane, 1975). In functional self-analysis, clients learn about themselves from their past successes, not their mistakes. Clients list ten specific accomplishments that they have both done well and enjoyed doing. Then clients analyze each accomplishment to determine the needs met and the skills used. After identifying needs and skills for each of the ten events, clients organize the results and, with the help of a counselor, identify and discuss their continuing pattern of needs and skills. Counselors may reinforce clients' newly articulated sense of identity by relating it to the present and future. The pattern can be related to the present by asking clients to give examples of things they have done during the current week that exemplify their continuing pattern. The pattern can be related to the future by explaining why individuals should choose an occupation that manifests their continuing pattern and implements their vocational identity.

3. Explain that people control their futures through actions in the time zone where the present and future circles overlap. The more people plan their actions in this time zone, the more likely they will achieve their goals. Persuade clients of the wisdom of

the "5 Ps": *prior planning prevents poor performance.* Point out that when people enact plans, they begin to feel the future emerging. Convince clients that the three rules of success are prepare, prepare, and prepare.

4. Tell clients what constitutes a good plan. A plan is an anticipated series of activities or path that leads to a goal. A path is contingent if success at one step on the path is needed to guarantee the opportunity to engage in the next step. If success at a step has no bearing on the next step, then the path is noncontingent. People who construct contingent paths to goals are more realistic and achieve better results.

5. Show clients an example of a contingent path to a career goal. For example, a contingent path to the occupational goal of physician may include the following steps: study hard in college, do well in courses, apply to medical school, get accepted into medical school, work hard in basic science courses, pass the courses, impress clerkship instructors, choose a medical specialty, apply to residencies, graduate from medical school, obtain a residency, succeed in residency, earn medical license, and set up practice.

6. Use the Future Plans Questionnaire (Pearlson & Raynor, 1982) to teach planning skills. Start by asking clients to select an occupational (or other life) goal for which they would like to construct a plan.

7. Give clients 15 blank sheets of paper and tell them to view each sheet as a "Step Page." Ask clients to think about the steps they must take to reach the goal they are using for this activity. Tell clients to write on each page a distinct step that they plan to engage in, the positive outcome of that activity, and any negative outcome that might occur. Explain that they should write only steps that require attainment of the positive outcome to continue along the path. When they have finished the Step Pages, ask clients to check their steps to make sure that they are sequenced in a contingent path.

8. When clients have completed their paths, analyze the steps to make sure that they are contingent. Next, discuss the plans and revise them if necessary. Revision could include making a step more specific and detailed, adding steps to further differentiate the future, making the plan more comprehensive, and building in alternatives.

9. Discuss achievement standards for each step in the path. Steps

on the contingent path define *what* they will do. Now ask clients to consider *how* well they will perform each step. Encourage effort and discuss why they should strive to do their best as they execute their plans. Review the steps in their plans and underline, in red ink, words that directly (e.g., good, better, best) and indirectly (e.g., earn, strive, responsible) indicate concern about quality. For steps that lack quality standards, use the red pen to add words that arouse the need for achievement.

10. Conclude the intervention by generalizing clients' newly gained planning skills to other goals. Teach clients that they need a plan for every important goal they set for themselves. Goals without plans are unlikely to be achieved.

Supplemental Activities

1. Hopkins (1977) described a brief exercise that shows clients how to overlap the present and the future time dimensions.

> I list five things that I need to do by Monday (these tend to be urgent) and then five things that I want to do during my lifetime (these tend to be important). My next task is to combine the lists into one imperative list of things both important and urgent. I can get at a big important thing by making a small part of it urgent (p. 2).

2. Games designed to increase time relatedness work well with high school students. "When I Grow Up I'm Going to Be Married" (Staff, 1972) is a game that illustrates how time and circumstances affect women. Ten girls can play at a time. Each girl is given a profile with four facts about her marriage, childbearing, education, and death. Participants are each asked to design an "ideal life" around her four facts and to indicate at which periods in her life she will be doing what. After each girl has designed "her" life, she is given a list of problems that occurred in her life. She must then cope with each problem and analyze how better planning might have prevented the problem or increased her ability to adapt to the problems. The "Life Career Game" (Boocock, 1967) provides a similar yet more structured experience in planning for the future.

LEARNING TO MAKE TIME PERSPECTIVE INTERVENTIONS

You may develop skill in applying the time perspective intervention by engaging in the following activities:

1. Evaluate your own time perspective. Do the exercises yourself and discuss the results with a friend or colleague.
2. Practice the time perspective intervention on counselors or students before you use it with clients. Ask these counselors or students to give you honest feedback about the intervention and the way you did it.
3. Familiarize yourself with the other time perspective interventions by reading *Learning for Tomorrow: The Role of the Future in Education* (Toffler, 1974)
4. Identify the time perspective of the organizational culture in the institution where you work (Ringle & Savickas, 1983) and consider how it influences your daily behavior and career plans.
5. Study the psychology of time by reading the references included in the foregoing discussion.
6. Learn more about the philosophy, history, and social meaning of time by reading such books as *Man and Time* (Priestley, 1989) and *Time: Rhythm and Response* (von Franz, 1978).

SUMMARY

Time perspective can be altered to increase future orientation, populate the future with probable events and personal goals, and link present behavior to future outcomes. Counselors who use time perspective interventions with their clients aim to make the future important, cause the future to seem real, and create hope that goals can be achieved. Clients with an extensive vista on the future display greater career awareness, more optimism, and increased motivation for life planning. The planning attitudes and skills that result from time perspective interventions may also generalize to empower individuals as they plan for other life roles.

REFERENCES AND SUGGESTED READINGS

Boocock, S. (1967). The life career game. *Personnel and Guidance Journal* 46: 328–34.

Cottle, T. (1967). The circles test: An investigation of perceptions of temporal relatedness and dominance. *Journal of Projective Techniques and Personality Assessment* 31: 58–71.

Crites, J. (1978). *Theory and Research Handbook for the Career Maturity Inventory* (2nd ed.) Monterey, CA: CTB/McGraw-Hill.

Haldane, B. (1975) *How to Make a Habit of Success*. Washington, DC: Acropolis Books.

Hopkins, W. (1977, Autumn). Urgent or important? *Learnings*, p. 2.

Hubley, J., & Hubley, F. (1975). *Everybody Rides the Carousel* [Film]. Produced by Hubley Studios; distributed by Pyramid Distributors.

Hughes, E. (1958). *Men and Their Work*. Glencoe, IL: Free Press.

Kastenbaum, R. (1961). The dimensions of future time perspective: An experimental analysis. *Journal of General Psychology* 65: 203–18.

Marceau, M. (1975). *Youth, Maturity, Old Age, and Death* [Film]. Produced by John Barnes Productions; distributed by Encyclopaedia Britannica Educational Corporation.

Maw, I. (1982). The future autobiography: A longitudinal analysis. *Journal of College Student Personnel* 23, 3–6.

Pearlson, H., & Raynor, J. (1982). Motivational analysis of the future plans of college men: Imagery used to describe future plans and goals. In J. Raynor, & E. Entin (eds.), *Motivation, Career Striving and Aging*, 115–24. Washington, DC: Hemisphere Publishing Corporation.

Priestley, J. (1989). *Man and Time*. New York: Crescent Books.

Ringle, P., & Savickas, M. (1983). Administrative leadership. *Journal of Higher Education* 54: 649–61.

Savickas, M. (In press). The use of career choice measures in counseling practice. In C.E. Watkins, Jr. & V. Campbell (eds.), *The Use of Tests in Counseling*. Hillsdale, NJ: Lawrence Earlbaum Associates.

Sheehy, G. (1976). *Passages: Predictable Crises of Adult Life*. New York: Dutton.

Staff. (1972). When I grow up I'm going to be married. *Impact* 2: 32–38.

Super, D., Thompson, A., & Lindeman, R. (1988). *Adult Career Concerns Inventory: Manual for Research and Exploratory Use in Counseling*. Palo Alto, CA: Consulting Psychologists Press.

Miller-Tiedeman, A., & Tiedeman, D.V. (1990). *Career Decision Making: An Individualistic Perspective*. D. Brown, L. Brooks and Associates. Career Choice and Development (2nd ed.), 308–37. San Francisco, CA: Jossey-Bass.

Toffler, A. (1974). *Learning for Tomorrow: The Role of the Future in Education*. New York: Vintage Books.

von Franz, M. (1978). *Time: Rhythm and Response*. London: Thames and Hudson.

Wallace, M. (1956). Future time perspective in schizophrenia. *Journal of Abnormal and Social Psychology* 52: 240–45.

CHAPTER 15

Gathering Occupational Information

Occupational information refers to a variety of facts about occupations, such as the nature of the work performed, education and training requirements for entry, employment prospects, work environment, earnings, and the like. Accurate occupational information is essential if clients are to select options that are compatible with their interests, values, lifestyles, and so on.

Clients differ considerably in regard to the kind and amount of information they need. For example, clients with little or no work experience may need a general orientation to the world of work to help them generate a list of options, while a client who has held several diverse jobs will want quite specific information about salary level, job duties, opportunities for advancement, etc. The following pages focus on the primary sources of occupational information and techniques the counselor can use to assist clients in their research about career options.

USES OF OCCUPATIONAL INFORMATION

Uses of occupational information include the following:

1. To clarify which occupational alternatives are congruent with client's interests, skills, values, and current needs or life situation
2. To generate new occupational alternatives

3. To narrow the number of occupational options currently under consideration
4. To help inexperienced clients become familiar with the world of work
5. To correct stereotyped or inaccurate impressions regarding specific occupations
6. To motivate career decision making by illustrating rewards associated with career choice

BACKGROUND

In the not too distant past, a course on occupational information was the only course in career counseling or development offered in many graduate training programs in counseling. Often entitled simply "Occupational Information," the course usually reflected the viewpoint that one of the most important tasks of the counselor was to be thoroughly familiar with the world of work, including labor market trends and the characteristics of a variety of occupations. As career development theorizing and counseling have progressed over the years, the training of career counselors has broadened considerably, and occupational information is more typically covered as one topic in a general course on career counseling and development. Moreover, the expectation that counselors are occupational encyclopedias has shifted to the more realistic view that counselors need a working knowledge of sources of occupational information so that they can direct clients to data that may be useful to them.

The appropriate use of materials is a necessary adjunct to successful career counseling. Unfortunately the best means of utilizing printed material has not been empirically tested, at least not extensively. A recent review of the bibliotherapy literature failed to turn up a single recent study that addressed this issue (Riordan & Wilson, 1989).

The use of computerized systems that facilitate occupational exploration both in conjunction with, and separate from, career counseling has come under empirical scrutiny, often with mixed results (e.g., Garis & Niles, 1990). The fact is that we are not certain what the best approach to delivering occupational information is at this time although we would speculate that the client's personality will be a key variable in deciding how this can best be accomplished. (For example "Social" personality types may want to interact with people to get information.) We believe that the nature of the client is important in determining what sources of information should be used, but we also believe that the best approach to information development is to engage the client actively in the process regardless of the clients personality characteristics.

Counselors, in order to help clients gather occupational information, need to be familiar with the common occupational classification systems (see Chapter 5), to know the general contents, advantages, and disadvantages of the various sources of information, to be able to adequately prepare clients for the data collection process, and to be prepared to help clients realistically evaluate the information they collect.

SOURCES OF INFORMATION ON OCCUPATIONS

The primary sources of occupational information are (1) print material, (2) computer-based systems, (3) audiovisual materials, (4) interviews with workers or experts, (5) direct experience, and (6) comprehensive statewide systems of occupational information. Which are used depends primarily on availability and accessibility. In addition, counselors will need to take certain characteristics of occupational information such as reading level, personality type, and handicapping condition of the client into consideration before deciding which sources of occupational information will be most effective. Clients who have a low reading level may have to access audiovisual materials whereas those with handicaps may not have the mobility needed to conduct interviews. Informal observations suggest that "Realistic" personality types may prefer computer systems to personal interviews. Still other clients may not possess the social skills needed to effectively engage in interviews with workers. In the latter instance, counselors can, and probably should, provide social skills training, (e.g., assertiveness skills, interview skills) prior to data collection interviews.

Print Material

Print material may be the most frequently used source of information about occupations. One of the most useful and detailed of these is the *Occupational Outlook Handbook* (OOH) (U. S. Dept. of Labor, 1988- 89). The OOH is revised every two years and contains information on approximately 850 occupations and thirty-five industries. Information provided on each occupation includes job duties, education and training requirements, places of employment, earnings, working conditions, employment trends, and sources of further information. The 850 occupations are organized into thirteen clusters of related jobs, an arrangement that enables the reader to review a large number of jobs within specific interest areas.

Another widely used book that contains detailed technical descriptions of practically all known jobs in North America (approximately 20,000) is the *Dictionary of Occupation Titles* (DOT) (U.S. Dept. of Labor, 1977) and the 1982 supplement. The DOT is a good source of information for occupations not included in the OOH, although the technical style and complexity of the format makes the information difficult to access.

Still another printed source of occupational information is *The Guide for Occupational Exploration* (GOE) (U.S. Dept. of Labor, 1979) which organizes occupational information around twelve interest clusters (e.g., artistic, scientific, mechanical), subdivided into sixty-six work groups and 348 subgroups. The format of the GOE enables the reader to obtain an overview of the world of work and identify alternatives that reflect his or her interests, abilities, and potentials.

In addition to these widely used books, literally dozens of commercial publishers produce materials of all types on a large number of occupations. For example, Chronicle Guidance Publications publishes more than 600 occupational briefs, as does Science Research Associates. Finally, many books ranging from comic books to autobiographies are available describing occupations in various fields (e.g., allied health, outdoor occupations, etc.).

The primary advantages of printed sources of information are that they are easily available and relatively inexpensive. Local libraries, for example, ordinarily keep current copies of the OOH. Career-information libraries or centers can be found in most colleges and universities and many high schools. Disadvantages of printed sources are that the material is often boring to read, may present only positive and neutral information, and becomes quickly out of date (Brooks, 1990; Yost & Corbishley, 1987).

Computer-based Information Systems

Computer-based systems of information have become increasingly popular in recent years. Although several systems are available, only three of the most commonly used are briefly described here. The Guidance Information System (GIS), operated by Time Share Corporation, a part of Houghton-Mifflin, provides national data on occupations (over 1000), four-year colleges, two-year colleges, graduate schools, financial aid, and armed services occupations. The DISCOVER system, developed primarily by Jo-Ann Harris-Bowlsbey, produced and distributed by the American College and Testing Program, consists of modules on values, decision making, career planning, and occupational information. Seven large data banks provide information on occupations, four-year colleges, two-year colleges, technical and specialized schools, apprenticeship programs, military programs, and graduate/professional schools. The System of Interactive Guidance and Information (SIGI) and SIGI Plus were developed at Educational Testing Service by a research group under the direction of Martin Katz. The SIGI Plus system offers a value-based approach, providing, for example, lists of occupations that meet the user's weighted combination of values. The system provides information on occupations and how occupations compare on a variety of criteria, estimates the chances for success in preparatory programs for occupations, and suggests occupations that best fit the user's values.

Advantages of computer systems are that clients usually enjoy using them, and information can be updated easily. Disadvantages of computer systems include a limited memory capacity, so that only broad categories of occupations can be covered, and a high initial financial investment.

Audiovisual Materials

Audiovisual materials are another source of information about occupations. Some universities, for example, maintain a collection of audio tapes on college majors. Videotapes describing various occupations are also available. The latest development in this area is interactive video, which provides many of the advantages of a computerized system but allows for more visual input (e.g., pictures of workers on the job). Audiovisual aids may engage the client's interest more readily than some printed sources, but they contain limited information, are expensive, are sometimes cumbersome to use, and appear more obsolete to the user than printed sources when the information is out of date (Yost & Corbishley, 1987).

Interviews

Interviews with experts or workers in the field have recently become a very popular method of obtaining information. Frequently labeled the "Information Interview," the method involves client interviews with individuals who are knowledgeable about the field from firsthand experience. Typical questions asked include: "How did you get into this work? What do you like most about it? What do you like least about it? Can you suggest other people in this kind of work that I might talk to?" Other questions may be important depending on the characteristics of the client. For example, those who value social interaction would want to inquire about the emphasis on teamwork and group cooperation. People who want to use their creative and inventive skills might ask about the flexibility of the work environment (Hirsh & McEvoy, 1986). (See their *Using the Strong in Organizations* for additional suggestions for questions of importance for certain types of clients.)

Clients are often reluctant to initiate an information interview because they feel it is an imposition on the individual worker's time. Many people, however, enjoy talking about themselves and what they do and welcome the opportunity to be helpful. Some counselors maintain a file of contacts in the community who are willing to participate in these interviews, and clients can be urged to check with their friends and family for names of contacts. If names of people employed in a field cannot be obtained through the resources of the client or the counselor, it is relatively easy to locate places of work using the Yellow Pages of the telephone book and calling the business to ask for the name of a person who is employed in the job.

A major advantage of information interviews is firsthand knowledge and direct observation of the worker and working conditions. Personal interviews can provide that "between the lines" information that cannot be gleaned from printed sources and can confirm or disconfirm various routes or paths into the field. Cautions about this source are that some workers interviewed may be atypical in the way they view or approach their work and may be overenthusiastic and point out advantages but not disadvantages. The possibility that only a worker with a skewed view is interviewed can be obviated by ensuring that the client meets with more than one person in the occupation.

Experience

Direct experience (e.g., job shadowing, volunteer work, internships) is also a common source of occupational information. Job shadowing involves literally following a worker around for a day, a few days, a week, or longer, to get a firsthand view of what the work involves. Many colleges and universities, and some high schools, have set up an extensive system for students to get experience through volunteer work or more formal internships. These kinds of experiences can be especially helpful for clients who have little or no work experience. This method has one major disadvantage: time. Employed clients may have little time to pursue these usually nonpaid opportunities and may be precluded from direct contacts.

Comprehensive Statewide Systems of Information

Instate career information delivery systems (CIDS) were initiated in the 1970s to develop and deliver career information. The National Occupation Information Committee (NOICC) assumed responsibility for these systems in 1979 and developed a series of State Occupational Information Coordinating Committees (SOICCs). Though the actual nature of the CIDS varies from state to state (and territories) they typically make available to users local and state occupational information that includes up-to-date job descriptions, wage information, and outlook data. They also provide educational information regarding public and private two-year and four-year colleges, vocational technical schools, and graduate schools, as well as information about the military, specific employers, and so forth. A similar set of information focused at the national level is offered by many CIDS. The actual method of delivering information to users, which consist of high schools, two- and four-year colleges, libraries, vocational technical schools, businesses, employment security agencies, vocational rehabilitation agencies, and correctional institutes, varies considerably among states. Typically, microcomputer files are available, along with microfiche and print materials (NOICC, 1986), but one needs to contact the SOICC director to determine exact delivery systems being used.

Information from the various CIDS has the advantages of being oriented to the local situation and being current because it is updated on a regular basis. User institutions must pay a subscription fee and an annual update fee, and this presents a barrier for some institutions.

HELPING THE CLIENT
GATHER INFORMATION

The main tasks of the career counselor in the information-gathering stage are to prepare the client to gather information and to help the client evaluate information. It is important for counselors to stay involved with the client insofar as possible throughout this stage, but counseling sessions are usually scheduled less frequently.

Preparing the Client

For clients to make effective use of occupational information, it is important that they approach the task with a schema to organize the information they obtain. Without such a schema, the information will simply be a collection of unrelated facts having no personal meaning for the client. The schema need not be elaborate and usually evolves naturally from the previous stages of counseling, providing that the assessment process has been thorough. By the time clients are ready to gather occupational information, they should have a reasonably clear picture of their interests, values, skills, needs, personality, and life situation. Thus, clients can gather information with this self-schema in mind and with an eye toward the extent to which certain occupations are or are not congruent with "who I am and what I want."

Three related strategies can be useful here. First, the client can be asked to summarize what has been learned thus far in the counseling process and what kinds of information are the most important. Second, depending on the client, the major points of this summary could be organized into a chart or checklist to be used in the information-gathering process. (e.g., "This is what I know, this is what I need to know"). Some clients, however, will find a chart or checklist too confining and structured, though others will welcome such concrete guidelines. Third, the counselor can explain the various sources of available information and help the client develop an information-seeking plan. The following dialogue between a college sophomore and her counselor illustrates the preparation of the client for gathering information.

Co: It seems to me that the work we've done on identifying your interests, skills, and values has come together into some consistent themes.

Cl: Yeah—I'm a lot clearer now than I was when I came in here the first time about what some possible areas are. I'm still not sure, though, exactly what I want to do. Like, I think I might be interested in public relations, but I still don't know much about it.

Co: Right. It seems to me that it's time to get some information about that and some other possibilities you've talked about. What do you think?

Cl: I agree. Are you talking about reading in some of those books you've mentioned in the career library?

Co: Yes, reading is one way. We've talked briefly before about some other ways, also. Remember?

Cl: Um-hmm. Doing volunteer work, talking to some people in the field.

Co: Yes. I suggest that we spend the rest of our time today developing a plan for getting the information you need, unless you have something else you want to talk about.

Cl: No, I don't think so. Let's develop a plan—I'm eager to get started.

Co: Okay. I suggest that we begin by reviewing the ideas you have about the areas you think you're interested in and then summarizing what you know at this point about your skills and values. Doing both of these activities could help us identify the most important points for you to look for.

Cl: Well, the list of possible jobs I listed the other day included public relations, director of guidance, dietitian, speech pathologist, foreign language interpreter, and marriage counselor. And I don't know much about any of them.

Co: Since you don't have much information about any of them, perhaps the best way to start is to do some reading about all of them. You might find after you get some preliminary information that some seem to fit you better than others, and then you could dig a little deeper into those by talking to some people in the field, doing volunteer work, and so on. How do you react to that idea?

Cl: Seems fine, except that I've heard it's real hard to find a job as an interpreter. But then, as you said the last time, I guess I shouldn't let that get in my way—if I decide that's for me, I'll just go for it!

Co: Good. You've listed the areas you want to start with. Let me just point out that when you start reading, you might see some other fields that sound like possibilities that you hadn't thought of, and I want to encourage you at this point to "follow your nose," so to speak. If some other possibilities catch your eye, read about those, too. Right now, I think it's important for you to look as broadly as possible and then narrow them down after you have more information.

Cl: That seems like a good idea.

Co: Let's talk now about what you want to look for when you do this reading. What characteristics of the fields are going to be important to you? What features would make you feel positive and negative about each field? Keep in mind here the values and skills exercises you did.

Cl: Well, I know I just couldn't stand a job where I have to sit at a desk all day. And I'd like to be able to travel some, although I wouldn't want to do that every day. And I need to be involved with people—either helping them or serving the public. And I'd rather not go to graduate school if I can avoid it.

Co: Okay—not being confined to a desk, some opportunity to travel, involvement with people, and preferably requiring a bachelor's degree. Anything else from the values and skills exercises that stands out?

Cl: Hmm—well, money is sort of important. I don't need to earn a lot of money—just enough so that I can support myself and don't have to be dependent on anyone. And—

skills . . . .Well, I'm good at managing and organizing and helping people. I'm not sure right now how important those things are, but I guess I'd want to check those out, too. And—that's it, I think.

Co: That seems like a good summary of the things we've talked about. Before I accompany you to the library and show you how to use it, I want to emphasize a couple of points. First, I want to urge you to take notes on what fields you read about and what you like and dislike about each one. There are two reasons why this is important. One is that sometimes people discover some things they hadn't thought about before as being important to them, and it can also happen that they realize that some things they thought were important are not. If either of these things occurs for you, then we have some new information that would be important for us to talk about. The second reason it's important to take notes is that sometimes the information is confusing and can be misinterpreted. If you have some notes, then we can review them together.

Cl: Okay, sounds good.

Co: Before we go to the career library, let's talk about when we'll meet again. How long do you think it might take you to do the reading we've talked about?

Cl: I'm kind of busy right now—two exams this week. It might take me a couple of weeks.

Co: So we might meet in two or three weeks?

Cl: I think two weeks will be fine.

(The counselor accompanies the client to the library, shows her the location of various sources, and generally explains their contents).

The preceding vignette illustrates several important points. First, the counselor helps the client summarize what has been learned in the assessment stage in order to provide some guidelines for the exploration process. In this case, the client has no work experience, so her knowledge of the world of work and her work values are quite limited at this point. Some direct experiences will probably be necessary later. Also, there appear to be no restraints on her options (as there might be with many adults who have friend or family obligations), other than a seeming lack of interest in education beyond undergraduate school. Second, the counselor conveys the expectation that counseling will continue by indicating the need to evaluate the information together and by scheduling another appointment. Third, the counselor encourages the client to continue to explore additional options rather than approaching the task with the aim of reducing the number of alternatives. Finally, the counselor provides an orientation to the printed resources. The counselor could use a similar, although slightly modified, process if the intention were to use one of the other sources of information (e.g., job shadowing).

EVALUATING THE INFORMATION

After the client gathers information, it is important to carefully process the findings. In particular, the counselor needs to pay close attention to the conclusions reached by the client and to inquire about the facts used to arrive at these conclusions. Younger clients in particular, who are inexperienced in the work world and have not been financially independent, can easily misinterpret information or have an unrealistic picture of it. For example, one college sophomore from an upper middle-class family, who had never held a job for pay, announced that the salary of receptionists was quite large. It was quite clear to the counselor that this client had a very limited picture of the amount of money it would take for her to live the life style she desired. The counselor's approach to helping the client develop a more realistic picture was to take her through a budgeting process. Specifically, the counselor first noted the expected amount that would be deducted from her paycheck each month for taxes, and then asked the client to fill in expected expenses (rent, food, clothes, car expenses, utilities, entertainment, etc.). The client saw in concrete terms that the purchasing power of the expected salary was indeed quite limited. In another instance of inaccurate impressions, a college freshman indicated that he was considering obtaining an undergraduate degree in education and then entering medical school. His mistaken idea was that he would need a degree in education to teach in medical school. These examples, although perhaps extreme, illustrate the need to query the client regarding his or her impressions of all of the information that has been gathered.

For clients who have sought information from sources other than print material, (e.g., information interviews or volunteer work), similar procedures should be used to discern if the client's evaluation of the information is realistic. For example, some workers are too enthusiastic about their field and may paint too rosy a picture. Others are too negative, and it is important to help the client evaluate these biased views with an eye to whether the bases for the biases are relevant to the client. A salesperson might put considerable emphasis on the excitement of working on a commission. Though the client might feel enthusiastic about the interview with the salesperson, the counselor needs to encourage the client to carefully consider whether working on a commission is an arrangement that would be exciting and motivating or too uncertain and anxiety-producing.

One technique to use to ensure that information gained by clients is realistic is to ask them to talk about both the negative and positive aspects of each occupation. This technique is especially important for clients who are either entirely positive or entirely negative. For some clients who have had considerable difficulty making a decision and are at long last expressing some enthusiasm about a field, it is tempting for the counselor to avoid encouraging a balanced evaluation. Nevertheless, such an evaluation is essential.

Ideally, the end result of the client's gathering and evaluating of occupational information is that the client is ready to make a decision and a plan for the future. Chapters 12 to 17 discuss tools and techniques to assist the client with decision making. For some clients, however, the initial information-gathering process (e.g., reading, interviewing workers) demonstrates that this process needs to continue for some length of time. Clients who have no work experience may decide that they need to become involved in some volunteer experiences. Currently employed clients, who are not desperate for another job and have little extra time, may need several months to complete the information-gathering process to their satisfaction. In these instances, it is unproductive and in some cases unnecessarily expensive to continue meeting regularly with the client. The door should be left open, of course, for the client to return at a later date. Before concluding the counseling, however, the counselor should engage the client in the termination process (see Chapter 22), which might include, among other things, some attention to developing a plan for further information gathering.

LIMITATIONS OF GATHERING OCCUPATIONAL INFORMATION

Gathering occupational information has some drawbacks and limitations.

1. Printed sources of information can be dull and may not provide the kind of life-style information desired by the client.
2. Counseling sometimes stops prematurely at the information-gathering stage.
3. Some clients need extra help in setting up and conducting

information interviews.

4. Clients can easily misinterpret information.

5. Some sources of information used by clients (e.g., friends, parents, workers new to a field) provide unreliable and inaccurate information.

LEARNING TO ASSIST CLIENTS WITH INFORMATION GATHERING

The following are suggestions for the counselor regarding learning to help clients obtain occupational information.

1. Become thoroughly familiar with the various occupational classification systems described in Chapter 5.

2. Review the major printed sources of occupational information (the OOH, DOT, and GOE) to become familiar with the kinds of information they contain.

3. Review several sources of audiovisual materials.

4. Select an unfamiliar field or occupation of interest to you and engage in the information-gathering process (e.g., find and read various printed sources, interview a worker, etc.). Pay particular attention to the kinds of information that are and are not provided by various sources. Think of additional methods to obtain information that is lacking; follow up on your ideas to check out their feasibility.

5. Spend a few hours with one of the major computerized systems of occupational information. Assume that you are a client and determine whether you are receiving the type of information you need.

6. Take advantage of opportunities in your everyday life to talk to workers in various fields so that you can expand your current knowledge. Ask family members, friends, and people you meet in social and or business situations such questions as: "What do you like and dislike about your work? What's the best preparation for going into your field? What advice would you give to people who are interested in a job like yours?"

SUMMARY

At some point in career counseling, clients will need to gather information about the world of work and occupations they have identified as possible alternatives. Five primary sources of information are printed media, computer-based systems, audiovisual aids, interviews with workers, and direct experience such as volunteer work. Each of these sources has advantages and limitations, and counselors need to be very familiar with all of them in order to effectively assist the client in this stage of career exploration. Two important tasks of the career counselor are to prepare clients to gather occupational information and to assist them in making a realistic evaluation of the options they have reviewed.

REFERENCES AND SUGGESTED READINGS

Brooks, L. (1990). Career counseling methods and practice. In D. Brown, L. Brooks, & Associates, *Career Choice and Development* San Francisco: Jossey-Bass.

Garis, J.W., & Niles, S.G. (1990). The separate and combined effects of SIGI or DISCOVER and a career planning course on undecided university students. *Career Development Quarterly* 38: 261–74.

Hirsh, S.K. & McEvoy (1986). *Using the Strong in Organizations.* Palo Alto, CA: Consulting Psychologists Press.

NOICC. (1986). *Using Labor Market Information in Career Exploration and Decision Making.* Garrett Park, MD: Garrett Park Press.

Riordan, R.J., & Wilson, L.S. (1989). Bibliotherapy: Does it work? *Journal of Counseling and Development* 67: 506–08.

U.S. Department of Labor. (1977). *Dictionary of Occupational Titles* (4th ed.). Washington, DC: U.S. Government Printing Office.

U.S. Department of Labor. (1979). *Guide for Occupational Exploration.* Washington, DC: U.S. Government Printing Office.

U.S. Department of Labor (1988–89). *Occupational Outlook Handbook.* Washington, DC: U.S. Government Printing Office.

Yost, E.B., & Corbishley, M.A. (1987). *Career Counseling.* San Francisco: Jossey-Bass.

16

Identifying Personal Transferable Skills

A skill is simply an ability to do something. It may be a natural ability or one acquired through training or education. When we say someone is "good at———"we are talking about a skill.

Though everyone has hundreds of skills, people often overlook many of their skills, taking them for granted or minimizing them in comparison with other people's. A request to identify one's skills is experienced as a very difficult endeavor for many clients. Thus, career counselors need techniques to facilitate this process.

In general, skills identification is most commonly used in career counseling for two different but related purposes. The first, which occurs near the beginning stage of counseling, is for general assessment (identifying interests, skills, values, etc.). The second purpose is to identify transferable skills—those skills that are usable in a wide variety of work settings and occupations (Bolles, 1990; Figler, 1979). Some examples are listening to others, writing clear reports, or sketching charts and diagrams. Transferable skills are different from technical or work-content skills, which are those competencies or abilities that enable one to perform the task of a specific job (Figler, 1979), e.g., to restore old paintings, write editorials, or repair small appliances. Transferable skills have received a great deal of focus from professionals involved in assisting people with the job search.

USES OF TECHNIQUES TO IDENTIFY SKILLS

Helping clients identify skills can serve a variety of purposes in career counseling. Among them are the following:

1. To identify strengths and abilities
2. To determine competencies or abilities that are important in one's work
3. To assess self-confidence and/or self-esteem
4. To increase positive self-evaluation for clients who doubt their abilities
5. To help career changers examine alternatives by focusing on skills
6. To formulate a career objective for writing a resume
7. To serve as the first step in creating a resume that uses a skills or functional (versus chronological) format

BACKGROUND

In recent years, those who have been involved in helping people find jobs have strongly urged a skills orientation to this task. This is in contrast to career counselors who more typically place a greater emphasis on assessment of interests. One assumption of the skills approach is that employers are looking for people with particular competencies, not with special interests. A second assumption is that many different job titles require similar (transferable) skills. For example, teaching and sales training both require instructional skills. A third assumption is that people want job situations in which they use the skills that are important to them. Given these three assumptions or conditions, the emphasis on skills identification as a first step in identifying the kind of work one would find desirable has intuitive appeal. If employers are looking for people with skills, then individuals need to be clear about their skills in order to market themselves well. Further, job-seekers might be less likely to dismiss certain jobs based on titles only, and might consider, instead, how skills needed for a job match up with their own.

The closest parallel to skills identification in traditional career counseling has been the interest in aptitude assessment (i.e., evaluating the client's capacity or ability to learn). Early work on developing specific aptitude batteries (e.g., music aptitude) yielded meager results in terms of predictive validity, however.

One of the reasons it has been difficult to develop measures of aptitudes that will accurately predict job performance is that motivation is not taken into account. Most of us, for example, can cite many instances within both ourselves and others where poor performance was related more to lack of motivation than to low aptitude or ability. Rather than ignore motivation, the skills orientation to the job-search process capitalizes on it. Haldane (1974), for example, labels his approach the "System to Identify Motivated Skills" (SIMS). Frequently, the process of skill identification begins with first listing several achievements (i.e., something that has been accomplished with success). The assumption is that certain strengths or skills are used repeatedly in these achievements and that use of those skills is motivating. In general, then, the purpose in skills identification is not simply to generate a list of skills that the client has developed; rather, the aim is to discover those skills that are important, enjoyable, and motivating to the person.

TECHNIQUES FOR SKILLS IDENTIFICATION

Identifying Skills for General Self-Assessment

Perhaps the simplest method of identifying skills is to provide clients with a list of skills and instruct them to mark with a check those skills they possess. Figler (1979) lists 91 skills found in a cross-section of occupations; Lock (1988) offers 195. Both Lock and Carney and Wells (1987) provide extensive lists organized according to Holland's six types.

A variation of the checklist approach is the card-sort technique. Skills are written on index cards, one per card. Clients are then taken through the following steps:

1. Cards are sorted into three piles: "Skills I have and want to use," "Skills I am indifferent to," and "Skills I don't have and don't want to develop."
2. Cards in the "Have and want to use" pile are grouped according to related job categories or according to something they have in common. Alternatively, skills that clients want to acquire or improve can be placed in a separate group. The latter may be helpful in identifying blocks to career choice or advancement (Hampl, 1983).
3. The client selects and ranks five to ten skills that he or she would most like to use in a job or career.

The results of the card sort might be used to brainstorm careers that would be most likely to require the skills that are most important to the client, to form the structure of a functional resume, or to help the client formulate a job objective (Hampl, 1983).

A slight variation of the card-sort method described above is used in the SKILLSCAN Professional Pack (1987, SKILLSCAN CO., Orinda, CA). The deck of sixty-four skill cards is first sorted according to competence and then according to preference for use in a career. The cards are color-coded according to seven marketability categories: Communication, Leadership/Management, Mental Creative, Mental Analytical, Physical, Humanitarian, and Creative Expression.

Advantages of the checklist card and sort methods are that they are time efficient and inexpensive. Counselors can readily create lists and card sorts from the sources noted .

Another method of skills identification is to instruct clients to keep a log of their activities for a week and analyze the skills and abilities used in each activity. Yost and Corbishley (1987) suggest that this method is particularly effective with clients who doubt their abilities or are skeptical about possessing any skills. One frequent result of completing these skills exercises is that clients realize that they have many more skills than they had previously acknowledged. Thus, the exercise can be very self-affirming. One client, for example, after completing a skills card sort exclaimed, "It never occurred to me that some of these things are skills. I feel real good about myself right now!"

Some clients, however, produce a very short list of skills, and the counselor quickly discovers that self-confidence needs some attention before career counseling can proceed. Other clients produce short lists because they minimize their skills. One client described numerous volunteer experiences that illustrated she had developed a remarkable set of skills. For example, she had taken over the fundraising efforts for the local symphony and increased contributions 60 percent over previous years. She had also created numerous ingenious products. Further discussion with this client revealed that she minimized her obvious abilities and accomplishments because they were all nonpaid experiences. It took considerable affirmation and support to persuade this client that those skills could be highly valuable in the marketplace.

Identifying Transferable Skills

A common approach to identifying transferable skills starts with instructing the client to list accomplishments or satisfying experiences. The assumption of this approach is that all people have some forms of excellence within them that will be expressed in experiences that are felt to be achievements or successes. Examination of these many experiences will reveal a pattern of skills that are used repeatedly (Haldane, 1974; Irish,

1987). Once clients have listed their accomplishments or successes, they then complete a series of steps that can result in a list of skills that are important and enjoyable. This method is outlined in some detail below. This exercise takes considerable time to complete, so it should be assigned as homework. Counselors can easily reconstruct the following directions into a "Homework Sheet," one version of which is produced in Table 16.1. The technique is probably best used with adult clients because they have many life experiences upon which to draw.

It is usually a good idea to provide clients some general orientation to the exercise before sending them away with the exercise to do on their own. Several specific points should be made. First, the counselor should explain that the overall goal of the exercise is to identify the skills that are most important to the client in his or her work on the job. In addition, the counselor should explain that the exercise starts with having clients list their achievements. An achievement is something that has been accomplished with a sense of success. The assumption is that all achievements involve the use of skills. For example, "I published an article" required writing skills, among others. Second, since the exercise is mentally taxing, the counselor should suggest that it be completed in several sittings. Third, the counselor should instruct clients to focus on their own standards of accomplishment and not what others think; that is, all experiences that clients feel good about should be listed, no matter how trivial they might seem to others. Fourth, the list should include accomplishments or successes from all stages of life. Fifth, clients should be asked to think of one achievement before they leave the counseling session, in order to see if they might have difficulty completing the exercise. Some people take their achievements for granted and have difficulty making such a list. These clients can be told that each day there is some one thing that they do that feels more satisfying than others—some activity that gives a greater sense of achievement (Haldane, 1974). Clients who trivialize their accomplishments can be assured that even the most minute accomplishment should be listed, provided it is important or satisfying to them, because the overall goal is to discover skill patterns and priorities. The following list suggests helpful instructions for the counselor to present:

1. List the experience(s). Various stimuli can be used to prompt clients to identify the experiences or accomplishments. Figler (1979) suggests the following possibilities: (a) personal achievements—experiences in which clients felt good about what they did and were satisfied with their behavior; (b) a happy role occupied—a position or role that made the person feel satisfied, such as Boy Scout leader, song leader at camp, and so on.; (c) a peak experience—an enjoyable moment or event.

TABLE 16.1 Motivated Skills

An achievement or success experience is something you feel you have done well, that you enjoyed doing, and that you are proud of having accomplished. Keep in mind that it doesn't matter what others think about these achievements. Only your opinion and feelings matter.

A. List below the first achievement that comes to mind from anywhere in your life: school, home, leisure, relationships, church, sports, community, work.

1. _____

B. Now list below nine additional achievements. To help you in your search for achievements, focus on each ten-year period of your life. Then, try to list at least two achievements for each of these ten-year periods.

2. _____

3. _____

4. _____

5. _____

6. _____

7. _____

8. _____

9. _____

10. _____

C. Look back over your ten achievements. Check the three achievements that you think are the most satisfying and meaningful to you. Write these below. Choose the one you consider most important and rank it 1. Rank the remaining achievements 2 and 3.

1. _____

2. _____

3. _____

D. Using one sheet of paper per accomplishment, give some details about each of these experiences in a way that will enable you to appreciate the skills you used to make them happen. State as clearly as you can what you did, as if you were writing a job description.

E. Now identify the skills it took to achieve the accomplishments.

Adapted from Haldane, B. (1974). Career Satisfaction and Success. New York:AMACOM.

Haldane's (1974) SIMS approach uses two stimuli to identify important experiences. The first is achievements that come from any part and time of the person's life—school, church, community, childhood, adolescence, adulthood. The second is to list the jobs one has held and then the most significant contributions at that job.

2. Describe the experience in some detail. Details should include what was done from beginning to end ("I did this, then I did this") in the simplest possible terms, with particular emphasis on the actions taken by the person. One way to ensure that sufficient detail is provided is to instruct clients to describe the experience as if they were writing a job description. Providing an example can also be helpful. "I published an article" is too terse, for example. Sufficient detail would break this accomplishment into specific steps, such as "I reviewed the research on the topic, identified questions that had not been addressed, designed a study, collected and analyzed the data, interpreted the results, and wrote an article using APA style."

3. Identify the skills used in each experience. Identifying the skills can either be accomplished by directing the person to simply analyze each experience and identify the skills, or more systematically, by having the client review a checklist of skills provided by the counselor. Both Haldane (1974) and Lock (1988) provide a skills inventory chart. Haldane's is simply a list of fifty-two one-word descriptors (e.g., artistic, analysis, or imagination). Lock's is more elaborate and categorizes seventy-two skills using Holland's six types. In each, the chart lists the experiences across the top and the skills down the left side. The client is instructed to check off the skills used in each experience. Table 16.2 provides an example of a format using some of the skills listed by Figler (1979).

4. Review the skills identified in No. 3 for patterns and priorities. Patterns are concerned with skills used more than once and priorities with which skills are most important. Patterns can be determined by totaling the rows; that is, the number of times the skill was checked off. Priorities can be discerned by instructing clients to list the skills that are most important and then assigning each a rank.

5. Summarize the skills or groups of skills that are most important and most enjoyable and that are "musts" in one's job or occupation. The next step depends on the goal of identifying the skills. If the purpose is to identify skills to market oneself, for example through a resume, then the most important ones can be selected and

TABLE 16.2 Skills Inventory

Check off the skills used in each of seven achievements.

Skills	1	2	3	4	5	6	7	Total
administering programs	—	—	—	—	—	—	—	—
advising people	—	—	—	—	—	—	—	—
analyzing data	—	—	—	—	—	—	—	—
appraising services	—	—	—	—	—	—	—	—
arranging social functions	—	—	—	—	—	—	—	—
assembling apparatus	—	—	—	—	—	—	—	—
auditing financial records	—	—	—	—	—	—	—	—
budgeting expenses	—	—	—	—	—	—	—	—
calculating numerical data	—	—	—	—	—	—	—	—
checking fat accuracy	—	—	—	—	—	—	—	—
classifying records	—	—	—	—	—	—	—	—
coaching individuals	—	—	—	—	—	—	—	—
collecting money	—	—	—	—	—	—	—	—
compiling statistics	—	—	—	—	—	—	—	—
confronting other people	—	—	—	—	—	—	—	—
constructing buildings	—	—	—	—	—	—	—	—
coordinating events	—	—	—	—	—	—	—	—
corresponding with others	—	—	—	—	—	—	—	—
counseling people	—	—	—	—	—	—	—	—
creating new ideas	—	—	—	—	—	—	—	—
deciding uses of money	—	—	—	—	—	—	—	—
delegating responsibility	—	—	—	—	—	—	—	—
designing data systems	—	—	—	—	—	—	—	—
dispensing information	—	—	—	—	—	—	—	—
displaying artistic ideas	—	—	—	—	—	—	—	—
distributing products	—	—	—	—	—	—	—	—
dramatizing ideas or problems	—	—	—	—	—	—	—	—
editing publications	—	—	—	—	—	—	—	—
enduring long hours	—	—	—	—	—	—	—	—

(continued)

TABLE 16.2 Continued

Check off the skills used in each of seven achievements.

Skills	1	2	3	4	5	6	7	Total
entertaining people	—	—	—	—	—	—	—	——
estimating physical space	—	—	—	—	—	—	—	——
evaluating programs	—	—	—	—	—	—	—	——
finding information	—	—	—	—	—	—	—	——
handling complaints	—	—	—	—	—	—	—	——
handling detail work	—	—	—	—	—	—	—	——
imagining new solutions	—	—	—	—	—	—	—	——
initiating with strangers	—	—	—	—	—	—	—	——
inspecting physical objects	—	—	—	—	—	—	—	——
interpreting languages	—	—	—	—	—	—	—	——
interviewing people	—	—	—	—	—	—	—	——
inventing new ideas	—	—	—	—	—	—	—	——
investigating problems	—	—	—	—	—	—	—	——
listening to others	—	—	—	—	—	—	—	——
locating missing information	—	—	—	—	—	—	—	——
managing an organization	—	—	—	—	—	—	—	——
measuring boundaries	—	—	—	—	—	—	—	——
mediating between people	—	—	—	—	—	—	—	——
meeting the public	—	—	—	—	—	—	—	——
monitoring progress of others	—	—	—	—	—	—	—	——
motivating others	—	—	—	—	—	—	—	——
negotiating contracts	—	—	—	—	—	—	—	——
operating equipment	—	—	—	—	—	—	—	——
organizing people and tasks	—	—	—	—	—	—	—	——
persuading others	—	—	—	—	—	—	—	——
planning agendas	—	—	—	—	—	—	—	——
planning organizational needs	—	—	—	—	—	—	—	——
politicking with others	—	—	—	—	—	—	—	——
predicting futures	—	—	—	—	—	—	—	——
preparing materials	—	—	—	—	—	—	—	——

TABLE 16.2 Continued

Check off the skills used in each of seven achievements.

Skills	1	2	3	4	5	6	7	Total
printing by hand	—	—	—	—	—	—	—	—
processing human interactions	—	—	—	—	—	—	—	—
programming computers	—	—	—	—	—	—	—	—
promoting events	—	—	—	—	—	—	—	—
protecting property	—	—	—	—	—	—	—	—
questioning others	—	—	—	—	—	—	—	—
raising funds	—	—	—	—	—	—	—	—
reading volumes of material	—	—	—	—	—	—	—	—
recording scientific data	—	—	—	—	—	—	—	—
recruiting people for hire	—	—	—	—	—	—	—	—
rehabilitating people	—	—	—	—	—	—	—	—
remembering information	—	—	—	—	—	—	—	—
repairing mechanical devices	—	—	—	—	—	—	—	—
repeating same procedure	—	—	—	—	—	—	—	—
researching in library	—	—	—	—	—	—	—	—
reviewing programs	—	—	—	—	—	—	—	—
running meetings	—	—	—	—	—	—	—	—
selling products	—	—	—	—	—	—	—	—
serving individuals	—	—	—	—	—	—	—	—
setting up demonstrations	—	—	—	—	—	—	—	—
sketching charts or diagrams	—	—	—	—	—	—	—	—
speaking in public	—	—	—	—	—	—	—	—
supervising others	—	—	—	—	—	—	—	—
teaching classes	—	—	—	—	—	—	—	—
tolerating interruptions	—	—	—	—	—	—	—	—
updating files	—	—	—	—	—	—	—	—
visualizing new formats	—	—	—	—	—	—	—	—
working with precision	—	—	—	—	—	—	—	—
writing clear reports	—	—	—	—	—	—	—	—
writing for publication	—	—	—	—	—	—	—	—

Skills from Figler, H. (1979). The Complete Job-Search Handbook. New York: Holt, Rinehart & Winston.

experiences that illustrate those skills can be described within each category. If the purpose, on the other hand, is to identify skills that are "musts" in one's occupation, then the list can be used to guide the occupational information-gathering process (see Chapter 15) or to begin the job search (see Bolles, 1990; Figler, 1979; Irish, 1987). Haldane (1974) also illustrates ways that skills can be used as a starting point for achieving greater career satisfaction, success, advancement, and even getting pay raises.

LIMITATIONS OF SKILLS IDENTIFICATION

Skills identification has some limitations, as follows:

1. Some clients have great difficulty identifying skills and/or taking credit for their accomplishments. Severe deficits in this regard will necessitate counseling on issues such as self-esteem or self-efficacy prior to completing skills exercises.
2. Some clients will find skills identification using the "Achievements" method to be tedious.
3. Younger clients with little life or work experience will be unable to identify which skills would be most to them in their career.

LEARNING TO IDENTIFY SKILLS

These techniques will help counselors learn the skills-identification process:

1. Complete the skills identification process on yourself, using the method outlined in this chapter.
2. Complete Bolles and Zenoff's (1975) Quick Job-Hunting Map.
3. Interview practicing career counselors and ask them about the methods they use to help clients identify skills.
4. Make and complete a skills card sort on yourself.
5. Ask several friends or family members to complete Table 16.1. Interview them about the benefits of the exercise.

SUMMARY

Everyone has many skills, defined as simply the ability to do something. Skills identification may be used in career counseling to assist clients in general self-assessment and/or in determining skills that are transferable to many jobs or occupations. Techniques that can be used range from checklists to a more elaborate system that begins with listing accomplishments or successes and works through to the identification of skills that are "musts" in one's job.

REFERENCES AND SUGGESTED READING

Bolles, R.N. (1990). *What Color Is Your Parachute?*. Berkeley, CA: Ten Speed Press.

Bolles, R.N., & Zenoff, V B. (1975). *The Quick Job-Hunting Map*. Berkeley, CA: Ten Speed Press.

Carney, C.G., & Wells, C.F. (1987). *Career Planning: Skills to Build Your Future*. Monterey, CA: Brooks/Cole.

Figler, H. (1979). *The Complete Job-Search Handbook*. New York: Holt, Rinehart & Winston.

Haldane, B. (1974). *Career Satisfaction and Success*. New York: AMACOM.

Hampl, S.P. (1983). The skills sort: A career planning tool. *Journal of College Student Personnel* 24, 463–64.

Irish, R.K. (1987). *Go Hire Yourself an Employer*. New York: Doubleday.

Lock, R.D. (1988). *Taking Charge of Your Career Direction*. Pacific Grove, CA: Brooks/ Cole.

Yost, E.B., & Corbishley, M.A. (1987). *Career Counseling*. San Francisco: Jossey-Bass.

CHAPTER 17

Using Decision-Making Aids

Decision making is the process of choosing from among two or more *unequal* alternatives to solve an immediate or long- range concern or to exploit an immediate opportunity. Career decision making typically involves choosing from among several options in order to solve an immediate problem (employment) while working toward a long-range career objective. In the process of choosing from among options, the decision maker can never have complete information about all immediate or long-range implications of a particular choice and, thus, the decision maker is always, to some degree, in a state of uncertainty. Not unexpectedly, career decision makers react differently to this uncertainty. Some proceed while others either avoid choice making or make the choice impulsively because of their uncertainty. Career decision- making aids are devices that can be used to structure the decision-making process and improve the process itself, or used to avoid the negative reaction to a poor decision (Janis & Mann, 1977) for many clients. Some clients cannot take advantage of career decision-making aids until the anxiety relating to the decision is allayed.

USES OF CAREER DECISION-MAKING AIDS

Career decision-making aids have two main uses: To teach new career decision-making skills and improve decision-making skills the client already has, and to provide one tool to diagnose career indecisiveness.

BACKGROUND

For decades, career counselors ignored the career decision-making process, apparently assuming that everyone possessed the decision-making skills needed to choose a career. In the 1960s, this perspective began to change (see Gelatt, 1962; Katz, 1969), and several models of career decision-making emerged, along with aids to assist the decision maker. Though these models varied to some degree, they were primarily based upon the fundamental paradigm provided by science: Identify the problem, identify realistic alternatives (based on characteristics of the individual), collect data about the alternatives, choose a career, implement choice, and recycle as necessary.

To a very large degree, the skeleton just described still underpins our approaches to career decision-making, although new approaches that are a bit more sophisticated have emerged as psychologists, mathematicians, economists, and others become increasingly interested in the decision-making process. The result of this interest has been the development of additional decision-making aids that have been designed to help career decision makers as they choose among various alternatives.

During the past twenty years, we have also recognized that some career decision makers cannot make career decisions even when provided assistance with career decision-making aids. These people are called "indecisive career decision makers." Goodstein (1970) points out that some people need fairly simple interventions such as assistance with decision making or information related to the career choice; these are undecided clients. Indecisive clients, on the other hand, cannot benefit from routine interventions because of their anxiety. Career counseling with indecisive clients must begin with treatment of the anxiety. In 1976, Osipow and associates published the *Career Decision Scale* (Osipow, Carney, Winer, Yanico, & Koschir, 1976). They suggest that a substantial number of people who come to career counseling cannot benefit from typical counseling interventions because of the presence of factors such as choice anxiety. Therefore, the use of decision-making aids with indecisive clients should not occur until the underlying problem associated with the indecisiveness is addressed. Unfortunately, there are times when the counselor may not be aware that a client is indecisive until he or she actually engages in the decision-making process and is unable to make choices.

DESCRIPTION OF DECISION-MAKING AIDS

There are a number of kinds of decision-making aids available.

Force Field Analysis:

The force field analysis aid (Lewin, 1951) is used widely to facilitate decision making. The assumption underlying this technique is that decision making takes place in a field of forces, some of which are working against problem resolution and some of which are moving or driving the decision maker toward problem resolution. Decision makers need to identify and eliminate or minimize restraining forces and to maximize those forces that are driving them toward problem resolution. The steps in this process can be followed by having the counselor ask questions that evoke responses similar to those provided here:

1. *Co:* Identify the problem as you now see it.

   Cl: I have no career goals and I just cannot seem to get motivated to choose a job, even though I know I should.

2. *Co:* Describe an acceptable solution to the problem you just described.

   Cl: I'd like to choose a career that would be exciting.

3. *Co:* Can you identify the barriers to reaching this solution?

   Cl: I don't know much about jobs.

   I'm not very motivated.

   I'm not sure I have the skills needed to look for a job.

4. *Co:* Can you identify the factors "moving" you toward solving the problem you described?

   Cl: My parents.

   I need money.

   I'm bored.

   I would like to feel like I'm going somewhere.

5. *Co:* Can you think of some action steps that will help you overcome these barriers we talked about?

   Cl: Learn more about jobs.

   Try harder.

   Look at my skills. Maybe plan to get more education. Set short-range goals.

6. *Co:* Can you list action steps that will strengthen forces that are moving you toward solving your problem?

   Cl: I could ask my parents to help me.

   I could try to find an exciting career option.

> I could set some goals.
>
> I could learn more about my interests.

7. *Co:* Now, review the list of barriers and forces moving you toward solving your problems. Select two or three of the most important ones from each group. Then look at action steps related to these forces.

   Cl: Well, one of the most important barriers is motivation. An action step I could take is to set short-term goals.

   One barrier is that I need information. I could talk to some workers about jobs to see if they interest me after I know more about them.

   I'm bored.???

   I need money. I guess I'd better try to identify an immediate employment opportunity.

   Co: Are the action steps you have outlined feasible? If they are, identify a series of action steps to move you toward solving your problem, starting with the one that seems most important.

   Cl: I'd say my first priority is to set some kind of short-term goal, to get a job of any kind and earn some money. Then I could begin to explore careers of interest so that I can set longer range plans. I could interview two workers per week to find out more about what they do and the training they need.

The force field analysis strategy is particularly useful in helping clients identify those forces that are restraining them from making decisions, as well as those that are moving them toward choosing a career. It can also be used at the point of actual career decision making with some alterations. However, the decision-making aids that are discussed next may be more useful in this regard.

Elimination by Aspects

The elimination by aspects approach (EBA) was developed by Tversky (1972) and adapted for career decision-making by Gati (1986) as a tool to help decision makers make simultaneous choices from among numerous alternatives. In this approach, the decision maker considers only one characteristic (aspect) of the alternatives available at a time. The process to follow (Gati, 1986) is suggested in this counselor–client dialogue:

1. *Co:* Let's begin by listing the characteristics of a career that are important to you.

    Cl: High income potential.
    Can get a job in the South.
    Little travel—I want to be with my family.
    Security.
    Potential for advancement.

2. *Co:* Now prioritize the list of characteristics, starting with the one most important to you and ending with the one least important to you.

    Cl:
    a.   Income potential high.
    b.   Potential for advancement.
    c.   Little travel.
    d.   Security.
    e.   Can get a job in the South.

3. *Co:* Make a list of the jobs you are considering. Now, using the list of important job characteristics that you have identified, see if you can eliminate any of the jobs you are considering

The client's list can be exemplified in the following table:

Jobs	Income	Advancement	Travel	Security	Job in South
Software sales	E	C	E		
Manager— Computer Sales outlet	C	C	C	C	C*
Consultant— Computer Systems design	C	C	C	C	C*
Instructor— Community college	E				
Programmer	C	E			

Important Characteristics

C = continue under consideration
E = eliminate from consideration
* = explore in more detail

The EBA model may be most useful as a tool to narrow choices rather than as an aid for making a final choice (Gati, 1986). The reason for this is that, ultimately, career choice should take place while considering the most important aspects of a job simultaneously. However, when the list of career opportunities is lengthy, it is virtually impossible for the decision maker to consider the entire list along with their numerous characteristics.

Balance-Sheet Approach

The balance-sheet approach was developed by Janis and Mann (1977) to help individuals make decisions under conditions of uncertainty. The utility of the balance-sheet approach in areas such as choosing a college or a career has been demonstrated by the developers as well as others (e.g., Mann, Beswick, Allouache, & Ivey, 1989). Interestingly, this decision aid was developed not only to help improve decision making but to help decision makers cope with failure. Janis and Mann (1977) have demonstrated that people who utilize the balance sheet are better able to cope if the decision reached is a bad one, because they come to feel that they did all that they could to make a good decision. A description of the use of the balance sheet follows:

1. Generate career alternatives and enter them in the balance sheet (Table 17.1). This first step is a crucial one. The balance sheet should not be begun until alternatives to be included are carefully considered. The EBA aid may be useful in this regard.

2. List personal gains and/or losses for self (utilitarian gains) that you expect to accrue as a result of making a career change.

3. Assign a weight to each aspect of gain expected ranging from +5 to -5 for each alternative.

4. List gains and/or losses others will accrue as a result of your choice (utilitarian gains for others).

5. Weigh the gains and/or losses others will accrue from -5 to +5.

6. List types of self-approval or disapproval as a result of making various career choices.

7. Weigh sources of self-approval or disapproval from -5 to +5.

8. List sources of social approval or disapproval resulting from choices from -5 to +5.

9. Weigh sources of social approval or disapproval resulting from potential choices from -5 to +5.

10. Compute value for each career alternative by summing positive and negative weights.

TABLE 17.1 The Balance sheet

	Alternative Courses of Action					
	Alternative 1		Alternative 2		Alternative 3	
	+	−	+	−	+	−
A. Utilitarian gains or losses for self						
1. Personal income						
2. Interest value of work						
3. Opportunity to live in preferred city						
4. Social status						
5. Educational opportunities						
6. Leisure opportunities						
7. Other						
B. Utilitarian gains or losses for significant other						
1. Personal income						
2. Interest value of work						
3. Opportunity to live in preferred city						
4. Social status						
5. Educational opportunities						
6. Leisure opportunities						
7. Other						
C. Self-approval or disapproval						
1. Moral or legal consideration						
2. Serving others						
3. Self-image (e.g., variable)						
4. Other						
D. Social approval or disapproval						
1. From wife/husband						
2. From close friends						
3. From colleagues						
4. Other						

From Janis, I. L., & Mann, L. (1977). *Decision Making*: A Psychological Analysis of Conflict, Choice, and Commitment. New York: The Free Press, p. 128. Reprinted with permission of the Free Press, a division of Macmillan, Inc. Copyright © 1977 by The Free Press.

The unique aspect of the balance sheet is that it has identified the categories of variables to be considered. The actual characteristics of the job and/or consequences of making a particular selection are generated by the client. For example, the utilitarian gains or losses for self would vary for each client, as would all of the other variables listed.

The Subjective Expected Utility Approach (SEU)

The SEU approach attempts to help career decision makers maximize the likelihood of making a good choice by considering two variables: the value (utility) of the benefits that will result from the choice and the probability of the value being realized as a result of the choice (Wright, 1984). Because actual values or probabilities cannot be ascertained, the "weights" used in this approach are subjectively assigned by the client.

The first step in the use of the SEU approach is to generate a list of positive and negative characteristics of a job, with positive characteristics relating to those aspects of a job that are desirable, and negative characteristics being those aspects of a job that take away from the attractiveness of the job. Once the list of characteristics is generated, they are to be weighed using a -10 to +10 scale. The following is an example of such a listing and the resulting weighting:

Job Characteristics	
Positive	*Values*
High income	8
Independence on the job	10
Security	4
Opportunity for leisure/family time	6
Opportunity for advancement	8
Opportunity for spousal employment	8
Located in a city with good schools	8
Negative	
Commuting long distances	−10
Strict deadlines	−8

It can be seen from this example that the negative aspects of a job could simply be mirror images of the positive aspects (short commute [+] long commute [-]). Clients should be made aware of this possibility and asked to avoid it.

Once the positive and negative characteristics of a job are delineated, alternative job choices should be identified, and the probability that the positive and negative characteristics will be associated with each job estimated by the client. For example:

Job Characteristics and Values		Probability of Achievement (Rate 0 to1)	
		Sales	Accounting
High income (8)	X	.9	.9
Independence (10)	X	.8	.2
Security (4)	X	.3	
Leisure/family time (8)	X	.9	.3
Advancement (8)	X	.4	.7
Spousal employment (8)	X	.7	.6
Good schools (8)	X	.8	.9
Long commute (-10)	X	.9	.5
Deadlines (-8)	X	.8	.9

Finally, the subjective expected utility of each career alternative being considered should be computed by multiplying values of job characteristics times probability of achievement, as follows:

Sales = .72 +.80+.12 +.72 +.32 +.56 +.64 + (-.90) + (-.64) = +2.90

Accounting =.72 + .16 + .24 + .27 +.28 +.42 + .72 + (-.50) + (-.72) = +2.01

The last step in the SEU approach is choosing from among the alternatives. In the preceding example, the client "should" choose sales based upon the calculations. However, it is suggested that the career counselor carefully review each alternative by reviewing each of the values assigned to the job characteristics and the probability of achievement.

As is the case with the balance sheet, the SEU approach can best be used after the client has developed a "short list" of alternatives. It should also be noted that the SEU approach adds a scientific air to a nonscientific process. In order for this approach to be useful, clients must carefully consider the values, weights, and the estimates of achievement carefully. The counselor's responsibility is to help the client develop the per sonal insight and information about self and careers that will make these estimates meaningful. Even given that these conditions are met, each characteristic of the job is being considered separately, which is not the manner in which careers are chosen. In other words, the final weights are indicative of the choice that will be reached if one variable is considered at a time. The result may be quite different if all variables are considered simultaneously.

PREVIEW AND AID SELECTION

Decision-making points arise at numerous times in career counseling. For example, clients must choose which occupations to explore. Then they must decide which, if any, of those explored are suitable. Finally, they must pick one or two career options from among the suitable occupations, usually selecting a primary option and then identifying some secondary or fallback positions. In all of these situations with almost any client, a decision-making aid can be useful. The question to be answered is "Which aid in which situation?" The following excerpt was taken from a session where the client was trying to select which career options to explore:

Co: What is your reaction to your Strong Vocational Interest Blank profile?

Cl: It's helpful, but a little overwhelming. There seem to be a lot of jobs that I'm similar to.

Co: Actually, your interests are similar to the interests of people in certain careers, and you did have quite a number of similar and very similar scores, particularly in the Social and Enterprising areas.

Cl: Yes, and that fits. I am extroverted and I want to work with people, but some of the jobs seem quite different.

Co: You seem a little concerned about the differences, and certainly being a manager is quite a bit different from some of the helping occupations.

Cl: And I don't understand how funeral-home director got in there.

Co: That throws a lot of people, but if you think more about

what a funeral-home director does, you'll probably see
why it's in your profile.

(More discussion of individual occupations.)

Co: Perhaps the best way to proceed is to identify which of the
occupations listed you want to explore further. I suggest
that we begin to identify some criteria by which you can
make that decision.

The counselor has come to the one choice point just mentioned. This
client is somewhat overwhelmed by the results of his or her interest
inventory, and there is a need to eliminate some of the alternatives. The
Elimination by Aspects aid described earlier could be used in this situation.
Another client at a different stage of career counseling presents a far
different problem:

Cl: I'm really stuck. One part of me says "Go ahead and be
the doctor's wife. He loves you. Your children love you.
And the life isn't bad at all." We travel a lot and we belong
to the best clubs, live in a lovely house. God, what's
wrong with me? I'm not really satisfied with all of this! A
lot of women would kill to be where I am and, believe me,
a few have tried.

Co: Sometimes it's hard for even you to understand why you
are unhappy. All in all, you've got a good life, one that
others would like, and it's one you don't want to lose.

Cl: That's right! And maybe that's the problem—I'm afraid of
losing what I have in order to pursue a foolish fantasy—
making my own contribution in this world.

This client is at a very important choice point in her life, and she is
feeling quite ambivalent about the alternatives. The force field analysis aid
can be utilized to help her look at those forces that are moving her toward
change and those that are restraining her. More important, the force field
analysis aid can be used to help her plan to deal with these forces in a
constructive manner. Another excerpt illustrates a different concern:

Co: I believe that what you have concluded is that there are
at least a half-dozen career choices that would be suitable.
My suggestion is that you try to pick a primary choice and
then prioritize the others as "fallback positions" in case
something doesn't work out.

Cl: Something doesn't work out?

Co: Well, let's say that you decide to pursue electronic technician, go on to technical school, and then encounter some difficulty. I believe it's a good idea to have another career alternative or two identified so that you could continue to move ahead.

Cl: I see what you mean, although I'm sure I can do the schoolwork for the jobs I'm looking at.

Co I'm sure that you can as well. . . .

Cl: But things happen. I never thought I'd be unemployed at thirty-two. I don't want that to happen again.

This client needs to make a career choice and begin to prepare for entering that career. As the counselor has suggested, this does not mean that other options will be discarded. It does mean some prioritization is in order, beginning with the first choice and then identifying two or three of the most viable alternatives as fallback positions. The balance-sheet method or the SEU approach could be easily used to assist the client with this process.

USING DECISION-MAKING AIDS

The counselor can better help the client make career decisions by following these suggestions:

1. Identify the type of choice confronting your client. Assess his or her decision-making skills and ability to make the choice without an aid.
2. Assess indecisiveness or undecidedness: If the client is indecisive, treat anxiety.
3. Select an appropriate aid with the client.
4. Follow the procedure for the specific aid as outlined in this chapter.
5. Analyze the results of the decision-making process with the aid to determine the client's reaction to the decision.
6. Help the client arrive at a final decision based both upon data derived for an aid-assisted decision-making process *and* more subjective client perceptions.

LIMITATIONS

A decision-making aid is not a replacement for a careful discussion and consideration of career alternatives between the counselor and the client; it is a supplement to the process. The successful use of a decision-making aid is dependent upon clients' awareness of his or her values and a client's ability to adequately estimate probabilities of certain events occurring as a result of making certain career choices. Therefore, self and occupational information must be available to the client prior to or during the use of a decision-making aid.

No decision-making aid currently available is well enough developed to serve as an aid that can be used with all clients in all situations. Therefore, a career counselor must be prepared to select from among the aids available to meet the needs of the client. It is likely that more than one aid will be used in career counseling with some clients.

LEARNING THE USE OF CAREER
DECISION-MAKING AIDS

1. Spend some time reading background material on decision-making. Chapter 1 in Janis and Mann's (1977) book, which is listed at the end of this chapter, would be a good starting place.
2. Review the concepts associated with indecisiveness and undecidedness. Discuss these ideas with practicing career counselors. Find out about their experiences with these two types of clients.
3. Use the aids to help yourself make various decisions.
4. Thoroughly familiarize yourself with the four career decision-making aids presented in this chapter. Then, with a friend, colleague, or fellow student, help reach a decision using one of these aids. These decisions do not have to deal with careers. They may involve buying a car, deciding where to live, or selecting a vacation spot. Practice using all of the aids at least once. Additional practice is recommended.
5. Practice with clients. Each time a decision-making aid is used, get feedback from your clients regarding their reaction to the aid.

SUMMARY

Career counseling involves numerous points where choices must be made. Some clients are psychologically ready to deal with these choices, and others are not. Those clients who can be classified as indecisive must first deal with their choice anxiety before they can engage in meaningful career decisions, whether it be with or without the use of career decision-making aids. There are numerous decision-making aids available for use by the career counselor, the simplest of which are based on the traditional scientific method of problem identification, generation of alternatives, information gathering, choice, and recycling as needed. The aids presented in this chapter are somewhat more sophisticated than this simplistic model because they attempt to engage the client in identifying forces related to the decision or in assigning values and probabilities associated with various choices. None of these aids is a substitute for the conversation between the counselor and the client.

REFERENCES AND SUGGESTED READINGS

Gati, I. (1986). Making career decisions: A sequential elimination approach. *Journal of Counseling Psychology* 33: 408–17.

Gelatt, H.B. (1962). Decision making: A conceptual frame of reference for counseling. *Journal of Counseling Psychology* 9: 240–45.

Goodstein, L.D. (1970). Behavioral views of counseling. In B. Stefflre & W.H. Grant (eds.), *Theories of Counseling*, (2nd ed.) 243–86. New York: McGraw-Hill.

Hesketh, B., Shouksmith, G., & Kang, J. (1987). A case study and balance-sheet approach to unemployment. *Journal of Counseling and Development*, 66 175–79.

Janis, I.L., & Mann, L. (1977). *Decision Making: A Logical Analysis of Conflict, Choice, and Commitment*. New York: The Free Press.

Katz, M. (1969). A model of guidance for career decision making. *Vocational Guidance Quarterly* 15: 2–10.

Lewin, K. (1951). *Field Theory in Science*. New York: Harper & Row.

Mann, L., Beswick, G., Allouache, P., & Ivey, M. (1989). Decision workshops for the improvement of decision-making skills. *Journal of Counseling and Development* 67: 478–81.

Osipow, S.H., Carney, C.G., Winer, J.L., Yanico, B.J., & Koschir, M. (1976). *Career Decision Scale*. Columbus, OH: Marathon Press.

Tversky, A. (1972). Elimination by aspects: A theory of choice. *Psychological Review* 29: 281–99.

Wright, G. (1984). *Behavioral Decision Making*. Beverly Hills, CA: Sage Publications.

18

Lateral Thinking in Career Counseling

Career decision making can follow many forms of reasoning, including deductive, inductive, and lateral. Deductive reasoning, also referred to as syllogistic reasoning (Gilhooly, 1982), proceeds from premises that are assumed to be true. For example, most people making career decisions have assumptions about themselves such as "I am good at math; engineers have to be good at math; therefore, I would make a good engineer." The problem with the use of deductive reasoning in career decision making is that, because of the number of premises that must be used, it is totally unlikely that all of them can be tested.

Inductive reasoning is the most common form of logic employed in career decision making and serves as the basis for the career decision-making aids discussed in Chapter 17. In inductive reasoning, certain hypotheses are generated (e.g., "On the basis of the data, I would make a good engineer") and then tested against several types of external data (e.g., getting feedback on performance in skills related to engineering) (Gilhooly, 1982).

In both deductive and inductive approaches to career decision making, data presumed to be false or invalid are eliminated at every step. This systematic exclusion of "invalid" data is one of the major problems with these approaches (de Bono, 1970), partially because it is almost impossible to distinguish valid from invalid data.

de Bono (1970) suggests that three types of problems arise in all decision making. One of these is that more information is needed or better techniques for handling available information are required. The career decision-making aids presented in Chapter 17 represent "better" techniques for handling the vast amount of information associated with career decision making. The second type of problem associated with decision making requires no new information but demands that the data available be rearranged in some fashion. For example, a career decision maker may have to rearrange data that suggest that interests are incompatible with aptitudes. The third type of decision making problem exists when the current situation is actually satisfactory (e g., "I have a good job"), but there are better alternatives available. The "good" situation actually blocks consideration of new alternatives because people are satisfied with their lives. de Bono indicates that even people who are satisfied with the status quo may need to look for new, better options.

Typically, human beings use vertical thinking methods based upon either deductive or inductive logic to solve their problems. These forms of logic entail an analytic, sequential, linear process that systematically excludes incorrect and irrelevant information and follows the most likely path to a solution (de Bono, 1970). A problem-solving process that is complementary to vertical thinking is lateral thinking, a strategy that focuses on generating as many alternatives as possible, does not necessarily follow a given path to a solution, is nonsequential, keeps "incorrect and irrelevant" data instead of discarding it, and avoids classifying or categorizing data or people. de Bono believes that the result of a lateral, nonlinear problem-solving approach is an increased likelihood of rearranging cognitive patterns, but he also stipulates that the process does not promise a solution. Lateral thinking can be used to solve the second decision-making problem, the need to rearrange data to develop alternative approaches.

ASSUMPTIONS AS BASIS FOR LATERAL THINKING

Lateral thinking is based upon certain assumptions, as follows:

1. "Lateral thinking and vertical thinking are complementary" (p. 50). de Bono believes that lateral thinking strategies are the preferred ways of creating ideas, solutions, and alternatives and that vertical thinking is the best approach to refining and developing a set of ideas once they have been generated.
2. Lateral thinking is useful in rearranging information stored in an individual's memory. de Bono believes that our information is stored and recalled in a predictable fashion and that, in order to be creative, it must be rearranged.
3. Information stored in our memory is recalled in a predictable, piecemeal pattern. Our recall is less than optimal because these

patterns develop in a piecemeal way. If the patterns that have developed gradually can be rearranged through lateral thinking, the result can be a more effective use of information.

4. Lateral thinking is a problem-solving strategy, but more important, it is an attitude that the patterns we perceive are not the only ones available to us. Adapting a lateral thinking attitude requires that we give up our rigid ways of looking at the patterns that emerge from our memories and look for alternate ways of arranging data.

5. Information is used in lateral thinking not for its own sake, but to change a pattern of thinking and to stimulate more information: It is provocative. Thus, lateral thinking encourages the utilization of unlikely (seemingly negative or neutral) information to provoke new patterns.

6. Once a way of looking at a pattern, problem or event is generated, it should be considered as one of many ways to look at the pattern, problem, or event.

USES OF LATERAL THINKING

Lateral thinking can be used in the following ways:

1. To generate career alternatives
2. To break from personal, environmental, and occupational stereotypes
3. To deal with mild injunctions
4. To foster creative exploration of alternatives
5. To preclude premature closure in the decision-making process
6. As an adjunct to lateral decision-making aids

BACKGROUND

Adams (1986) examined the roots of creative problem solving and traced them to psychology, advertising, business, private consulting firms, and education. Much of this chapter is based on the work of Dr. Edward de Bono who focused a great deal of his efforts on teaching creative problem solving to school-age youngsters. In 1970, he published a provocative book entitled *Lateral Thinking: Creativity Step by Step* to which we have already referred in this chapter, and he has published several other books dealing with the subject. The premise of de Bono's 1970 book is that the vertical thinking employed by most problem solvers is inadequate to generate creative solutions to problems. Adams (1986) supports this position and identifies what he terms "blocks to problem-solving," including reliance upon traditional, logical problem-solving paradigms. Adams also suggests that people's fear of taking risks, their unwillingness to trust their feelings and intuition, their reliance on "tried and true" methods, and their thoughts that using fantasy, reflection, and playfulness in problem solving need to be avoided, are all blocks to creativity.

Some career counselors have incorporated techniques that stimulate creative problem solving strategies into their approaches. For example, brainstorming, which Adams (1986) reports was first developed by an advertising executive, is a commonly used strategy. Recently, Gelatt (1989) has recommended that we abandon the rational-objective approach to decision making and replace it with an approach he calls "promoting positive uncertainty." This new approach calls on counselors to help their clients prepare for change and continuous ambiguity associated with continuous change. Gelatt also suggests that counselors help clients learn to use their intuition and accept other nonrational approaches to decision making.

In support of his recommendation that counselors encourage positive uncertainly, Gelatt (1989) posits that decision making is a nonsequential, nonsystematic, nonscientific human process, and that there are three guidelines that should direct it. The first of these is "treat your facts with imagination, but do not imagine your facts" (p. 254). Gelatt notes that facts become obsolete quickly, that the more information we get about possibilities and options, the greater our uncertainty, and that all information is modified by the sender and/or the receiver and is therefore not objective. He goes on to suggest that people who are making decisions need to know that their information is not objective, and thus it has limitations.

Decision makers need to be in a constant state of seeking new information and to be aware of their own impact upon information as they process it.

Gelatt's (1989) second guideline is "know what you want and believe, but do not be sure" (p. 254). For Gelatt, counseling is not a process of helping clients set goals and then pursue them. For him, decision making involves a continuous process of discovering goals. For that reason, clients should learn to be in a continuous state of positive uncertainty about their goals by keeping their options open at all times.

Gelatt concludes that the decision maker should be rational unless there is a good reason to be nonrational. In this third guideline, Gelatt is, in a sense, supporting one of de Bono's basic premises, which is that rational thinking should not be discarded. de Bono (1970) sees suspending traditional logical thinking as complementary to logical thinking. Gelatt (1989) has not really discussed the relationship of nonrational and rational thinking in his decision-making paradigm, but his third guideline suggests that, while he encourages the use of nonrational approaches, he has not discarded rational thinking.

LATERAL THINKING TECHNIQUES

Alternative Views

de Bono (1970) outlines a number of techniques for teaching people to think laterally, including having them generate alternative ways of looking at a geometric figure such as a triangle. As can be seen in Figure 18.1, a triangle can be viewed in a number of ways.

Figure 18.1   Alternative Views for Triangle

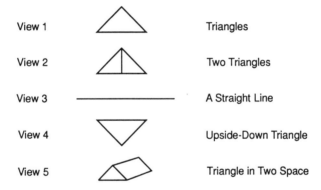

de Bono (1970) also suggests that parts of pictures can be shown or portions of stories read, and individuals can be allowed to generate alternative parts of the pictures or endings to the stories. However, for career counselors, his techniques for challenging assumptions (the "why" technique), suspended judgment strategies, fractionation, reversal procedures, and brainstorming strategies seem most promising. Clients who have a great deal of difficulty breaking out of old patterns may also need to be taught the use of po.

The "Why" Technique

Many clients who come to career counselors never challenge their own patterns of thinking. Counselors can begin the process of teaching them the "why" technique by simply indicating that they are going to begin by asking them why they believe as they do (e.g., men cannot be nurses) and that, gradually, they are to assume that role of asking themselves why. For maximum effectiveness, de Bono (1970) recommends that the "why" technique be focused on a specific aspect of a communication. For example:

Cl: I've always just assumed that I would attend this university.

Co: Why have you made that assumption?

Cl: Well, both my parents attended this university. They met here and they wanted me to come to school here.

Co: Why did they want you to come to school here?

Cl: Because they were happy here and, of course, they've done well.

Co: Why do you think they have done well?

Obviously, there is a limit to how many "why" questions can be asked in a sequence, but in the excerpt above, the client is operating on a number of unexamined assumptions. The counselor is trying to foster an exploration of these assumptions to help her develop new ways of thinking about herself.

Suspended Judgment

Suspending judgment requires the client to deliberately delay making a decision. de Bono (1970) believes that, too often, decision making goes awry because people believe that they have to be right at every stage of the process. He believes that this concern about "rightness" leads to an inhibiting fear, which in turn leads to decisions that are less desirable than those that would be produced by what he terms a "self-maximizing memory system" (p.108).

Judging requires the client to *evaluate* the relevance of information, their own thought processes, and ideas offered by others. On the other hand, when clients suspend judgment, they allow themselves to consider the implications of information, stop censoring their own thinking processes, and consider the possibilities inherent in the suggestions made by others. The following conversation between a career counselor and a client illustrates these ideas.

Cl: I'm a paralegal and I'm quite good at it, but my father

thinks I should go to school for something else. I'm here
to get him off my back. For God's sake, I'm twenty-eight
and just because he's a successful lawyer doesn't mean
that I should be. I know that's what he has in mind even
though he never comes out and says it.

Co: Sounds like you've rejected your father's ideas without
giving them much thought and that you're a little angry
because he's pushing them.

Cl: Well, I'm not the brightest person in the world. I flunked
out of school, although Ill admit I didn't study much. I'd
never get into law school even if I wanted to.

This client has rejected her father's advice because of some assumptions she has made about herself. The counselor could have followed up
this last disclosure with the following:

Co: What if I asked you to suspend judgment on two things:
your father's thought that you ought to be a lawyer, and
your own conclusion that you couldn't get into law school
even if you wanted to?

If the client agrees not to eliminate law from consideration, then this
entire area can be explored.

Fractionation

Clients confronted with critical career-development problems often
look at them as a whole and feel overwhelmed by what they see.
Fractionation is a process of breaking problems into parts, rearranging
those parts into new patterns, and even creating new parts. de Bono (1970)
stresses that the problem solver is not searching for the right way to
arrange the parts, only new and creative ways of looking at the concern.
Consider the following case:

A thirty-seven-year-old woman reports to her counselor that she has
decided that it is time to choose a career. She also reports that she had
never really liked school, had held down a clerical position for a number
of "unhappy" years, and had no definite interests. She also reports that she
is happily married, enjoys housekeeping, and although she and her
husband live a moderate lifestyle, they are happy with it. Her husband is
reportedly supportive of her interest in a career, but has also told her that
he is quite content for her to stay in her role of homemaker. The couple
has no children.

When a group of career counselors was presented with this case and asked to make suggestions for counseling the woman, they immediately began to generate ideas about interest and personality inventories, homework assignments to explore careers, and volunteering to develop career interests and/or leads. Fractionation would have required an approach such as the following:

	Career	Few successful life experiences
		No interests
		No goals
		No motivation
Life/Career Problem		
	Life	Likes staying at home
		Happy marriage
		Husband supportive
		Likes life as housewife

The same approach could have been used with the client to help her look at subpatterns. She could then have been encouraged to visualize the fractions in terms of their relative size (importance). In this case, the woman elected to stay in her current role rather than pursuing a career. The concern about choosing a career had grown out of her observation that most of her female friends and relatives were working. However, when she placed the degree of her discontent about not working beside her contentment with her current role, it became apparent that a change might not only be unnecessary but might lead to a degree of unhappiness.

Reversals

Reversals, like fractionation, are designed to help the client look at new patterns. Often in career counseling, we try to project the correct path. But what if we asked clients to reverse their life patterns and try not to reach the sought-after vice-presidency, or to consider what it would be like to be the worst employee. Out of these types of exercises can come new ways of looking at problems.

Brainstorming

Brainstorming is a procedure that is used in a variety of decision-making strategies. It is typically used in a group situation, but can be adapted for use with individuals as well. Brainstorming requires suspending judgment about the "goodness" or "badness" of ideas, relies upon the stimulation of others (in a group), and begins with induction into the strategy (de Bono, 1970).

The induction begins when the counselor suggests that one way the group might help one of their colleagues is to generate a series of options for him or her to consider. For example:

> *Co:* Jim's been debating about the wisdom of leaving a rather secure position to take what is admittedly a riskier but more attractive job. I wonder if we could brainstorm some ways that he might make this transition. Two things are very important about this process. One is that we not censor our own thoughts. Any idea, no matter how ridiculous you think it is, should be shared. Two, we should not censor each other. Keep in mind that everyone is trying to help Jim, and that while an idea may seem odd or silly, it may be useful.

Brainstorming also requires that someone take notes during the actual idea-generation stage, and that once ideas have been generated, they be carefully evaluated. de Bono (1970) suggests that at the end of the evaluation session, ideas that have immediate usefulness should be identified, as should suggestions that require further exploration. Perhaps most importantly, suggestions that provoke new ways of looking at the problem should be discussed and their implications explored.

Avoiding Polarization

Polarization is the process by which many people classify themselves. "I'm a people person." "I don't have math skills." "I hate everything about geometry." "I'm ugly." "I'm worthless." Unfortunately, when we create polarized ways of thinking about ourselves, we tend to sort information into those categories and process it using the words that we have attached to those categories. For example:

> *Cl:* I only scored at the 70th percentile on the math section of the SAT. I couldn't possibly be an engineer with a score that low.
>
> *Co:* The 70th percentile seems pretty high to me. Tell me why you concluded that you cannot be an engineer.
>
> *Cl:* Because engineering requires that you be good in math. Only people who have SAT scores above the 90th percentile are going to be good engineers.

This client seems to have a view of himself as not good in math. Some people are good at math (90th percentile on the SAT), and because of his perception of himself he has to interpret his SAT score (70th percentile) as confirming the fact that he is not good in math.

Career counselors need to identify the polarizations that clients have created, challenge the labels that have been attached, challenge the way data are placed into those categories, and stimulate clients to create new labels and new categories. For example:

Co: It seems that along the way you have developed the perception that you are a poor math student. I'm wondering why you have that perception when your grades have been B's or better in all of your math courses, and your SAT score places you at the 70th percentile among all college students.

Cl: I'm not sure. I think because I have to work so hard at math.

Cl: Does that make you a bad math student? You do seem to experience some success.

Cl: Not really success. I'm getting along, but I have to work so hard.

Co: So you've decided that you are a bad math student because you have to work so hard. 1 wonder if you are really being fair to yourself. Isn't there something between a good math student and a bad math student? Aren't you a pretty good math student?

Cl: Average, I guess I'm not bad, just average.

Co: Average is the 50th percentile, if I remember my math. Aren't you being a bit hard on yourself? You have to concede that you are at least above average.

Cl: But not good.

Co: Let's look at what good means to you.

Teaching Clients to Say Po

Vertical thinking involves the process of saying no, no to information, and no to alternatives. "Po is to lateral thinking what no is to vertical thinking. No is a rejection tool. Po is a restructuring tool" (de Bono, 1970, p. 226). Just as the other techniques discussed in this chapter have been aimed at cognitive restructuring, so is po. It is a language device that can be helpful in creating new patterns and challenging old patterns by provoking new thought patterns, disrupting old ways of thinking, and allowing the thinker to link parts of patterns together that could not logically be linked using vertical thinking.

In career counseling, clients are often exposed to a great deal of new information. Their first inclination is to label that information and say "Yes, it is important," or "No, it is not important." Po permits clients to retain information and to delay judgment about its utility. In effect, when a client receives a new piece of information, he or she can classify it as acceptable, unacceptable (no), or *maybe* acceptable or unacceptable (po). Clients should be encouraged to say po to all new information, at least until that information can be examined in the context of other related and unrelated information.

The use of po also allows clients to link two unrelated facts or elements together. Work and leisure seem unrelated but are not unrelated, at least once one gets beyond the stereotypical definitions of the two roles. Commuter and marriage also seem unrelated, but many couples have held the two ideas together long enough to allow them to associate.

Po can also be used as permission to be wrong. Many clients apologize when they feel they are about to make a mistake by prefacing their statements with, "This may sound silly." One response to this is, "Say po to your idea—not yes, not no—po." Po gives you permission to be wrong—but many good things have come from mistakes.

Po instead of yes or no allows clients to retain information that might otherwise have been discarded prematurely, to link unrelated and often illogical ideas so that their association can be tested and they can make mistakes, because sometimes mistakes or illogical ideas lead to better solutions to problems.

Explaining Po:

Some clients have a great deal of difficulty breaking out of their conceptual boxes. The techniques discussed earlier in this chapter can be useful in assisting some of these clients. It is suggested here that the counselor paraphrase the popular drug slogan and introduce the client who is burdened by premature judgment and stereotypes with a new slogan. "Just say po!" Clients should be encouraged to just say po to new information, at least long enough to consider its consequences. For example, clients often dismiss low inventory or test scores as nonrelevant, but if judgment about these ideas can be postponed until their implications can be fully explored, new patterns might emerge.

Earlier in this chapter, we presented a brief interaction between a client and a counselor discussing a SAT score. That client dismissed engineering because of a "low test score." However, if success in engineering and low math ability can be considered, there is at least an opportunity to explore the possibilities associated with a desired career and a barrier to its achievement. Recently, the senior author chatted with a prominent surgeon about his route into the medical field. He had been an average high school student, had been dismissed from college once for academic reasons, and barely achieved the necessary 2.0 to graduate with a social science major from a "mediocre" college. During his senior year, he began thinking about medicine because of his grandfather's success in the field, and he began to consider ways to get into medical school. He ended up in a medical school in Spain, transferred to an American school, managed to get a desirable residency, and the rest is history. A 2.0 average in a social science undergraduate major and medical school. Just say po.

Figure 18.2   The Rules of Po

THERE ARE NO RULES WHEN MAKING DECISIONS

Using Metaphors

Adams (1986) indicates that the use of metaphors to stimulate creative decision making has been in use for nearly thirty years. de Bono (1970) suggests that metaphors may be a useful means of stimulating thinking about the problem and avoiding an obvious train of thought. Gysbers and Moore (1987) recommend the use of metaphors as a means of enhancing communication and stimulating reluctant and/or naive clients. They also suggest that metaphors are best used with some degree of planfulness while also allowing for spontaneity.

What is a metaphor? It is a story, a joke, a picture, or a fantasy that in some way is analogous to a real-life situation. de Bono (1970) and Adams (1986) discuss metaphors as being generated by the person or persons working on the problem. Gysbers and Moore (1987) present metaphors that can be used by counselors when working with clients.

In simplest terms, a metaphor is an analogy that helps clients develop new ways of thinking about their career or life style. The metaphor can be introduced by the counselor, or the counselor may ask the client to generate the metaphor. As Gysbers and Moore (1987) suggest, counselors may draw upon their own experiences or the experiences of other clients as the basis for metaphors. Family counselors often ask families to generate stories (metaphors) that describe their family or to compare their family situation to novels they have read, nursery rhymes, and/or television programs (Goldenberg & Goldenberg, 1985). What follows are some examples of the uses of this technique.

Gysbers and Moore (1987) reported the following metaphor, which was used with a client who had trouble leaving home and taking a job in another city.

> METAPHOR
> Because you grow plants in your house, you will understand my concern. I had this cluster of plants in a large pot They seemed to be getting along all right. I watered them and took care of them, but they didn't seem to have a healthy look. They were crowded together. So in spite of their apparent satisfactory survival, they didn't seem to be able to grow. I decided to separate them into several pots. I repotted them. At first they looked kind of lonely and puny. But after proper care, they began to grow. They did not have to share the water and nutrients in the common pot. Now they had their own pots. Even the plant I left in the original pot prospered. Everything grew better. Eventually, they were all equally strong and prospering. It may difficult to imagine how a cluster of plants can be divided and then each one become a strong separate potting. But it happened to me. (pp. 25–26)

After reading this metaphor the client could be asked simply to react to the story as it applied to his or her situation, or the client could be asked to generate her or his own story.

> *Co:*   You seem stuck. You'd like to move out of your parents' house, but something, perhaps fear, keeps holding you back. Can you think of a novel you've read or a movie that you've seen that has a common theme?
>
> *Cl:*   (Generates story)
>
> *Co:*   How did the actual person in the story handle the problem, and what were the consequences?
>
> *Cl:*   (Responds.)
>
> *Co:*   Can you see any similarities between yourself and your situation and the person in your story?

As de Bono (1970) points out, a metaphor is just a story until it is applied to the problem at hand. The process for doing this is (1) generate the metaphor, (2) have the client examine the themes, and (3) stimulate self-exploration by having the client draw parallels between his or her own situation and that of the central figure in the metaphor.

Six-Hat Thinking Technique

In 1985 de Bono suggested that decision making can be facilitated by having people put on different colored thinking hats. One hat, the blue one, is the control hat, and its wearer directs the person to wear other colored hats. In career counseling the counselor may actually "wear" the blue hat and encourage the client to put on the other hats that include the following:

White hat: Examines only the verifiable facts about self and careers (e.g., grades, job trends, hiring requirements, etc.)

Red hat: Uses unjustified hunches, impressions, and/or intuition about self and career. Takes into consideration how one feels about self and career

Black hat: The pessimistic view; critical, looks at why things (such as a career change) will not work

Yellow hat: Optimistic, positive thinking that focuses on the benefits; on why things will work. The opposite of the black hat

Green hat: Generates new thoughts, new alternatives, and new ways of viewing the problem. Decision making focuses on creative (lateral) approaches to change

The six-hat method of decision making can be used in association with the other techniques and as a separate strategy to help clients sort out their thinking about the career choice or change problem confronting them. de Bono (1985) suggests that decision makers may benefit from a process that takes them through the various thinking hats. For example, the counselor might proceed as follows:

Co: Let's put on our white hats and examine the facts regarding you and your potential career choice. In so far as you are able suspend your emotions and your judging qualities, try not to think about the goodness or badness of the data. We will do that later. Wear your white hat for awhile.

(Subsequently) OK, let's ignore the facts for the moment. Put on the red hat. How do you feel about yourself and the options open to you? What does your "gut" tell you about your options?

(Subsequently) Tell me why this isn't going to work. Be logical but pessimistic. Be as critical as possible while you wear your black hat.

> (Subsequently) Now review your black hat thinking and put on the sunny yellow hat. Be an optimist. Think logically, but optimistically about what is infinitely you. (Subsequently) Now let's see if we can create some new alternatives. Start by brainstorming (or) Let's take the information generated by your black hat and yellow hat thinking and examine them together to see if these associations change your perspective.

The foregoing order was selected at random and thus should not necessarily be imitated. The important thing is to have the client experience each of the "thinking hats." After clients' exposure to the thinking hats, counselors may wish to ask a client to identify the hat that he or she is wearing to sensitize the client further to the different ways of thinking about the problem.

USING NONRATIONAL DECISION-MAKING STRATEGIES

Nonrational aids to decision making are meant to stimulate the generating of alternatives, help clients who are stuck become unstuck, allow clients to break down stereotypes, and free clients from limiting decision-making strategies. Their use requires the career counselor to determine when problems are occurring (e.g., stereotypes are limiting decision making) and then introduce appropriate techniques. It is recommended here that the counselor not get too tied up in the selection of the appropriate technique, however. In a very real sense, the counselor and the client will have to experiment with these techniques to see what works at the moment.

LIMITATIONS

We must take a phrase from Gelatt (1989) and approach the use of lateral thinking strategies with an attitude of "positive uncertainty." Practically nothing is known about their utility or their potential impact on goal setting, the decision-making process, or outcomes.

It is not suggested here that nonrational techniques and strategies should replace rational decision-making approaches. de Bono (1970) has posed his strategies as complementary to logical approaches. Brainstorming is a means of generating potential solutions to which a logical selection process can be applied The "why" technique delays judgment, and reversals and the other techniques discussed in this chapter can best be thought of as strategies for developing different and better data relating to the career choice problem. However, all decision-making processes reach a choice point. The trick is to maximize what occurs at that choice point. Nonrational approaches may maximize the information about possible choices, but it is doubtful if anyone is ready to suggest that we encourage nonrational choice making; thus, some rational approach to the decision-making process is the only option. Despite the temporariness of our data and the subjectivity of our perceptions, approaches that rely upon the principles of vertical thinking are probably to be preferred no matter how limited they might be.

LEARNING THE USE OF NONRATIONAL DECISION-MAKING STRATEGIES

1. Read *Lateral Thinking. Creativity Step by Step* and *Six Thinking Hats* by Edward de Bono. Reading Capra's *The Turning Point* may also be helpful.

2. Examine your own decision-making style by looking at how you have made recent decisions. Was your style systematic and rational or nonsystematic and nonrational? Did you set goals and pursue them? Did your goals change as you pursued them?

3. Practice using po in your next decision-making endeavor. Be particularly sensitive about saying po to information and ideas that do not seem to fit together. Also, try to avoid closure on the problem until at least some irrational arrangements are examined.

4. Use nonrational approaches in making some routine decisions, such as choosing a restaurant. Try this sentence in your decision making: It makes no sense, and therefore we should look at it. Also, try generating a list of reasons why you should not make a decision along with the reasons why you should do something. Put these together as follows: "I should do this because. . ." and "I should not do it because. . ." See if the ideas coalesce into a new pattern of thinking.

5. Start using the following statement in your decision making: "I'll suspend judgment."

6. Interview other students about their decision-making strategies. Look for nonrational approaches.

7. Join with a small group of your peers and brainstorm the virtues of using nonrational approaches.

8. Try to generate metaphors that describe the situation in which you find yourself. Nursery rhymes and jokes may be useful and humorous

ways of finding analogous situations. Try to determine how the following metaphors could be applied to certain kinds of clients in career counseling.

Metaphor	Client Type
a. Between a rock and a hard place	_____
b. Up the proverbial creek	_____
c. The wisdom of Solomon	_____
d. The grasshopper and the cricket	_____
e. The three little pigs.	_____
f. There was an old woman who lived in a shoe	_____
g. Donate	_____
h. Walden's pond.	_____
i. Three blind persons and the elephant	_____

9. Under supervision, try some of the nonrational strategies described in this chapter.

SUMMARY

Recently there has been an assault on logical decision-making strategies; some people suggest that we discard them altogether. However, most persons concerned with decision making are suggesting that nonrational or, as de Bono calls it, lateral thinking, be used to complement vertical and rational thinking. A number of strategies have been suggested that can aid clients who are limited by stereotypes, injunctions, or decision-making methods to enrich their career decision making. Brainstorming is a means of generating potential solutions to which a logical selection process can be applied. The "why" technique may be helpful in helping clients question their own judgments. Reversals and the other techniques discussed in this chapter can best be thought of as strategies for developing different and better data relating to the career choice problem. However, all decision-making processes reach a choice point, and at this point vertical or linear strategies seem to be useful. The trick is to maximize the data that will be useful at the choice point.

REFERENCES AND SUGGESTED READINGS

Adams, J.L. (1986). *Conceptual Blockbusting: A Guide to Better Ideas.* (3rd ed.). Reading, MA: Addison-Wesley.

Capra, F. (1982). *The Turning Point.* New York: Simon & Schuster.

de Bono, E. (1970). *Lateral Thinking: Creativity Step by Step.* New York: Harper & Row.

de Bono, E. (1985). *Six Thinking Hats.* Boston, MA: Little, Brown.

Gelatt, H. B. (1989). Positive uncertainty: A new decision-making framework for counseling. *Journal of Counseling Psychology* 36: 252–56.

Gilhooly, K.J. (1982). *Thinking: Directed, Undirected and Creative.* London: Academic Press.

Goldenberg, I., & Goldenberg, H. (1985). *Family Therapy: An Overview* (2nd ed.). Monterey, CA: Brooks/Cole.

Gysbers, N.C., & Moore, E.J. (1987). *Career Counseling: Skills and Techniques for Practitioners.* Englewood Cliffs, NJ: Prentice-Hall.

CHAPTER 19

Guided Fantasy

Guided fantasy is a five-phase process, including induction, relaxation, fantasy, reorientation, and processing, that is structured and directed by the career counselor to assist clients to deal with various aspects of career choice and adjustment problems. It can be used either with individuals or groups, and it can be used at any stage of career counseling.

USES OF GUIDED FANTASY

There are eight uses for guided fantasy in career counseling, as follows:

1. To develop self-awareness
2. To overcome here-and-now time orientation
3. To develop awareness of masculine and feminine sides of personality
4. For values clarification
5. For goal setting
6. In problem solving
7. To generate career alternatives
8. To examine career aspirations

BACKGROUND

Apparently, some form of guided fantasy has been in use for over sixty years (Skovolt, Morgan, and Negron-Cunningham, 1989). Its early use was primarily with adults, and it is a technique that is often associated with some forms of behavior therapy (e.g., Wolpe, 1982). However, career counselors have long recognized the potential of guided fantasy as a useful technique (see Skovolt and Hoenninger, 1974), and there are few, if any, of the myriad self-help books on career exploration and choice that do not contain guided fantasy exercises. In some instances, these exercises can be adapted for use with individual clients and groups, but effective career counselors need to have the facility to develop guided fantasies that will help their clients cope with the problems confronting them.

There are some clients who cannot, or will not, participate in guided fantasy experiences. In some instances, inability or unwillingness to participate may be related to a sense of loss of personal control. We have also observed situations in which some low-ability students had difficulty generating fantasies but could participate if fantasies were described in great detail. Unwillingness to participate seems to be linked more to the relationship to the counselor and proper explanation of the guided fantasy than to any other variables. It is unrealistic and unethical to expect all clients to participate in guided fantasy. However, fantasy has been used successfully with children, women, rehabilitation clients, black clients, and others according to a literature review conducted by Skovalt et al. (1989).

DESCRIPTION OF THE TECHNIQUE

Induction

Guided fantasy has five phases. The first of these, induction, involves introducing the concept of fantasy to the client and exploring the appropriateness of the technique for them. The use of guided fantasy *should not proceed* unless it is fully understood and accepted by the client. The following script provides an overview of how fantasy might be introduced:

> *Co:* You seem to be having trouble projecting yourself into the future, and this is hampering your ability to do even short-range planning. I want to suggest that we try using a guided fantasy to help you think about yourself in the future. Guided fantasy involves several aspects, including relaxation and imagining a number of scenes that I will describe. For example, I might direct you to imagine a series of future scenes where you are continuing in your current job and then I will alter those scenes and describe

some other alternatives based on what I know about you. What do you think?

Cl: I'm not very good at imagining things.

Co: Tell me more about that.

Cl: I just don't seem to have a very vivid imagination.

Co: I believe that I can help you with that, but I'm wondering how comfortable you feel about imagining or fantasizing about your future.

Cl: I'm quite comfortable with the idea, but I just wonder if I can do it.

Co: Are you willing to try? We can break it off anytime you wish.

Cl: Ok.

In this situation, the counselor has introduced the technique of guided fantasy as a means of helping the client overcome his "here-and-now" orientation and has encountered some uncertainty. Richardson (1981) reported that three-quarters of the students in studies could engage in fantasy on the first attempt. The authors have found that considerably more than 75 percent of students and adults can engage in fantasy, but that some people *cannot* engage in fantasy. If one of these individuals is encountered, the fantasy should be abandoned and alternative strategies sought to deal with the problem at hand.

During the induction phase, certain points should be made. These are:

1. Fantasy is natural.
2. Fantasy is powerful.
3. Some fantasies can arouse emotion, which is natural.
4. In fantasy, you can go anywhere, do anything. It is not bound by time or perceptions of personal limitations.
5. You are in control of your fantasies.

Some individuals who resist fantasy may be doing so because they believe that it is an unnatural process. In life career planning groups, one career counselor found it helpful to introduce fantasy with music that elicited fantasies, and then to involve the group in guided imagery. Others who resist fantasy seem to do so because of a fear of losing control. It is important to stress that while our fantasies transcend time and personal limitations, we can control them.

Finally, our clients need to be prepared for the possibility that a fantasy may elicit powerful emotions. Lifeline, a future fantasy that takes clients from their current life situation through adulthood and even to the point of writing their own epitaphs can be engaged in by most individuals without difficulties. However, for individuals who have lost a spouse or experienced a traumatic divorce, thinking about the future may elicit tremendous feelings of loss and depression. Clients should be prepared for these feelings, and the counselor must be prepared to help clients cope with them once they are elicited.

Relaxation

Guided fantasy requires that one induce a slightly altered state of consciousness through relaxation. Before relaxation exercises are introduced, the counselor does the following:

1. Make sure that you will have audio or visual privacy (e.g., no telephone calls).
2. If it is a group situation, ensure against fantasy voyeurs. This is done by telling all individuals that even if they cannot get "into the fantasy," they are to keep their eyes closed.
3. Ask that uncomfortable shoes be removed (e.g., high heels).
4. Make sure that everyone is seated comfortably.
5. Have objects such as books, soft drink cans, notepads, and pencils put away so that they will not inadvertently fall on the floor and disrupt the fantasy.

Once the above chores have been completed, the counselor induces relaxation using deep breathing exercises as follows, and in a soft voice, says:

Co: Okay, close your eyes and get very comfortable. Just begin to relax. Let your tensions flow from your body. Just relax deeper and deeper, getting more and more comfortable. I want you to take a very deep breath—breath in—hold it—hold it—breath out, and just feel yourself relax more and more. Take another deep breath—hold it—hold it—exhale—feeling yourself relax more and more.

The above procedure should be continued until the client is totally relaxed. The counselor may wish to have clients signal when they are relaxed by raising an index finger. If this is the procedure of choice, clients should be so instructed at the beginning of the fantasy.

Fantasy

Fantasies are used for specific purposes and should be tailored to meet the needs of the individual or group. In career exploration groups or classes, this may be somewhat difficult because the individuals in these groups may be at different phases in their career development. Answering questions such as "What is the purpose of this fantasy?" "Where are my clients developmentally?" and "What gender and ethnic group considerations need to be considered?" will help decide which fantasies to use. The following guidelines should be followed in constructing guided fantasies:

1. Clients should be given indication of what they are to experience. (E.g., this fantasy will involve personal power.)
2. Fantasies should begin with anchor points, typically blank "mental screens" or peaceful scenes. If peaceful scenes are used as anchor points, each individual should construct his or her mental peaceful scene, because no scenes are relaxing for everyone.
3. Fantasy should have a logical progression through time, life stages, roles, and so forth.
4. Transitions from time period to time period or role to role require that adequate time be provided so that the client can mentally make the shift.
5. Descriptors such as adjectives and adverbs should precede nouns. If a workplace is to be described, the counselor should say: "It is a noisy, dusty, dark setting," *not* "Imagine a workplace. It is noisy, dusty, dark." The reason for this is that the client may have "filled in" the characteristics of the workplace and then will have to change thoughts, all of which interrupts the flow of the fantasy.
6. The directions must allow enough time for clients to fully experience each scene in the fantasy.
7. Fantasy should end with the anchor scene and should be followed by reorientation.

The following is an example of a fantasy that can be useful in helping clients explore the limitations they place on themselves because of their gender:

Co: (After relaxation is achieved) Now imagine that time and place when you are most at peace—most relaxed. Just imagine that scene and continue to relax. Now, slowly dissolve that scene and get a picture of yourself as a male or as a female. Think about yourself as a man or a woman—getting a clear image of yourself. You are going into your future and you are going to imagine the totality of your existence—all of your life roles. Your role as worker, child, your relationship with friends and significant others. Maybe these significant others will be wives and husbands—maybe not. Maybe you will become a parent, maybe not.

(Pause)

Co: Now, begin to move into your future: One year—two years—three years—five years. It's 199—, five years into the future—look at yourself. Where are you working— living? What is your life style? Now it's ten years into the future—look at your life again. (It's twenty years, etc.) Now you are standing at the end of your life looking at what you have done—what you have accomplished. What do you feel proud of? What are your regrets? Think about your life as you have lived it.

(Pause)

Co: Now begin to come back down the path you have travelled—back to the present—back to this room and back to your peaceful scene. Get that scene vividly in your mind and hold it—hold it.

(Pause)

Co: Begin to dissolve that scene and begin to imagine yourself as a member of the other sex. Work very hard to imagine yourself as a man or a woman. Feel the bodily changes as they occur. Look at your hair, your eyelashes, your clothes. Work very hard to get that image.

(Pause)

Co: Now we are going to explore your future again. To retrace our steps to the end of your life. (Repeat the fantasy up to the return to the peaceful scene as outlined before.)

The crucial point in that fantasy is the "sex change" scene. Although clients would have been prepared for this scene in the induction phase, some will still have problems. While there is no research in this area, our experience suggests that men have more difficulty changing to women and whites have more difficulty changing to ethnic minorities than the reverse. Even this difficulty in making the change can produce meaningful insights in the processing stage.

Reorientation

The reorientation phase of the fantasy involves regrouping the individual in the here and now. Failure to do this phase properly can result in diminished mental alertness, atypical mood swings, altered body perceptions, and a feeling that the counselor is still in control (Heikkinon, 1989). The following steps should be followed in the reorientation phase:

1. Return to the anchor scene.
2. Reorient to the immediate environment.
3. Ground by touching objects or people.
4. Do physical movement such as stretching, "jumping jacks," or other mild exercises.

The following excerpt illustrates those points:

Co: Just imagine your peaceful scene. Now I want you to begin to dissolve that scene and to imagine this room. Feel your chair pushing into your body. Think about the curtains, my desk, the books, the clock on the wall. (Pause)

Co: Now I am going to begin to count backwards from 10. At 0, I want you to open your eyes and look at the room. Okay, 10–9–8–7–6–5–4–3–2–1–0. Open your eyes. Look at the room. Stand up, stretch. Shake off the cobwebs. Clear your mind.

Once clients have opened their eyes and moved around, each one should be asked how he or she is feeling to determine alertness and readiness for the processing phase.

Processing

Processing involves asking clients to share thoughts and feelings experienced during the fantasy and puts them in the context of career planning. The following are some thoughts and feelings that have been elicited as a result of the gender reversal fantasy described above.

Cl: I felt that I could be much more aggressive as a woman.

> My father was passive and my mother was the aggressive one. I wonder if I have been limiting myself by only looking at careers that require nonaggressive people?
>
> I felt much freer as a man. I pursued my educational goals much sooner than I did as a woman. I didn't feel restricted by my family.
>
> I felt a tremendous weight on my shoulders when I became a man. It felt as though I needed to do more to be successful. It was a terrible feeling.
>
> I couldn't imagine myself as a man, but I could imagine myself as my husband. I just couldn't imagine myself being as independent as most men are.
>
> As a woman, I lived out my life as a mother and homemaker. As a man, I went to Harvard, did an MBA at Oxford, and pursued a very successful career on Wall Street. I realize that I am limiting myself too much because of my sex.
>
> I took on an entire new appreciation as my "wife." I wanted a career, but I was always being disrupted by my husband and my children. I'm not quite sure how she does it.

It is extremely important to help clients make "sense" out of their experiences during the guided fantasy. The guiding imperative: Use what has been learned to enhance your career planning and choice-making. Even more important, negative emotions should be explored with clients. Some examples of these follow:

> *Cl:* I simply could not get into the fantasy. I thought it would be easy. But when you asked me to think about the future all I could think of was losing my job. I got really depressed and just wasn't with you the rest of the way.
>
> I realize that I have got to get a job because my husband is gone. But when 1 thought about how my work would interact with my role with significant others, I got very angry. I'm still angry!

Both verbalizations illustrate how personal problems impinge upon career planning. Though both situations were handled within the context of career counseling, it is entirely possible either that the focus of the counseling sessions may need to be altered to deal with the depression or anger or that a referral to another counselor will be necessary. It is outside the scope of this book to discuss techniques for dealing with these situations.

SUMMARY OF GUIDED FANTASY PROCESS

The following steps represent a summary of the process of using guided fantasy:

1. Introduce: "Guided fantasy involves. . . ."
2. Assess willingness to participate: "How do you feel? Some people are uneasy about participating. "
3. Relaxation: "Begin by closing your eyes."
4. The peaceful scene: "Begin by imagining a peaceful scene."
5. The fantasy: "Start your journey through time."
6. Return to peaceful scene: "Now switch on your peaceful scene."
7. Reorientation: "Get a vivid picture of this room. Now, as I count backwards from 10. . . ."
8. Grounding: "Open your eyes. Touch the furniture."
9. Processing feelings: "How did you feel?"
10. Applying knowledge learned: "What did you learn that will be helpful in career development?"

EXAMPLES OF OTHER FANTASIES

Fantasies can be designed to deal with a wide variety of problems in career counseling. A few illustrations of fantasies follow:

Client Problem: Low self-efficacy regarding asking supervisor for a raise.

Fantasy: Get a vivid image of your supervisor in her office. Imagine how she is dressed. Imagine her desk. Her chair. Now imagine what she is thinking as the time for your appointment approaches. The time for your appointment is near, and you leave your office to go to the meeting. You are a little nervous because you know what she is thinking. But you become very calm. Very serene. You clench your jaw. Square your shoulders. You walk with confidence. You are saying to yourself, "I can handle this situation. I am a good employee. I do good work. I contribute. My fellow employees know I'm good. My god, I am good."

I enter the office, shake hands, and give my supervisor a confident smile. She knows I'm confident. I am. I look her in the eye and tell her why I'm there. She begins to put me off. I listen attentively. I then begin to make my case. I show her my evaluations, I tell her what I've been told by others—of my loyalty to the company. I am calm. I am convincing. I am magnificent.

Client Problem: Inability to clarify values.

Fantasy: Imagine yourself in a house filled with the following rooms. One room is filled with money, one with music, one with laughing playful children, and one with an adoring audience of well-wishers. Now you can go into any of those rooms. You can count your money until your heart is content, you can listen to music, play with the children, and be adored by a group of loving followers. Your life is at peace.
(Pause)
But a bad thing happens. An order comes that you can have only one room in your house and you must eliminate them one by one. Think about which room you would eliminate first, next, next, and now you are standing in one room. Which one is it? How do you feel about your losses? Do you want to change your mind?

Client Problem: Goal setting.

Fantasy: You are going to take an imaginary journey. We are traveling to a wonderful city that has all the things we enjoy. You really want to get to that city, and you are speeding down the highway when there is an unexpected fork in the road. You are puzzled because the left fork is the road you have always taken. It is comfortable but boring. The sign on the right says "to the city" but provides no other information. You've got to choose. The comfortable but boring way or a way that you have never traveled. If you take the left road, you will get to the city and you know when it will be. If you take the other road, you may get to the city faster or slower. You are not sure. There is even a possibility that you could get lost if you take the wrong road. Which road will you take?
Questions to ask during processing include the following:

1. Did you have difficulty getting into the fantasy? At what point? What were your emotions like when you had trouble? Were there "outside" difficulties (e.g., noise)?
2. How did you feel as you moved through each stage of the fantasy? Were there high and low points emotionally? Were there points where you had trouble staying in the fantasy?

3. What were your strongest positive emotions? Negative emotions?
4. Were there key people in your fantasy? Who were they, and what roles did they play?
5. What did you learn about yourself or your problem that you can use?
6. Are there any unresolved issues that were generated by the fantasy?

LIMITATIONS OF FANTASY

Guided fantasy has five limitations, as follows:

1. Some people cannot participate in guided fantasy for a variety of reasons. These may relate to risk taking, fear of losing control, or other reasons.
2. Guided fantasy in career planning probably should not be used with individuals who have current traumatic emotional problems such as a traumatic divorce or recent death.
3. Counselors using fantasy should be equipped to deal with emotional outbursts either directly or through referral to other helpers.
4. Some fantasies require a great deal of time to introduce, direct, and process.
5. Guided fantasies are not substitutes for reality testing. They are best used as preparation for real life.

LEARNING GUIDED FANTASY

In addition to making certain that the counselor fully understands the foregoing discussion, the following steps should be taken to learn guided fantasy:

1. Evaluate your own reactions and/or beliefs about fantasy. Do you use fantasies to solve your problems? Many people do. You should not introduce a client to a technique that you cannot personally endorse.
2. Review some of the self-help career decision-making books and identify fantasy exercises. Determine if these can be adapted to guided fantasies in career counseling using the guidelines suggested here.

3. Participate as a client in a guided fantasy.
4. Practice on other counselors or students before you use the technique on clients. Get feedback from colleagues or a supervisor about the following elements:
   a. Is your voice soothing? If not, get the fantasy taped by another.
   b. Is your presentation logical? (Are adjectives and adverbs inserted appropriately, etc.?)
   c. Is the speed of the presentation of your fantasy appropriate?
   d. Did you program the reorientation process correctly?
   e. Were the questions posed during the processing helpful?
5. Under supervision, try the technique with clients. Get feedback from the client as well as a supervisor.
6. Read suggested readings at the end of this chapter.

SUMMARY

Guided fantasy is a counselor-designed and -directed experience using the imagination of the client to deal with various career development problems. The process involves five stages: induction, relaxation, fantasy, reorientation, and processing. At the outset, it is extremely important that clients understand the nature of the experience and agree to it. Failure to reorient can lead to a variety of problems, and this must be seen as an essential stage. The final stage, processing, involves helping clients to apply what they have learned to the career choice and adjustment process.

Guided fantasy cannot be used with all clients and should not be attempted by all counselors unless they are equipped to deal with the emotional and cognitive side-effects that may develop. Preparation to use guided fantasy includes (1) becoming first a counselor who is able to handle personal as well as career counseling and (2) practice with other students and/or counselors prior to using the technique with clients.

REFERENCES AND SUGGESTED READINGS

Heikkinon, C.A. (1989). Reorientation from altered states: Please, more carefully. *Journal of Counseling and Development* 67: 520–21.
Richardson, G.E. (1981). Educational imagery: A missing link in decision making. *Journal of School Health* 51,: 560–64.

Skovalt, T.M., & Hoenninger, R.W. (1974). Guided fantasy in career counseling. *Personnel and Guidance Journal* 52: 693–96.

Skovalt, T.M., Morgan, J.I., Negron-Cunningham, H. (1989). Mental imagery in career counseling and life planning: A review of research and intervention methods. *Journal of Counseling and Development* 67: 287–92.

Wolpe, J. (1982). *The Practice of Behavior Therapy.* (3rd ed.). New York: Pergamon.

CHAPTER 20

Homework

Homework consists of systematic assignments developed collaboratively by counselors and clients and represents a deliberate attempt to intervene in the clients' problems by involving them in appropriate action. Homework assignments can be made at any stage of career counseling. They should grow out of the immediate context of the counseling session and must appear relevant to the client. According to Shelton and Ackerman (1974), effective homework assignments are specific in that they tell the client what to do and how often to do it.

USES OF HOMEWORK

There are a great many uses of homework in career counseling, including the following:

1. To assess client motivation by examining follow-through on relevant experiences
2. To increase self-awareness by having clients compare themselves to workers and others or by involving clients in self-exploration activities
3. To enhance awareness of occupational facts, including the contextual factors that can only be discerned through first-hand observation of workers
4. To engage the client in problem-solving activities that are the culmination of the career counseling process, such as job interviews
5. To enhance the client's feeling that career counseling sessions constitute a process rather than a series of discrete sessions that are only marginally linked

6. To keep the client continuously involved in growth-producing activities so that the momentum developed in the career counseling session will not be lost

7. To develop an active, as opposed to a passive, stance on the part of clients so that there is a sense of accomplishment at all stages of counseling

BACKGROUND

Homework has become such an accepted technique in all counseling approaches that it is taken for granted by many authors or simply left out of their discussions. Some (e.g., Cormier & Cormier, 1985) discuss it as a means to generalize or transfer what has been learned in counseling to the outside world by first identifying low-risk situations in which the client can be successful in trying out what he or she has learned and then gradually applying what has been learned to more complex situations. A person who is learning job interviewing skills might first practice with the counselor, then practice with a friend, interview a "friendly" employer, and finally test the newly acquired skills in a variety of real settings.

The concept that homework is used only to help the client generalize what has been learned to the real world, or if one prefers, the natural environment, is too restrictive for career counseling. Homework assignments can and should be made at any stage of career counseling, beginning with the first interview and continuing until the client has accomplished his or her objectives. However, the suggestion that homework assignments should specify exactly what is to be done and how often it is to be done is relevant (Shelton & Ackerman, 1974), although to the "what" and "how often" statements should be added "where" and "when" statements. An effective homework assignment should specify what is to be done, how often it is to be done, when (time) it should be done, and where it should be done. Finally, Cormier and Cormier (1985) report that the addition of a self-monitoring statement such as "I did my homework, and I was satisfied with it" is important in helping clients attribute success to their own efforts. The acronym 3 WHSS may help the reader remember that an effective homework assignment includes *w*hat, *w*here, *w*hen, *h*ow often, and *s*elf-*s*tatement components.

In Chapter 2, it was suggested that a collaborative counselor-client approach may be more effective in developing clients' self-perceptions of independence. As was noted in the definition, effective homework assignments are collaboratively designed. This collaboration should not include designing the components (3 WHSS) of the homework assignment but, perhaps more important, by "giving" the client the authority to determine whether he or she will actually follow-through on the home-work assignment. In the final analysis, clients need to feel that they are ready to complete a homework assignment prior to attempting to complete the assignment. If that readiness is not present, an abortive attempt may result, and the career counseling process may actually be damaged.

Using homework assignments, like the use of many other techniques, involves preparing the client for the assignment by previewing the technique, designing the assignment, preparing the client to complete the assignment, and then reviewing the success or failure of the assignment in the subsequent section.

PREVIEW AND DESIGN

As was noted at the outset, homework grows out of the context of counseling, has multiple uses, and must be relevant to the client. The nature of the preview will be dependent upon the stage of the counseling process, the nature of the counseling interview, and the ability and willingness of the client to complete the assignment. Generally speaking, the preview of the homework assignment should include the following:

1. Explain the homework technique and why it might be useful at this particular stage of the counseling process.
2. Relate possible homework assignments to the context of counsel-ing and to the "goal" being pursued at that time.
3. Stress that the client can accept or reject the homework assign-ments.

The following excerpts from career counseling interviews illustrate how these three aspects are covered at various stages of the counseling process.

Excerpt One—End of Session One

Co: It's become clear that you would like to engage in a great deal more self-exploration prior to actually starting to look at career alternatives.

Cl: That's right. I feel like I've been in the dark serving others, and while it's my turn to do something with my life, I really don't know much about who I am, what I can do or, really, what I would like to do.

Co: There are a variety of ways that you can find out more about yourself, and we'll talk about some of those next time. However, I would like to suggest the possibility of using homework assignments that may help you begin the self-discovery process.

Cl: Homework. That sounds a little like school.

Co: To a certain extent, it is. Homework involves trying to help you achieve your goals by having you do things outside the counseling interview.

Cl: That sounds reasonable. What do you suggest?

Co: You said that you need to know more about yourself as something other than a wife and mother. One way to explore your values and interests is to look at the decisions you make.

Cl: I don't really make any decisions, so that will be very hard.

Co: Well, maybe you make more than you think. I wonder if you would mind keeping a daily log (how often) of what newspaper articles you *choose* to read and what television shows you to *choose* watch (what). Don't keep a record of shows you watch to accommodate your husband or children. Just those you choose to watch. This record should be made at the end of every day (when). Every time you make an entry, give yourself a mental pat on the back by mentally saying, "I'm moving forward at last. I'm actually doing something." (self-statement) (Note: The "where" is somewhat superfluous in this assignment.)

Cl: Let me get this straight; you want me to keep a record of the newspaper articles I read and television shows I watch. What about magazine articles? I read several of those.

Co: That's great! We are trying to get at the types of things you decide to do.

Cl: The mental pat on the back may be hard. I usually don't say those types of things.

Co: If you are uncomfortable doing that or it seems irrelevant, don't do it. Remember, it's your choice. But try to keep the log every day if possible. But here again, you have the final say.

Cl: I think I've got the idea, and I guess I do make some decisions.

Co: Let's think through something that might happen during your homework assignment before you leave today.

Excerpt Two—Session Three: Goal Setting

Co: We are getting down to the point where you need to choose between staying in your current job or making a switch to another company.

Cl: Yeah! (sigh) It's a really big decision. I'm doing well where I am, but I feel like I'm wasting my potential. But I don't want to seem disloyal. The company has been very good to me and my family.

Co: After our first two sessions, you engaged in two homework assignments. I'm wondering if you could think of something you could do outside of counseling that would help you resolve your ambivalence about your choices.

Cl: A part of it is my concern about the impact a mistake might make on my family. My wife works, but she only makes about half as much as I do. If I make a mistake, it could be a disaster. She encourages me, but I'm just not sure.

Co: One bit of homework might be to really get your wife's opinion.

Cl: And I guess I'm not sure what my future is in my present job. I've been afraid to ask because my boss might think I'm unhappy. (laughs) Of course, I am unhappy, but I don't want to jeopardize my future if I do decide to stay in my current job.

Co: So, another possibility is to find out more about your future in your current job by talking to your boss.

Cl: And then, of course, I'm a bit of a coward. I never did like to take risks. I guess I'm just the type of person who would rather stay with the tried and true than jump into the unknown.

Co: That makes a third thing that you could work on: to try to confront your own inability to take risks. Which area seems to be most important to you right now?

Cl: I guess I would really like to know what my future is likely to be in my current job. If it looks good, I will not have to take any risks.

Co: Interviewing your boss to get his ideas about your future in your present job is where you would like to start (what).

Cl: Yes.

Co: Let's talk about when and where you might conduct this assignment.

Cl: Well, the "where" could probably be in his office because that's where he conducts his business. The "when" could be next week. I know he's going to be in town.

Co: So we have the "when" and "where" nailed down. Think about how you might feel as you approach your interview. Can you visualize it?

Cl: Sure. I get a little nervous just thinking about it. I told you I'm no risk taker.

Co: Can you imagine what you might be saying to yourself?

Cl: Run! (laughs) No, really, I'd be a little scared. I'd probably be trying to talk myself out of doing it.

Co: So you'd be a little frightened and your self-talk might be negative. Let's think of some self-talk that might keep you on track toward the interview.

Cl: I'm not sure what you mean.

Co: Most of us "talk to ourselves" when we are approaching scary situations, and we say things that will keep us on track. Whether it's an important business engagement like meeting with your boss or a dreaded tee shot over a large body of water, we usually say things that keep us psyched.

Cl: Now I know what you mean. I always say "Keep your eye on the ball, stupid" when I have a big shot in golf. I usually keep reminding myself to keep calm, move ahead, and things will be okay, in other situations.

Co: What about a specific statement?

Cl: Let's see—This is very important. You've got to call the boss and get into that interview. It's time to get on with your future" (self-statement).

Co: That's good! Now, let's think through the strategies you might use when you sit down with your boss. Just think out loud about how you would approach your boss, what types of questions you would pose, and what types of answers you might receive to your questions.

Excerpt Three—End of Session Five: Acting on a Decision

Co: You've decided to enter OCS after college in spite of your parents objections to the military.

Cl: It just seems right to me. My major in Art History is going to take me nowhere. I realize that mom and dad protested against the Vietnam War, and they are involved in all of these world peace organizations. I'm for peace too, but I believe that a strong military ensures the peace. Besides, I think that four years in the military will help me get ready for a career in business. I just don't believe that I'm ready for the business world right now. But mom and dad are going to throw a fit

Co: You're concerned about how they will react to your decision.

Cl: That's right! Maybe we could spend a little time getting me ready to deal with them.

Co: This would be your last piece of homework and it sounds to me like getting you ready to deal with your parents' disappointment, and maybe anger, is in order (what).

Cl: Yeah. Let's just think about what I'm going to say.

Co: First, why don't you tell me what you expect. You might begin by setting the scene in your home when you tell them.

Cl: They are always glad to see me when I come home from college (when, where), so usually the first night home we spend together. Lately, they have been pushing me about my plans after college. The topic will certainly come up again. Things have been a little tense when this subject comes up lately. They know I'm considering OCS.

Co: Tell me what you are going to be thinking as you approach that fateful night.

Cl: They're going to hit the ceiling. They hate war. They may hate me. Maybe I'm stupid. Nope, got to tell them—got to tell them.

Co: Will the "Got to tell them" (self-statement) statement keep you on task?

Cl: Yes. I think so.

Co: Then it's important to keep saying it whenever doubt appears. Okay, let's look ahead to the scene at your house and practice a bit. I'll be your tense mother. (Note: "How often" is not relevant in this situation.)

Preparing the Client to Complete the Assignment

Preparation for completion of homework assignments involves rehearsal and building confidence. Rehearsal may involve mentally reviewing what is to be accomplished or role playing situations involving the use of social skills. In excerpt one, one homework assignment involved keeping a log of decisions made to read newspaper and magazine articles and television shows viewed. Preparing the client to complete this assignment might involve (1) helping her design a log sheet, (2) mentally reviewing a recent day to look at the decisions she made regarding television viewed, and (1) practicing recording the decisions made.

Excerpt two dealt with preparing a client to interview his boss to discern what his future might be if he stayed in his current job. After some mental rehearsal, preparation for this interview might very well require role-playing the actual interview with the counselor starting the practice session as the boss. Role-playing as a strategy to develop social skills is discussed in detail in Chapter 21.

One aspect of preparing clients to complete a homework assignment should be an assessment of their confidence that they can perform the homework. One can assess readiness to complete homework by asking clients to rate their ability to complete the assignment on a 1 to 10 scale with 1 being little or no confidence and 10 being great or complete confidence. If a homework assignment has a number of interrelated parts, the client should be asked to rate each of the parts, because failure on one aspect of the assignment may (and probably will) spell failure on the entire assignment. For example, clients who have accepted the assignment of identifying, applying for, and interviewing for one job should be asked to rate their ability to perform the following tasks:

1. Identify a job opening using friends, relatives, newspaper ads, and so on.
2. Make a telephone or in-person request for a job application using proper grammar while making the request.
3. Fill out a job application form requesting personal, education, career, and related information.
4. Dress appropriately for a job interview, using as a guideline the usual dress of the persons working in the job.

5. Conduct a job interview, including fielding difficult questions, questions about work history, and asking pertinent questions about the job being interviewed for and the company offering the job.
6. Perform interview follow-up procedures, including writing a follow-up letter.
7. Deal with disappointment should the interview be unsuccessful

Another culminating step in preparing clients to follow up on a homework assignment is to prepare them to self-reinforce for successful completion of various aspects of the homework. These statements should be designed using the client's usual methods of self-reinforcement. If the client typically says to himself or herself: "You did great!" then that statement may be chosen as the self-reinforcing statement for completing homework. In some instances when a variety of homework is to be completed between sessions, a number of self-reinforcing statements may be used.

Finally, it may well be as Goldfried and Davison (1976) suggest, that a daily log sheet will be helpful in ensuring that homework will be completed. However, a log sheet such as the one in Table 20.1 will be useful only if (1) the client believes that an aid of this type of useful, and (2) the homework assignment is to be done periodically. Many homework assignments in career counseling are to be performed once, and thus log sheets are unnecessary. The log sheet shown in Table 20.1 was developed with the homemaker who was to make daily records of newspaper and magazine articles read and television shows viewed.

TABLE 20.1 Daily Log of Decisions Made

	Mon	Tues	Wed	Thurs	Fri	Sat	Sun
Television programs watched							
Newspaper articles read							
Magazine articles read							

FOLLOW-UP/PROCESSING

During the sessions following homework assignments, the outcomes of the assignments should be carefully processed. If clients successfully negotiate assignments, it is important to know the following:

1. What they learned about themselves as a result of doing the homework assignments.
2. What they learned about others as a result of engaging in the homework.
3. How confident they are that they could perform the same act in other situations.
4. What reteaching, if any, is necessary.

If clients fail to perform homework assignments, several questions also need to be answered, including the following:

1. Was lack of motivation a problem? If yes, was it because the assignment did not seem relevant or because of lack of self-confidence?
2. What additional skills will be needed before the homework can be completed successfully?
3. What did the clients learn about themselves and others as a result of failing to complete the homework?
4. In retrospect, how could the preparation for the homework have been altered to enhance the chances for success in performing the homework?
5. Should work on this homework assignment be continued in this session or should it be delayed? Was the sequencing of the homework inappropriate?

It is conceivable that our college student arrived at his parents' home, sat down with them, and then simply could not tell them of his decision to attend Officers Candidate School. In this situation, the following explanations are possible:

1. He did not possess the skill to express his wishes to his parents.
2. He possessed the skills but had not practiced enough and, thus, his self-confidence was low.
3. Contextual variables such as an aunt being present were not anticipated in the preparation for the communication.
4. A degree of uncertainty exists about the decision.
5. The client had too much fear of the consequences of displeasing his parents.

These all need to be considered as the client pursues his objective of acting on a career decision.

SUMMARY OF THE HOMEWORK PROCESS

1. The homework assignment should grow out of the context of the counseling session.
2. The homework assignment should be designed *with* the client.
3. The client should be "given" final authority in determining whether to follow through on homework assignments.
4. If the client does not follow through, reasons for failure to do so should be carefully assessed.
5. If the client does follow through, the experience should be thoroughly discussed in order to ascertain what has been learned, what needs to be relearned, and what new learning needs to occur.

LIMITATIONS OF HOMEWORK

1. Homework is an extension of processes begun in the context of counseling. If those processes (e.g., the development of awareness of the utility of the homework) are not performed competently by the counselor, homework is likely to fail.
2. In some situations, in vivo homework assignments are not possible (e.g., interviewing with NASA) and, thus, contrived role playing will have to suffice as preparatory experiences for real-life encounters.
3. Homework involving the use of social skills requires the ability to engage the client in meaningful role-playing activities. Thus, the successful use of homework depends on the counselor's mastery of another technique—role-playing.

LEARNING TO USE HOMEWORK

The following suggestions for performing homework assignments will help the counselor understand the process and better use it in career counseling sessions:

1. Remember the 3WHSS (what, where, when, how often, self-statement).
2. Role-play designing homework assignments with a colleague or fellow student.
3. Master role-playing as an adjunct to homework.
4. Read case studies and imagine what types of homework assignments could be devised, the problems that might arise, and what might be done about them.
5. Contrast the homework assignments made by teachers and professors with those used in career counseling. How are they similar? Different?
6. Practice with a client.

SUMMARY

Homework is included in the strategies employed by almost all kinds of counselors. It is a counseling technique that almost everyone believes he or she understands, and to a certain extent, that is true. However, contrary to the analogy with classroom-related homework assignments, homework in counseling should be collaboratively designed. Like its classroom counterpart, homework in career counseling has certain specifications. These include: what is to be done, when it is to be done, and where it is to be done (3Ws); how often it is to be done (H); and a self-statement in which the client gives himself or herself a pat on the back for doing the homework (SS). Like most techniques, homework should be previewed with the client, the client should be prepared to follow through on the homework, and then the results should be reviewed.

REFERENCES AND SUGGESTED READINGS

Cormier, W.H., & Cormier, L.S. (1985). *Interviewing Strategies for Helpers: A Guide to Assessment, Treatment, and Evaluation* (2nd ed.). Monterey, CA: Brooks/Cole.

Goldfried, M.R., & Davison, G.C. (1976). *Clinical Behavior Therapy*. New York: Holt, Rinehart, & Winston.

Shelton, J.L., & Ackerman, J.M. (1974). *Homework in Counseling and Psychotherapy*. Springfield, IL: Charles C. Thomas.

CHAPTER 21

Role-playing

Role-playing, or behavioral rehearsal, is a technique involving modeling and systematic feedback that is utilized to develop or remediate underdeveloped or inappropriate social skills. It can be used with individuals or groups, and though it is presented here as an intervention strategy, it can also be used in the assessment of social skills deficits.

USES OF ROLE-PLAYING

Role-playing is a technique that can perform the following functions:

1. Assess weaknesses in social skills
2. Develop job interviewing strategies
3. Develop assertive behavior with supervisors and others
4. Remediate aggressive or other inappropriate behavior
5. Develop networking skills that require interpersonal behaviors
6. Develop self-confidence

BACKGROUND

Role-playing is a strategy that has been used in psychotherapy for decades (see Moreno, 1953), but it was the behaviorally oriented counselors such as John Krumboltz and associates (e.g., Krumboltz & Schroeder, 1965; Krumboltz & Thoreson, 1964) who demonstrated that behavioral rehearsal could be effective in developing career-related behaviors, particularly if the behavior to be developed was modeled and reinforcement was provided for successful practice.

Role-playing involves a number of steps, but can be broken down into five general stages: preparing the client, assessment, modeling, practice, implementation, and follow-up. To be effective, the assessment must be carefully conducted so that both the counselor and the client are aware of the deficits to be remedied. It is also important that the behavior(s) being developed relate to the goals that the client has set.

DESCRIPTION OF THE ROLE-PLAYING TECHNIQUE

Preparing the Client

It is a common error for neophyte counselors to launch into role-playing without properly preparing the client for the experience. The result is usually confusion and, at best, reduced learning. Role-playing must be presented in the context of the client's problems and his or her goals to deal with those problems. The following excerpt illustrates how role-playing might be introduced:

Co: You've been waiting to ask your boss for a raise, but you just cannot get up the courage to do it?

Cl: That's right. I get cold feet every time I approach his office. It's beginning to bother me because I know I deserve a raise.

Co: I can tell that you're very frustrated. One way that we might get you ready to deal with your boss is by rehearsing what you might do and say when you approach him. We would begin by me acting in the place of your boss and you trying to create how you would approach him. Then we would do some role reversal, and I would be you and you might be your boss. How does that sound?

Cl: OK, I guess. I'm not quite sure what I'm going to do though.

Co: Try to be spontaneous. I'm sure you have gone over the scene where you actually ask for a raise a number of times.

Cl: (Nervous laugh) Yeah, well, and I never get it.

Co: Are you willing to try it again?

Cl: Sure.

Assessment

Assessment involves having clients act out how they would deal with a particular concern. In order for the assessment to be accurate, the counselor must develop a good picture of the individual with whom the client is to interact. In the foregoing situation, the boss is the stimulus person. Two techniques can be utilized to assess the boss's behavior: having the client describe the boss or having the client role-play the boss to illustrate how he or she thinks the boss will respond in the conference in which a raise will be requested. Once this picture is developed, assessment of the client's behavior can begin.

Co: OK, I'll be the boss and you be yourself. Let's set the stage. You are coming down the hall to my office. You are going to enter my office, shake my hand, greet me, and then proceed with the conference.

Cl: I think I have the picture. I'm a little nervous already.

Co: Go out of the room and let's begin.

Cl: (leaves room and knocks on the door)

Co: Come in.

Cl: Hello, Mr. Hogan. (They shake hands) It's good to see you.

Co: It's nice to see you again, too. It's been a little while since we talked. How have you been?

Cl: Fine. (Tense)

Co: What can I do for you?

Cl: I, uh, I was wondering if it would be possible to, uh, talk about my salary. (Avoids eye contact)

Co: Sure, what about it?

Cl: I, well—I think I should be making more money.

Co: Really? It seems to me that you are paid about the same as others doing the same work that you are doing.

Cl: I suppose you're right, but I just think I should make more.

Co: You're a good employee, but I'm not sure we can justify giving you more money.

Cl: OK, I guess I should get back to work now.

After the assessment role-play, the client should be asked if the behavior acted out was typical of the way they interact or *would* interact in this situation. If the answer is yes, assessment should go on to the next step, which involves role reversal.

In role reversal, the counselor assumes the role of the client or, in the foregoing case, the nonassertive employee. The client becomes the stimulus person or, in this case; the boss. The counselor prepares the client for role reversal and then demonstrates how the client has performed.

> *Co:* You seem to think that how you just acted would be typical of you. Let's reverse roles, you become the boss and I'll be you. I want to show you how you appeared to me.
>
> *Cl:* All right. I can be the boss.
>
> [Repeat role-play as above, then have client evaluate behavior.]
>
> *Co:* What did you think of yourself?
>
> *Cl:* I wouldn't have given me a raise either. I seem so uncertain, so wishy-washy. Ill have to do better than that.
>
> *Co:* What could you have done better?
>
> *Cl:* Everything.
>
> *Co:* Let's be specific.
>
> *Cl:* Well, I stammered, I didn't look at him, and I didn't make my case. I didn't tell him why I should get a raise. I just folded.
>
> *Co:* Your posture also needs to be improved. You slumped a bit. You need to assume a posture that makes you look confident.

Once the client has assessed his or her behavior, it is time to move to the next stage.

Modeling

In the modeling phase, the counselor, if it is individual counseling, or another client, if it is group counseling, will demonstrate more effective behavior. The objective at this stage is to show the client how to overcome deficiencies that have been identified.

> *Co:* Let's continue the role-playing at this time. I'm still you, and you are still the boss.
>
> *Cl:* All right. Go out of the room and let's start.
>
> *Co:* (Knocks)
>
> *Cl:* Come in.

Co: (Firm handshake) Good morning, Mr. Hogan (smiles).

Cl: It's good to see you again. It's been a while since we talked.

Co: It has. I believe that we chatted briefly at the Christmas party.

Cl: What can I do for you?

Co: I scheduled this appointment so that we could discuss my salary. I very much enjoy working for this company, but I believe that I am underpaid.

Cl: Really? As I recall, you are paid about the same as the others doing the same job.

Co: To a certain extent that's true, but there are some circumstances that you might not be aware of, such as that my performance appraisal has been in the top 5 percent for four years running. I also want to point out that I have been given more responsibility than others in my general area. I must make summary reports of the sales from each division of the company and analyze the trends for each division director. That takes skill and time. As I said, I really enjoy working for this company, but I do believe that I deserve a raise to recognize my performance and my extra duties.

Cl: You are right. I wasn't aware of your performance appraisals and your extra duties. Ill take your request for a raise under advisement.

Co: Thank you very much. I really appreciate your willingness to listen to me. I'm looking forward to hearing your decision.

Once modeling is completed, the client is again asked to assess his or her behavior.

Co: What did you think of the new you?

Cl: That was great. I might have a chance to get a raise if I performed in that way.

Co: Now I want you to try it the way I did it.

Practice

Practice requires first having the client imitate what has been modeled and receiving feedback on the effectiveness of his or her practice.

Practice should continue until both the client and the counselor feel that they have mastered the behaviors to be used in resolving the problem at hand. Once mastery has occurred, then the situation should be varied and made more difficult. In the situation above, the boss was rather compliant. The situation could be varied by having the boss reject the raise request outright and then having the client persevere, or by having the boss ask for more information. Practice should continue until overlearning has occurred; that is, the client's responses are somewhat automatic, and he can vary his behavior in response to the changing conditions of the interpersonal interaction.

Implementation and Follow-up

In the implementation phase, the social skill being learned is taken out of the realm of "playing" and practiced in the real world. This occurs only when the client and the counselor agree that the client is ready. Clients' readiness can be assessed by asking them to rate their ability to perform the skill being learned to solve their problem on a 1 to 10 scale, with 1 representing low ability to perform the skills and 10 representing high ability to perform the interpersonal situation in real life. Once the rating of efficacy is high (7–10), a specific homework assignment is made to practice the skill. The following excerpt represents how this assignment might be made:

> *Co:* You have a high degree of confidence that you can go out and ask your boss for a raise, and I agree—you are ready.
>
> *Cl:* I feel much better about my chances. I'm not sure I'll get the raise, but it won't be because I didn't ask in the right way.
>
> *Co:* So, during the next week you are going to make an appointment and ask for a raise. I would introduce one caution. You and I believe that you are ready. However, if you get close to the time and your self-confidence gets low, it is probably a good idea to scrub the interview with your boss and wait until your confidence is high. You may only get one shot at getting a raise.

Note that the counselor tried to build in a mechanism that would preclude the client from failing, that is, the client was cautioned against proceeding if his or her self-confidence waned as the time for the conference with the boss approached. Generally, these types of precautions are good practice simply because failure may mean that the ability to get the client ready to tackle the situation again is reduced. As the counselor pointed out, the client may have one only shot at attaining his or her objective, and it is better to wait than waste the opportunity.

During the session following the homework assignment, the counselor and client would assess the client's performance. If he or she got the raise, then the objective has been accomplished, but the client may still wish to improve his or her performance in similar situations. If the client decided not to proceed with the assignment, then an assessment of why that decision was reached is in order, and reteaching through modeling and more practice is called for. Finally, if the client failed, a careful analysis of why the failure occurred should be conducted. If the failure was due to inappropriate behavior on the part of the client, then reteaching is called for. If, however, the client performed well, but circumstances embedded in the situation (the boss refuses raises to everyone) are responsible for the failure, then reteaching is not called for. The implications of the refusal on the client's failure in that company may become the focus of career counseling at this point.

SUMMARY OF THE ROLE-PLAYING PROCESS

The following steps represent a summary of the role-playing steps described in this chapter:

1. Begin with assessment: "Show me how you act in this situation."
2. Reverse roles: "Let me show you what I saw."
3. Get feedback on your imitation of the event: "Was my portrayal accurate?"
4. Assess appropriateness of client's behavior: "How well do you think you did?"
5. Determine willingness to learn new behavior: "Would you like to learn a different way?"
6. Model new behavior: Reenact role-play with appropriate behavior.
7. Assess your modeling: "How did I do?"
8. Reverse roles: "Now you try what I did."
9. Feedback: "Your role-play was. . . ."
10. Practice until mastery: "You were perfect."
11. Vary situations: "Let's make this situation a little different."
12. Increase difficulty: "We are going to try some more difficult situations."

13. Assessment: "On a 1 to 10 scale, how confident are you that you can perform the behavior we have been practicing?"
14. Homework, if self-efficacy rating is high: "Now you go out and try behavior in that situation."
15. Follow up: "How did you do?"
16. Relearning as necessary: "Let's practice some more."

LIMITATIONS OF ROLE-PLAYING

Role-playing is most effective when the counselor is aware of the following:

1. Some clients are embarrassed by the process of role-playing and may have difficulty portraying their "true" behavior. Generally speaking, these clients need more support and encouragement.
2. Role-playing is most effective when the model is of the same general status and background as the client. Middle-class counselors may not be good models for low-SES clients, and white counselors may not be good models for ethnic minorities. Videotaped models can be substituted effectively for live models, but this limits the ability of the counselor to design an intervention for the client.
3. When there are cognitive antecedents such as irrational fears of stereotypes that preclude effective behavior, these may have to be addressed before the behavioral rehearsal will be effective.
4. It is sometimes difficult to get an accurate picture of the stimulus person (e.g., boss) because of distorted descriptions by the client. This situation may require that the client be assigned to make more careful observations of the stimulus person.

LEARNING ROLE PLAYING

The suggestions that follow will help the counselor use role-playing successfully with clients:

1. Begin by reviewing the process outlined in this chapter and make sure that you have it fixed firmly in your mind. The acronym *PAMPI* may help you in this regard. These letters stand for *P*review with client, *A*ssess client's functioning, *M*odel new behavior, *P*ractice, and *I*mplement newly learned behavior.

2. Help a fellow student or a colleague work on a new behavior using a role-playing strategy.
3. Identify a personal social skills deficit. Write out a role-playing strategy for remedying the deficit you have identified.
4. Imagine that you have encountered a client who is afraid to take the risks involved in role-playing. How would you convince him or her that it is a good idea? What would you do if you could not convince the client that it was a good idea?
5. Write out a role-playing scenario for an individual who needs to learn the following:
   a. Job interviewing skills
   b. Dealing with a colleague who does not do his share of the work
   c. Making telephone contacts with prospective employees

SUMMARY

Role-playing has long been used as a counseling strategy, and we have had empirical support for its effectiveness for over twenty-five years. It is a technique that is especially useful in developing social skills and should be a part of every career counselor's repertoire. The role-playing process involves previewing the strategy for the client, assessing client deficits, modeling new behaviors, and then having the client implement newly learned behaviors in his or her real-life situation. Some clients may have difficulty engaging in role-playing situations, and, thus, alternative strategies need to be available for these people. With all clients, the choice of models with which they can identify is a key factor in the success of the process.

REFERENCES AND SUGGESTED READINGS

Hutchins, D.E., & Cole, C.G. (1986). *Helping Relationships and Strategies*. Monterey, CA: Brooks/Cole: 235–43.

Krumboltz, J.D, & Schroeder, W.W. (1965). Promoting career planning through reinforcement. *Personnel and Guidance Journal* 44: 19–26.

Krumboltz, J.D., & Thoreson, C.E. (1964). The effect of behavioral counseling in group and individual settings on information-seeking behavior. *Journal of Counseling Psychology* 11: 324–33.

Moreno, J.L. (1953). *Who Shall Survive?* New York: Beacon House.

Terminating Career Counseling

Termination is the last stage of the counseling process. Ideally, clients achieve their goals—decide to leave a dissatisfying job, choose a training program, decide on a college major, work out a more satisfying arrangement with spouse regarding work and family roles—and the client and counselor mutually agree that it is time to stop meeting. Experienced counselors know, however, that termination often occurs under less than optimal circumstances—clients abruptly and unexpectedly stop coming for counseling; external factors require that counseling end (e.g., geographical moves, counselor leaves the agency, the end of the school year arrives, counselors, although not clients, believe it is time for clients to be on their own). No matter what the circumstance of the termination, the viewpoint taken here is that termination is an integral part of the counseling process. Thus, every effort should be made to spend some explicit time with the client on the termination phase of counseling.

In general, the tasks of termination are to (1) review client goals and consolidate learning, (2) resolve affective issues and bring about closure of the client-counselor relationship, and (3) prepare the client for self-reliance and transfer of learning (Ward, 1984). Each of these tasks may receive different emphases, however, depending on the circumstances of the termination and the length and intensity of the counseling. In this chapter we discuss techniques for achieving each of the three tasks of termination, as well as ways to handle termination that comes about for reasons other than mutual client-counselor decision.

BACKGROUND

The topic of termination, has received little attention in the career counseling literature. A scanning of several books on career counseling reveals that only two devote any space to termination. Raskin's (1987) book contains a chapter on termination, and Gysbers and Moore (1987) devote three paragraphs to evaluating the impact of the intervention and closing the counseling relationship. On the one hand, this gap in the literature is not surprising. Career counseling has traditionally been viewed as a short-term, topic-limited endeavor that emphasizes methods and outcomes rather than the client-counselor interaction (Osipow, 1982). The view of career counseling as entailing a *process* with specific stages, from goal setting through termination, is probably uncommon. Thus, in traditional career counseling, attention to the termination task of resolving clients' affective issues and bringing closure to the client-counselor relationship is often irrelevant.

On the other hand, the termination tasks of client consolidation and transfer of learning seem especially important in career counseling. Moreover, at times, career counseling can and often does evolve into a complex process involving an intense client-counselor relationship. Termination can then trigger significant client dilemmas involving such issues as loss and abandonment or dependency and self-reliance. In short, termination is an important stage in career counseling as well as in longer term personal counseling. Thus, it behooves career counselors to be skilled in all three of the termination tasks just noted.

TERMINATION TASKS AND TECHNIQUES

The tasks of termination can often be achieved during one counseling session, although it may take longer in those cases in which the process has evolved into an intensive relationship or when the client is reluctant to leave. An important first step in managing the termination process is to prepare the client for the termination session. Thus, clients should be prompted to reflect on their counseling experience, giving specific attention to what they have gained, what they see as their next steps, how they feel about leaving counseling, and so on. An adequate review requires ample time; thus, the termination process should seldom be completed in the session in which it is initially introduced (Ward, 1984). Rather, a specific date should be planned sometime in the future. For example, suppose the counselor and client agree during one session that the goals of the counseling have been achieved and there is no need for any further sessions. It would seldom be effective to then try to complete the termination process during that session because the client needs time to review his or her experience. It would be better to schedule one more session—perhaps the next week—to allow the client (and the counselor) more time to prepare for the termination session.

Although the three tasks of termination can overlap considerably, they are discussed separately for purposes of clarity.

Review Client Goals and Consolidate Client Learning

The review of client goals and learning should be mutual but primarily the responsibility of the client (Ward, 1984). Thus, when it is appropriate during the session, the counselor could introduce the discussion of termination as follows:

> *Co:* Today is our last session and as I mentioned last time, I'd like for us to review what's happened for you since we first met. So why don't you begin by talking about what your concerns were when you first came? And then talk about how you view your current status.

One of the goals of prompting clients to review their goals and assess their current situation is to work toward a final, consolidating summary statement (Brammer, Shostrom, & Abrego, 1989). Such a review might reveal to clients that they have made more progress than they realized and thus provide a greater sense of mastery. At times, counselors need to help fill in the gaps when clients minimize or are unclear about their gains, as the following vignette illustrates:

> *Cl:* When I first came here I was dead set on going to medical school. Even though I told you that I wanted help figuring out what career to follow, what I really hoped was that you could help me figure out a way to get into med school, even though I knew my grades were probably not good enough. It was really hard to give up a dream I've had ever since I could remember. But I feel OK about that now. I've accepted that it doesn't mean I'm a total failure, and I'm excited about pursuing a career in health education.
>
> *Co:* You've come a long way—from facing the inevitable and dealing with the anger and sadness involved in losing a dream, to finding a different direction for yourself. I think you've worked very hard, and I feel good about where

you are right now. I'm curious, though—if you had to give someone a summary of what you've learned, what would you say?

Cl: I guess I'd say that I learned a lot about myself. That I didn't realize before that one of the main reasons that I wanted to go to medical school was that I wanted to make a contribution to people's lives, and there are other ways to do that that are just as worthwhile and valuable and that I can feel good about. And I have to admit that the prestige of being a doctor was grabbing me, even though I like to think of myself as someone who isn't caught up in status.

Co: Those are important learnings. Any other learnings come to mind?

Cl: Can't think of any.

Co: What about the influence of your father?

Cl: Hmm—I'm not sure what you're getting at.

Co: It seems to me that you were worried about disappointing him. It was his dream too that his son would become a doctor.

Cl: That's true. I was worried about letting him down.

Co: Yes, and you seem less concerned about that now. What has made the difference?

Cl: That's true, it doesn't bother me like it did. I suppose that once I found another alternative that I felt good about, then I felt better about myself, and disappointing Dad seemed less of an issue.

Co: It's almost as if your worry about disappointing Dad was confused with your disappointment in yourself.

Cl: I hadn't thought of it in quite that way. But that seems right.

Though the vignette illustrates a client who is pleased with his progress, it would not be unusual for a client to express dissatisfaction with counseling. At times, the dissatisfaction is a way of communicating a natural reluctance to leave. Others suffer a "relapse" as a way of delaying the end. The counselor, of course, should encourage further exploration of the dissatisfaction in order to better understand its bases and devise effective interventions. In some cases, for example, clients simply need the counselor's reassurance that they can make it on their own. Other clients may need help in gaining insight into the purpose of the "relapse." Still others need to explore their feelings about losing the counseling relationship—a topic that is discussed in the following subsection.

Affective Issues and Closure of the Relationship.

The relationship with the counselor may not be an especially meaningful aspect of the experience for some career counseling clients. Still, the client may have feelings about leaving counseling, and the counselor needs to inquire about them. Open encouragement of exploration of feelings is the main strategy to use here. An inquiry from the counselor such as "I'm wondering how you're feeling about not coming here any longer?" should be sufficient to begin the exploration. Naturally, the counselor needs to be alert to those situations in which the client is experiencing a significant loss and assure the client that it is important to explore those feelings. In any case, an important goal, regardless of the intensity of the relationship, is to "lead toward the expression of an appropriate and meaningful good-bye at the actual conclusion of counseling" (Ward, 1984, p. 23).

Preparation for Postcounseling and Transfer of Learning.

Given that the average person changes job seven or eight times, transfer of learning is an especially important issue in career counseling. Career issues are seldom settled for life, despite the common myth that "there is one right occupation for me that I can do for the rest of my life." Given this reality, the counselor will often want to ensure that the client has learned something about the process of decision making to be used at a later stage m life. One technique that can be used is to ask the client to speculate about what he or she might do at some later time if career problems or uncertainties arise again. For example, the counselor could say, "Suppose it's ten years from now, and you're feeling dissatisfied with your job. What do you think you would do in that situation?" Counselors who have not been explicit about the process of career decision making before this time may want to do so now if clients seem confused about the steps they might take to help themselves.

Another important topic to address in many cases centers on the client's plans or "next steps." Here the counselor can help the client be specific about the remaining tasks. A self-contract that identifies time lines and specific actions to be taken could be suggested to help keep the client involved in problem-solving. For example:

Co: Let's talk about what you see as your next steps. You've decided that you want to pursue a career in electronics. What do you think you need to do to make that become a reality?

Cl: First, I need to finish the training program at ABC technical college. While I'm doing that, I need to find out more about how to break into the field.

Co: Yes, and how might you do that?

Cl: I could do some reading in some of those books you mentioned, like the *Occupational Handbook.* I also need to talk to my instructors to see what suggestions they have. Other people in the training program probably have some ideas, too. And I need to find some other women who are working in the field so I can find out what kinds of issues have come up for them and how they have handled them.

Co: Sounds like a good plan—get more information about the field, as well as issues that come up for women, so you can develop a game plan. Sometimes it's helpful to get a plan in writing—specific actions you will take and the dates by which you will achieve them. It's a kind of self-contract to keep you active and motivated. What do you think of that idea?

Cl: Hmm——a good idea, but I don't think I need to do that. I'm feeling good about this decision and enthusiastic about following up, so I'm reasonably certain that I'll just naturally do what I need to do.

Co: You do seem very motivated. It's difficult for you to imagine that you won't take the next steps. Can you think of anything that might get in your way, if not now, sometime later? It's always good to be prepared.

Cl: The only thing that occurs to me is that I might get discouraged being the only woman in the training program. Sometimes I feel the guys think I'm sort of strange and they leave me out—sort of ignore me. Also, as we have talked before, my family thinks I should go to graduate school and get into a profession of some kind. So they will have some difficulty accepting this decision. That might tip me back into the conflict between what I think I should do versus what I want to do.

Co: You can imagine times when the external situation—the attitudes of your classmates or your family—might dampen your enthusiasm. Can you think of some things you can do to prevent that from happening, or if it does, what you might do to regain your motivation?

Cl: Hmm—uh—I'm not sure. Well—I think it would help a lot if I knew other women in the field. If I can find some, maybe I could call them up for a pep talk every once in awhile (laughs).

Co: Actually, that's an excellent idea. It's real important to have that outside support—someone who can help you affirm your choice when the going gets rough. You might also look around for a women's support group—the local Women's Center has support groups. You might even suggest they start one for women in nontraditional occupations—the Center is always looking for ideas for programs that are needed by women in the community. Also, though we've finished our work together right now, you could come back here for a booster. I feel good about where you are now and confident that you can finish the process on your own. Some unexpected issues could come up, though, and coming back here won't mean you've failed!

Cl: Good! I'm glad you said that—you know how hard it is for me to ask for help.

Co: Yes, and hopefully it will be easier now that you've asked once and survived with yourself intact.

In this excerpt, the counselor clearly felt it unnecessary to encourage the client to develop a written plan. Nevertheless, the idea gives the client a tool she might use in the future. Because the counselor had learned during her work with the client about some of the external pressures, she wanted the client to prepare herself for any relapses in motivation that might occur in the future and help her think about ways to cope with them. Finally, the counselor left the door open for future sessions. In this situation, the counselor was not worried that the client would return for counseling before trying things out on her own, as her need for self-reliance was a strong motivator ("I have trouble asking for help"). In other cases where the client is more dependent, the counselor would want to leave the door open but more strongly urge the client to develop self-reliant coping strategies. Cognitive strategies can be hopeful here, as illustrated in the following:

Co: One thing you're telling me is that you're very anxious about sticking to your plan. Maybe, next week, for example, your parents will start telling you this is a bad idea, and the guys in your class will tell you outright, "This is no field for a woman." And if those things happen, you're afraid you'll start wavering.

Cl: Right. I feel very certain now, but I've got you to reassure me.

Co: Okay, let's talk about some ways you might reassure yourself. What might you be saying to yourself when you're wavering?

Cl: Oh, things like "Maybe they're right—this *isn't* a field for a woman; if all men in the field are like them, I don't know if I could cope with it; maybe I should find something else that will be less trouble and also please my family."

Co: You might let it snowball. Suppose that happens. It would be important for you to notice that as soon as it starts and then substitute some more positive thoughts. What might be some effective substitute thoughts?

Cl: Hmm—that's a hard one. I suppose I could remember that I've looked at this issue from every angle and I know it's the right decision for me now, no matter what anyone else thinks. So I could say something like "It doesn't matter what anyone else thinks, I know this is right for me. This is what I want. I've spent too many years of my life doing what others want rather than what I want. I'm going to change that and I'll feel much better about myself."

Co: Good! One thing you might want to do real soon—like today, perhaps, while you're feeling strong—is write down a bunch of positive thoughts that will help you get through the rough times. It seems inevitable that you're bound to get discouraged at times because you're doing something that others don't understand and may find threatening. If you have an ammunition list of positive thoughts readily available it should help. Of course, you can always come back here if you need a boost, but I'd like to see you try things out on your own for awhile. How does that sound?

Cl: Okay—I can try that.

Co: You can try?

Cl: I can do it!

In this excerpt, the counselor helps the client develop some self-reliant coping strategies, and though she leaves the door open, she also expresses confidence in the client and urges her to be on her own for awhile. The counselor has also prepared the client for relapses and helped her develop some coping strategies.

TERMINATION WHEN COUNSELING IS INCOMPLETE

Ward (1985) observes that a major challenge for the counselor is terminating when clients wish to end counseling before the counselor believes they are ready. What Ward has in mind is the situation when the client abruptly and unexpectedly ends the counseling, often by simply failing to show up for the next scheduled appointment. As Ward rightly notes, the research on such so-called premature termination has been inconclusive, providing no definitive guidelines for preventing these occurrences. A variety of factors is undoubtedly responsible for premature termination. Among the possibilities are clients' judgment that they have achieved their goals, although the counselor may not agree; clients' fear of what might be uncovered in counseling; failure of counseling to meet clients' expectations, and/or lack of clients' commitment to counseling in the beginning.

Premature termination due to client's unmet expectations and lack of commitment might be prevented with adequate structuring at the beginning of counseling (see Chapter 2). For example, counselors need to elicit client expectations regarding the counseling process and the length of counseling so that any misconceptions can be corrected or renegotiated.

We suggest, however, that often it is not the client but rather the career counselor who unwittingly "prematurely terminates." For example, the seemingly common practice of assigning an interest inventory and then telling the client to schedule an appointment when the results have been returned from the scoring service may be perceived by the client as a lack of commitment on the part of the counselor, and may also imply that career counseling is indeed a limited enterprise—not a process, but a test interpretation. Similarly, telling clients to engage in occupational exploration by referring them to the occupational information file without scheduling a follow-up appointment is also an example of "premature termination." This failure to integrate occupational information into the counseling process has been lamented similarly by Crites (1976). He cites an unpublished study that shows that only 5 percent of the clients in a university counseling center actually used the file. Crites proposes that clients need to be reinforced for gathering information for themselves outside the interview hour. To this we would add that they also often need help evaluating the information they gather, particularly because they commonly misinterpret what they read. Some provision leading clients to expect that the counselor will continue to work with them throughout the exploration process is warranted. One method would be to set up a contract that specifies both the client's and the counselor's responsibilities and makes an explicit commitment to clients to work with them from self-assessment through deciding upon and implementing alternatives (Brooks & Haigler, 1984). First, however, counselors (and clients!) and must conceive of career counseling as a process rather than something that stops with a test interpretation.

Ways of handling two problematic termination situations: (1) The client has been engaged in counseling for more than two or three sessions and abruptly stops coming, and (2) the client needs to be referred to another counselor, are discussed in the following subsections.

When the Client Terminates Abruptly

Clients typically terminate abruptly by failing to show up for the next appointment. As Ward (1984) notes, providing the best treatment possible means that an effort should be made to extend the counseling beyond the time the client expects. "The major purposes of this extended work are to help clients to resolve any negative feelings resulting from counseling itself, to invite clients to continue counseling if they wish, and to work toward an appropriate referral to another counselor or type of treatment or toward increasing the likelihood that the client will reengage in some type of counseling or facilitative experiences at a later date" (Ward, 1984, p. 24).

A common strategy that is used when the client misses an appointment is to telephone the client three or four days later. Some clients may be testing the counselor's concern or may have reached a difficult time in counseling, and a contact may be all that is needed to resume counseling (Ward, 1984). Whether counselors have the agency receptionist make the telephone contact or make it themselves will depend on counselor judgment regarding the client's response. For example, if the counselor suspects that the client feels uncomfortable with or negative about the counselor, it might be best for the receptionist to make the call so that the client might feel freer to express any discomfort or dissatisfaction. In these instances, the receptionist should be instructed to mention to the client that a referral can be made to another counselor. Another method that can be used is a note from the counselor. Whatever method is used, the message should be conveyed to a client that the counselor is interested in him or her and that one more session would be used to help the client with any lingering concerns, to discuss a possible referral, and to help the counselor better understand the reasons for terminating (Ward, 1984). Also, the counselor should convey respect for the client's decision.

When the Client Is Referred to Another Counselor.

The need to refer a client to another counselor can occur in a variety of situations. Chief among them are external events (e.g., graduation, counselor leaves agency) or client need for another kind of service (e.g., financial counseling, individual or group psychotherapy) (Raskin, 1987). In addition, a referral might be made because progress has stopped and the counselor and client agree that another career counselor might be more appropriate (e.g., one of the same gender or ethnicity). How the referral is made will be determined by the independence of the client and the nature of the relationship between the client and the counselor. For example, less dependent clients simply need the name and telephone number of the person to whom they are being referred. Others may be better served by arranging a joint meeting, if possible, with the new counselor to help with the transition. Though counselors might in some instances make an appointment for the client, too much effort on the client's behalf may represent an overinvolvement in the case (Raskin, 1987) and/or some unresolved feelings on the part of the counselor (e.g., guilt for not being able to be more helpful). Counselors should remind themselves that all counseling pairs do not work, due to no particular fault of the counselor. Also, as Ward (1984) notes, client maintenance of negative feelings toward the counselor can sometimes increase the effectiveness of the referral. "Although it is difficult for counselors to end counseling while unappreciated and unliked by clients, it is sometimes in the client's best interest" (Ward, 1984, p. 25).

LEARNING TO TERMINATE

The following suggestions will prepare the counselor for facilitating the termination process in the career counseling situation:

1. Complete additional readings on termination: this is particularly relevant when counseling has involved a mixture of personal and career counseling and has extended over a period of time.
2. Counselors who have difficulty with good-byes in general might profit from readings on loss. Supervision or personal counseling should be sought if the problem continues.
3. Many writers and supervisors have noted that it is not uncommon

for counselors to experience difficulty in effectively terminating clients due, for example, to their own anxiety about loss. Martin and Schurtman (1985) discuss the sources of termination anxiety for counselors and therapists and the various defense maneuvers they might use to deal with the anxiety. Their article is recommended for counselors who find termination a persistent problem.

4. If you are in a supervised field experience, ask your supervisor to set aside some time for discussion of termination issues.

5. Talk to other experienced counselors regarding the various ways they handle termination.

6. Remember, sometimes it is in the client's best interest to terminate, even if you don't think he or she is ready.

7. Examine your own method of conducting career counseling to identify ways that you may "prematurely terminate" career counseling.

SUMMARY

Career counseling, like personal counseling, is appropriately viewed as entailing a process with several stages, of which termination is the final stage. The topic of termination has been neglected in the career counseling literature, no doubt because of the traditional view that it is a time- and topic-limited endeavor that focuses more on method than process.

The tasks of termination are to (1) review client goals and consolidate learning, (2) resolve affective issues and bring about closure of the client-counselor relationship, and (3) prepare the client for self-reliance and transfer of learning. These tasks are important when the counseling is deemed either finished or unfinished. If the client abruptly stops coming for counseling, the counselor should make efforts to extend the counseling so that attention can be given to the termination tasks. If counseling must end due to external circumstances or the client needs another kind of service, then termination involves making an effective referral.

REFERENCES AND SUGGESTED READINGS

Brammer, L.M., Shostrom, E.L., & Abrego, P.J. (1989). *Therapeutic Psychology* (5th ed.). Englewood Cliffs, NJ: Prentice-Hall.

Brooks, L., & Haigler, J. (1984). Contract career counseling: An option for some help-seekers. *Vocational Guidance Quarterly* 33: 178–83.

Crites, J.0. (1976). Career counseling: A comprehensive approach. *The Counseling Psychologist* 6: 2–13.

Goodyear, R.K. (1981). Termination as a loss experience for the counselor. *Personnel and Guidance Journal* 59: 347–50.

Gybers, N.C., & Moore, E.J. (1987). *Career Counseling*. Englewood Cliffs, NJ: Prentice-Hall.

Maholick, L.T., & Turner, D.W. (1979). Termination: That difficult fare-well. *American Journal of Psychotherapy* 33: 583–91.

Martin, E.S., & Schurtman, R. (1985). Termination anxiety as it affects the therapist. *Psychotherapy* 22: 92–6.

Osipow, S.H. (1982). Research in career counseling: An analysis of issues and problems. *Counseling Psychologist* 10(4): 27–34.

Raskin, P.M. (1987). *Vocational Counseling*. New York: Teachers College Press.

Ward, D.E. (1984). Termination of individual counseling: Concepts and strategies. *Journal of Counseling and Development* 63: 21–5.

CHAPTER 23

Career Counseling Techniques: Epilogue

In the foregoing twenty-two chapters, we have offered a skeletal outline of the career counseling process, discussed traditional and clinical counseling assessment, and defined and illustrated the use of a number of specific counseling techniques. Throughout this discussion, we have tried to caution that mental health problems that result in diminished cognitive clarity need to be considered while career counseling is being provided. We have also stressed that counselor-client interaction, race, ethnicity, and gender are all important considerations in the career counseling process. In short, we have tried to clinch the point we made in Chapter 1: the stereotype of career counseling as a simple process is fallacious.

We are aware that it would be possible, even after reading this book and completing the exercises that we have outlined, to regress to a "test 'em and tell 'em" mind-set, for we have seen it happen. However, we sincerely hope that the counselor will not fall into this trap. If we may be allowed one medical metaphor, assisting persons with career choice and adjustment problems using the narrow approaches of the past is roughly equivalent to treating a heart attack with bloodletting. The patient may live, but it will not be because of the treatment.

It must also be admitted at this point that we have much to learn about career counseling. For example, Kivlighan (1990) asserts that "the effects of group career interventions are similar to or greater than the effects of other types of career interventions" (p. 64), one of which is individual career counseling. However, the latest in a series of analyses of the research on career interventions by Oliver and Spokane (1988) suggests that career-development classes were the most effective intervention but required the greatest number of intervention hours, whereas individual counseling produced the greatest gain per client hour.

Even though Oliver and Spokane (1988) admit that there are some methodological problems with their analyses, some of their conclusions are worth citing. For example, they conclude that observations such as those by Holland, Magoon, and Spokane (1981)—that career classes and counseling make no greater impact than procedures such as self-directed assessment—were not supported. They also suggest that increasing the number of hours of an intervention increases the likelihood that the outcome will be favorable. Although one would presume that there is some limit to this recommendation, their recommendation that counselors work to avoid premature termination seems quite appropriate. Finally, they observe that diagnosis seems to be lacking in career interventions and recommend that counselors engage more actively in this process, a recommendation that supports one of the premises of this book.

TECHNIQUES AND THEORY: IS THERE A RELATIONSHIP?

Oliver and Spokane's (1988) suggestion that career counselors engage more actively in diagnosis raises the issue of the relationship of theory to the career counseling process. It is certainly the case that diagnosing a client's problem requires making some assumptions about the *causes* of problems (e.g., inability to make a career choice is related to lack of occupational information). We would also suggest that one way to increase career counseling effectiveness is to adopt a personal theory to guide the process.

In 1981, Crites set forth six theories of career counseling based primarily on major models of counseling and psychotherapy (e.g., a psychoanalytic model). Our observations and our interactions with leading career-development theorists (Brown, Brooks, & Assoc., 1990) suggests that, except for trait-and-factor theory, no theoretical approach to career counseling has emerged as a favorite of large numbers of career counselors. Rather, it seems that career counselors are quite eclectic in their approaches to dealing with career clients with some inclinations toward placing the trait-and-factor perspective at the heart of their eclecticism.

We have purposely not taken a stand favoring a particular theory in this book. We have warned against the use of the narrow trait-and-factor perspective of the 1930s. However, we do recommend that all career counselors develop a theoretical framework to guide the assessment and intervention process. The development of this framework should begin with an examination of personal assumptions held about the nature of human beings (e.g., intrinsically good, bad, neutral). This personal philosophy should then be tempered by what we know about normal and abnormal aspects of human behavior. There are, of course, rival hypotheses regarding why humans behave as they do, and personal philosophy is often the basis for choosing "acceptable" explanations. Once a general conclusion about how human behavior is acquired and changed is reached, then prospective career counselors should complete their theories by determining how their general perspective applies to career development processes such as the development of stereotypes, the acquisition of values, decision making, and so forth.

The process just outlined above should enable career counselors to articulate a position on how career planning and adjustment counseling should occur and should provide the basis for selecting techniques to increase the likelihood that it will be effective.

The metaanalytic research cited earlier (Oliver & Spokane, 1988) suggests that many types of career interventions are effective, and by extrapolation, that many theoretical perspectives can be employed in promoting career development and intervening with clients who need assistance.

A FINAL WORD

Books such as this provide a beginning for developing career counseling skills. Graduate courses continue this development. However, many exciting skills-building workshops are offered each year by local and national professional associations, continuing education centers, school districts, mental health centers, and so forth. In order to be apprised of these offerings it will be important join these associations so that the announcements of these workshops will be timely.

We also recommend that a counselor regularly consult professional journals, because information about career counseling is developing at an increasingly rapid pace. *The Career Development Quarterly, Journal of Counseling Psychology, Journal of Career Development,* the *School Counselor, Journal of Employment Counseling, Rehabilitation Counseling Bulletin,* and *The Counseling Psychologist* are important sources of information about career counseling, although some of this material will be slanted toward specific kinds of counselors or counselors working in specific settings. This array of journals indicates widespread interest in career counseling. It also is indicative of the magnitude of the task of keeping abreast of an area as dynamic as career counseling. However, we believe that because of the changing nature of the field, the effort to keep current is not only necessary, but will be an exciting task for the dedicated career counselor.

REFERENCES AND SUGGESTED READINGS

Brown, D., Brooks, L., and Associates (1990). *Career Choice and Development: Applying Contemporary Theories to Practice* (2nd ed.). San Francisco: Jossey-Bass.

Crites, J.O. (1981). *Career Counseling: Models. Methods and Materials* New York: McGraw-Hill.

Holland, J.L., Magoon, T.M., & Spokane, A.R. (1981). Counseling psychology: career interventions, research and theory. *Annual Review of Psychology* 32: 279–305.

Kivlighan, D.M., Jr. (1990). Career group therapy. *The Counseling Psychologist* 18: 64–79.

Oliver, L.W., & Spokane, A.R. (1988). Career-intervention outcomes: What contributes to client gain? *Journal of Counseling Psychology* 35: 447–62.

Index

359